AF252170

The Role of Computer Education in the Social Empowerment
of Muslim Minority Women in Greek Thrace

EUROPÄISCHE BILDUNG IM DIALOG

WISSENSCHAFT - POLITIK - PRAXIS

Herausgegeben von Wassilios Baros und Solvejg Jobst

BAND 12

Keratso Georgiadou

The Role of Computer Education in the Social Empowerment of Muslim Minority Women in Greek Thrace

Bibliographic Information published by the Deutsche Nationalbibliothek
The Deutsche Nationalbibliothek lists this publication in the Deutsche
Nationalbibliografie; detailed bibliographic data is available in the internet
at http://dnb.d-nb.de.

Library of Congress Cataloging-in-Publication Data
Names: Georgiadou, Keratso, author.
Title: The role of computer education in the social empowerment of Muslim
minority women in Greek Thrace / Keratso Georgiadou.
Description: Frankfurt am Main ; New York : Peter Lang, [2017] | Series:
Europäische Bildung im Dialog, ISSN 0947-6849 ; Vol. 12 | Includes biblio-
graphical references.
Identifiers: LCCN 2016052567 | ISBN 9783631714447
Subjects: LCSH: Muslim women–Greece–Thrace, Western–Social condi-
tions. | Muslim women–Education–Greece–Thrace, Western. | Computers
and women–Greece–Thrace, Western. | Social participation–Greece–Thrace,
Western.
Classification: LCC HQ1725.5.Z8 T475 2017 | DDC 305.48/697094957–dc23
LC record available at https://lccn.loc.gov/2016052567

Printed by CPI books GmbH, Leck.

ISSN 0947-6849
ISBN 978-3-631-71444-7 (Print)
E-ISBN 978-3-631-71445-4 (E-PDF)
E-ISBN 978-3-631-71446-1 (EPUB)
E-ISBN 978-3-631-71447-8 (MOBI)
DOI 10.3726/b10710

© Peter Lang GmbH
Internationaler Verlag der Wissenschaften
Frankfurt am Main 2017
All rights reserved.
Peter Lang Edition is an Imprint of Peter Lang GmbH.

Peter Lang – Frankfurt am Main · Bern · Bruxelles ·
New York · Oxford · Warszawa · Wien

This publication has been peer reviewed.

www.peterlang.com

To my mother

[a childhood with forbidden choices]

for her unwavering encouragement and support in all of my endeavours.

Acknowledgements

This research would not have been possible without the help, support, and active interest of many people around me. I hope that I managed to include everyone in the following section and ask forgiveness of those who feel they should have been mentioned. I would like to express my appreciation for the kind support of the Faculty of Educational Sciences and the Department of Primary Level Education that have allowed me to complete this research. I am most grateful to a supportive and cohesive committee. My deepest appreciation goes out to my advisor and committee chair, Prof Gerassimos Kekkeris for his valuable assistance, and by doing so, encouraged me to perform at higher levels than I thought possible. He made me believe in myself while continually giving me chances to enter in the scientific community from the very beginning of our collaboration. In particular, I thank the members of the scientific committees Prof. Eleni Taratori and Prof. Christina Metaxaki for intellectually challenging me and my work. I am deeply grateful to Prof. Mary Kalantzis at Urbana-Champaign Illinois who has an incredible amount of knowledge in the field of education. She took the time to share her knowledge and to articulate a respect for my own experiences during my research. I highly appreciate the time she has invested in this. I am grateful to Assoc. Prof Sabahat Sansa at the Bogazici University Istanbul, my Turkish "mother", who has been supporting me for the last decade. She read several drafts of the proposal and offered concrete suggestions holding me to a high standard. Her optimism, spirit and vision helped me recognise potential as well as limitations. I am obliged to thank with gratitude Assoc. Prof. Panagiotis Antoniou for his advices, Assoc. Prof. Georgios Tsomis for providing me material from libraries in Germany and also his encouragement through the preparation of my thesis and Mr Stergios Deliakidis who helped with the labyrinth of the statistics. My thanks do also go to all the people who have supported me in editing and improving the written work.

I am mostly grateful for the educational opportunities my parents have provided me with in the past. Without my mother's emotional and financial support I would not have been able to start this in the first place.

List of contents

Chapter 1: Introduction

1. Introduction

This study seeks to explore the phenomenon of social empowerment of Muslim minority women in Greek Thrace through Information and Communication Technologies (ICTs). The purpose of this multi-case study is to explore, with two samples of women of the Muslim minority living in the area of Thrace, their perceptions of how the computer education can lead them to pathways for their social participation and moreover the contribution of members of their community in administrative positions in this respect. It was anticipated that the ideas, the observations and the conclusions generated from this study would bring new insights on this subject.

This research employed qualitative and quantitative study methodology to illustrate the phenomenon under examination. Participants of the study included three purposefully selected groups of 137 women for the quantitative part of the research, 28 women and 30 key informants for the qualitative part of the research. This chapter begins with an overview of the context and the background that frames the study.

Following, the initial research as a starting point is quoted. The purpose and the need of the study, the problem statement, the statement of purpose and the research questions also. The research approach, the rationale and the significance of the study, the researcher's contribution to the research, and finally the structure of the thesis and the outlines of the chapters are included.

1.1 Background and Context

In the Greek part of Thrace, a Muslim minority has been living next to a Christian majority in the past years, sharing the same land, the same problems of living, and the same agony for the future. It is commonly observed and reported that minority women often find themselves marginalized and face exclusion within their own communities and in the wider society alike. They have limited opportunities for education and for political participation, decent work and income generating opportunities, social and financial capital, and basic social services. Women are also frequently discriminated against with regard to ownership and inheritance of property (UN Report, 2005b).

According to Latimer (2001), social gaps in society cause the digital divide; but the digital divide, in turn, may intensify existing social gaps and create new ones. Because members of minority groups and people from lower socioeconomic groups have less access to technology, they are likely to be even further disadvantaged from attaining some of the higher positions in tomorrow's economy, widening the economic divisions that already exist. Societies that discriminate by gender pay a high price in economic growth (World Bank, 2001). When women are excluded from learning, health care, and public sphere, the world looses the creativity and productivity of half its population (Sharma, 2003).

It is generally accepted that education helps women achieve their empowerment as it increases their capability, it arises their self-confidence, it provides them with knowledge to confront problems and situations that arise in their domestic life and gives them opportunities to contribute and act equally as men do (Moulton, 1997). Information and communication technologies as an educational tool promote women's empowerment and advancement in any society. We cannot expect that ICTs offer a panacea for social and economical development or can work as a wonder-working magic wand to eliminate the discriminations women have faced through centuries, but we can expect ICTs to prevent further ones.

The author's interest in investigating the connection of women of the Muslim minority to ICTs acted as the motive for her recent researches on this subject (Georgiadou et al., 2007a, b). As (2006:9) claims, being interested in others is the key to some of the basic assumptions underlying the research. In addition, the author was greatly involved to figure out the "Do related to ICTs" of the Muslim minority women in Greek Thrace and connect it with the "Do related to ICTs" of the women living in the Muslim world in order to extract ideas from efficacious applied programs and afterwards generate motives for the implementation of these programs in the local Muslim society. It can be said that one of this study's purposes is to indicate proper choices and suggestions for the improvement of the status of these women and finally to justify the fact that the resilient communities can only exist when women are playing a full and active part.

1.2 Initial Research

An initial study that took place between 2006 and 2007 was accordingly qualitative in nature: a case study survey using an ethnographical approach, which aimed to obtain an in-depth understanding of the relationship between women who belonged to the communities described below and ICTs. The research was conducted with the structured interview method for the Muslim women as well as the Pontian immigrants from former Soviet Union, one-on-one; using a questionnaire with a total of 59 questions, (both open- and closed-ended questions as well as scale items). All interviews were tape recorded and subsequently transcribed in full. More specifically, for the Roma women, the body of data was also semi-structured interview-based. While interviewing the Roma women, we chose the "vacuum-cleaner" technique and did not interrupt them even when they deviated from the main theme as interviews and narrations from such individuals and on such topics are rare (Goldstein, 1964).

1.2.1 Demographics of Participants

The research took place in the province of Rodopi (Xanthi and Evros provinces are the two other parts of Greek Thrace). It involved a non-probability sample of a total of 74 individuals of the so called "socially vulnerable" groups of the population in the area (32 Muslim women of Turkish origin, 35 Greek Pontian immigrants from former Soviet Union and 7 Roma).

The first two populations were identified and recruited by the snow-balling method and by the convenience sampling the third was simply available to the researcher by virtue of its accessibility. In this exploratory study phase, in order to achieve an understanding of the role of the interviewees' culture in the use and adoption of ICT, the sample was guided by the principle of maximum variation in terms of age, educational background, occupational background, parents' educational and occupational background, marital status, native country, and women's education and profession. Their age ranges for the Muslim women were 18–29 (12), 30–39 (16) and 40–49 (4). It was not possible to find women in the fifties involved with ICTs.

While conducting the group of Pontian women in the survey, we had to deal with a cultural group concentrated in a particular area of the city known as the "Russian neighbourhood". Their age ranges were 18–29 (11), 30–39 (11), 40–49(11) and 50–59 (2). Few women in their fifties involved with ICTs could be found. The seven Roma interviewees lived in a district of Komotini, called "Alan-Koyu" or "Tin Neighbourhood", in 50 sheds or other simple structures with communal toilets, with no land ownership; electricity, running water, and sewage provided; not easily accessible but with satellite antennas over all the roofs. Their age ranges were 18–29 (2), 30–39 (4), and 40–49 (1).

Most of the Muslim women we approached are graduates from Turkish universities as almost no minority students were enrolled in a Greek university prior to the positive discrimination measure of 1996 for entering Greek Universities (Dragonas & Fragoudaki, 2006). Due to this measure taken by the Greek government, an increasing interest in Greek universities can be mentioned. Collected data evidenced that young women of the minority show a great interest in receiving education, improving their skills, becoming more fluent in speaking the Greek language and being equally prepared for their future entrance to the labour market.

As for Pontian immigrants from former Soviet Union, most of them at the age of 18–29 had graduated from Greek high schools and were thus able to receive the same qualifications and skills as members of the local community. The great majority of women over 30, 40 and 50 years of age had graduated from high schools in the former Soviet Union. All had received secondary education, and twenty-six of them had received tertiary education, either in Greece or in the former Soviet Union. Although from data collected we have evidence that more of the interviewees over 30 who grew up in countries of the former Soviet Union were educated in the hard sciences; after their settlement in Greece they had to work in low-profile jobs unrelated to their initial studies in order to survive as Russian University degrees had problems in recognition or did not readily correspond to diplomas from Greek universities.

Finally, it has to be mentioned that none of the seven Roma women received any education and were totally illiterate. All of them spoke the Romani, most of them Turkish and some Greek although unable to read or write it. Only one of them, the eldest, whose family was travelling around Greece, was able to read Greek newspapers. Consequently, they could not compete with their classmates.

1.2.2 Relation to ICTs

A small number of open-ended questions asked participants to explain where or how they first learned the computer use; how they felt and feel in front of a computer; if the family encouraged them to use the computers; how many hours they used the computer every week and for what reason.

Data showed that most of the Muslim women at the age of 18–29 learned the use of computers at the Greek state high school or lyceum, where the lesson of computing science has been taught since 1994 while in minority schools started almost a decade later. Data also demonstrated that most of the Pontian women in the 18–29 age range learned to use computers in the Greek state middle or high schools, where computer science classes have been taught since 1994. Following their settlement in Thrace, nineteen of the interviewees attended EU funded seminars provided either by the prefecture of East Macedonia and Thrace, the Municipality of Komotini or the Greek Ministry of Labor, and conducted in private occupational education centres. For the Roma women, the 400 hour EU funded seminar for computer use they attended was their first experience with computers. They had never found themselves before in a schoolyard and had never attended lessons in a classroom. Even the keys on the keyboard were recognized as an image and not with the sense of the letters.

As illustrated by the data, most of the Muslims who possess a PC have Internet connection, have email accounts, and all of them own mobile phones. Among the group of Pontians, majority of the interviewees possesses a computer but have no Internet connection as they rarely have land phone connections due to the cost. Nearly all of them however own a mobile phone. Almost half of them have an email account. According to the data collected, most of the Muslim women do not frequent Internet cafes due to social reasons and structures of their society. The Pontians, at the age of 18–29, do not frequent Internet cafes since they own a computer at home or it is provided in their working area. The older Pontian women do not frequent Internet cafes due to their age for social reasons and their community structures; but some of them have access to the Internet at their workplaces.

Tele working is a more flexible way of work for women with domestic and family duties, and thus is more preferable for at least half of both Muslims and Pontians. As for the long working hours demanded by the ICT sector, half of the women from both groups felt positively. About on-line studies, most of the women felt as well, thinking that in this way family, marriage, domestic duties, dropping out of school, relations with family could be combined, affording them the opportunity for a "second chance" in their lives to improve their skills, abilities and prospects. They believed that in this way they would find jobs, become more educated and cultivated, and have more comfortable life with the ability to establish better relations with others.

Also commendable is the fact that both Muslim and Pontian women in the ages of 30–39 and 40–49 felt more comfortable than younger ones to function with men in groups in computer classes. The Roma women of all age ranges had also no problems being in groups with men. All of them had cell phones. They did not know what tele working was but when it was explained to them, they were positive in finding a job through this procedure as finding a job was their main problem mentioned several times during the interviews.

One of the things observed during the seminar attended by the seven Roma women was the good relations developed among members of the group. All the Roma women mentioned the fact that they were treated politely by their classmates, all members of the Christian majority.

As for the question that detected the reasons they used the computer, it was obvious that most preference was given by the Muslim women to the Internet,

Microsoft Office[1] applications and communication with friends followed by email and web surfing. Studies, games and telemarketing were not high priorities for these women. As for the Pontian immigrant women, most preference was given to the Internet, email and web surfing followed by Microsoft Office and communication with friends. On-line studies and telemarketing were not high priorities, also for these women.

All the interviewees were of the opinion that the use of ICTs is not only the realm of men. Most of the interviewees agree that computer knowledge was a necessity in today's world. Half of the Muslim women and most of the Pontian women responded positively when asked if computer illiteracy corresponded to non-computer use thus affirming the importance of being technologically literate today, but the rest were negative claiming that literacy was connected to education, university study or reading books. Nevertheless, most of the interviewees prefer reading from printed material to electronic.

Among the most commonly used ICT appliances, the Muslim women prefer traditional mass media such as mobile phones, television and computers and the Pontians mostly prefer television followed by mobile phones and computers. All the Roma interviewed, as mentioned above, owned cell phones and watched satellite TV. All Muslim interviewees and Pontian interviewees believe computer can facilitate their lives; ICTs can help in acquiring new knowledge and allow easier and faster communication and exchange of opinions but on the other hand do not believe that one must have particularly high qualifications in order to learn to use a computer.

For the Roma women, the material selected suggests that at the end of the seminar they recognized that the computer could facilitate their lives as they could see that things were done in an easier and quicker way. As visualization of information through images, demonstration and simulation is offered by computers in high quality, knowledge can be acquired in a better way (Kárpáti, 2004). This opened their eyes to positive changes. "Is this a mouse? You should see the mice I have in my house!" It was the first thing said when the tutor was demonstrating the hardware of the computer. Provided that the Roma women during the seminar showed increasing excitement for the computer day by day, that could be their first step towards climbing the stairs of literacy or facilitation of their everyday life as reading and writing, computer lessons for driving license, developing communication skills, etc. Their willingness to learn seemed obvious; when they understood what they were taught, they demanded more knowledge. If someone

---

1   Trademark of Microsoft Co.

willing to help them was showing something new, they could understand easily and apply it on the computer. They would no longer be afraid to press the buttons of the keyboard. All these was a good start for Roma women but if it ends after receiving the 2000euros subsidy, then everything will have been in vain.

Feelings of fear, stress and anxiety towards first computer use were reported by a small number of the interviewees. Most expressed feelings of interest, creativity and pleasure. Even women in their 30s, 40s or even 50s were positive towards new technologies, interested in learning how to use computers, and aware of their usefulness though they were aware of the difficulty of learning something new or the isolation that its use might bring.

1.2.3 Places to Gather

A significant problem for the women of the Muslim minority is the lack of a place where they can meet and exchange their views. Sometimes places like these exist due to private initiative and not due to municipal. Participants describing the place said they would like it as an area where they could meet over a cup of coffee and talk about problems that concern them, a place which would provide several facilities such as Internet connections, a library, lessons in chess and other games, newspaper and magazine subscription, sports, a theatre stage, collections of CDs and DVDs, or even conversations with psychologists and other types of consultants.

An Internet café in a commercial centre near the Pontian immigrants' quarter answers their needs for Internet connection when needed. The younger interviewees tend more to use the small municipal library. The elders, on the other hand, express a wish for the availability of Russian literature in this library, in which case they will visit it more frequently. Notable also is the absence of a place for women to gather. Most of them expressed the opinion that the place should host men also. Indeed, interviewees from all the age groups agreed that this place should be an inviting area with computers, a library with Russian literature, music, Internet access, DVDs, video, fax, newspapers, magazines, a coffee-shop, flowers, and classical music. Doctors, psychologists, and counsellors could be present to provide advice or give lectures on cultural, gynaecological and psychological issues. The data selected show that the great majority of the Pontian interviewees are subscribers to newspapers or magazines and are fond of books. Half of them said they would participate in programmes provided by the municipality solely for women although most of the interviewees were not informed about such programmes. Half of them were aware of EU funded programmes for increasing women's participation in business too. On the other hand, the majority of them were not informed about the existence of Europe Direct Information Relay of Komotini[2], which provides information on the EU in Komotini.

The Roma women were encouraged by their husbands to participate in this programme just to receive the subsidy; they even would bring them to school by car. Although most of them expressed that they wanted to communicate with other people, become skilled, and evaluate their lives, just be able to "have money and go to a cafe", they never participated in the local Romani association, since this is permitted only to men in their community. They had no idea of an Internet café or a library, or programmes offered by the municipality, solely for women.

1.2.4 Conclusions

This research due to the small sample, it could not provide in-depth answers to all the aspects of the questions that were raised and needed more thorough investigation. However, it was estimated that presenting preliminary findings on the Muslim women of Turkish origin, immigrants from former Soviet Union, Roma and their relation to ICTs, would contribute to the dialogue, that the results of the research could be announced so that some general comments would contribute toward identifying the problem more clearly and support the further studies of the questions raised. The themes that emerged from the qualitative data might also shed light on some of the many problems that these women living in this specific area of Greece face.

For the Muslim women of Turkish origin, to our initial questions whether women of the minority use the ICTs, the answer is positive although we cannot expect all women of the Muslim minority in general relate to technology in the same way. The women interviewed expressed their intention to be or become computer literate, to improve their knowledge of the Greek language, to continue their studies and to become qualified in order to be able to find a job. A continuous worry on this matter was expressed several times during the interviews with the women of different ages. The marital status of the participants was not an obstacle to the use of new technologies as many of them were supported and encouraged by their husbands to learn how to use a computer. Participants of the research showed a preference for mobile phones, TV, and then computers. When asked, they were negative to the mobility demanded by the ICT labour sector; but long working hours, telecommuting and online studies are accepted and generally welcomed. Women with domestic responsibilities particularly welcomed this flexibility. Influenced by the way Internet cafes function in the particular area, women of the

---

2   http://www.docstoc.com/profile/EuropeDirectKOM

Muslim minority are not comfortable with visiting them, although they exist in their neighbourhoods and villages. However, they do visit them when they are in Turkey, where anonymity is afforded. From the interviews it became evident that relation with and access to technology depends on education, income, and to some extent on the personality of the person who tries to become digitally literate.

For the immigrants from the former Soviet Union, interview results indicate that an overwhelming majority of the interviewees, both younger and older, consider ICTs to be of rapidly increasing importance. ICTs and the Internet offer obvious benefits as a means of communication. Immigrants have begun to use ICTs, especially email, cell-phone connections and cell phone text messages as valuable means of sustained contact with relatives in the former Soviet Union with the distinct advantages of low costs and immediacy of connection. Online newspapers greatly improve the immigrants' access to the traditional media in their former homelands.

Findings suggest that nearly two thirds of the participants welcome the mobility demanded by the ICT labour sector; long working hours, telecommuting and online studies are accepted and generally welcomed as new lifestyles. Particularly women with domestic responsibilities welcome this flexibility. The interviews indicate that immigrant women from the former Soviet Union, having made the decision to move to a higher-wage economy, aspire to gain access to the earnings and lifestyles available here. Most of them being highly educated, they generate a positive feedback effect.

Furthermore, it is a necessity to hold seminars according to the age, past ICT experience and specific needs of the participants. These seminars should also provide a broad range of computer knowledge from computer literacy to more specific programmes on demand in the labour market so that trainees may become more specialized. The results of past seminars on computer literacy should be disseminated in order to attract new trainees. The benefits of past computer literacy training programs should be evaluated. In order to pursue the goal of spreading the benefits of the information society to all residents of Greece, members or representatives of immigrant communities must be included as interlocutors, as subjects and not only as research objects in the information society implementation organs, overcoming in this way problems of expression and inclusion they usually face. This would assure that the views of these groups would be more effectively incorporated into policy formulation and implementation. Living conditions, problems and social exclusion faced by women immigrants from the former Soviet Union and other countries as well as refugees have barely been studied. The study and research on women's migration issues have gained new priority in efforts to decide upon new political and strategic targets with the aim of confronting the problems faced by migrant women, the betterment of their living conditions and social and economical inclusion in the receiving country.

For the Roma women, the interviews have indicated that their language skills must be improved as their oral and written comprehension is poor and insufficient for efficient learning. For this, we suggest that learning methods for seminars approaching the Roma and generally illiterate people must be improved and specialized, and knowledge processing strategies must be more diversified. Seminars with useful services driven by the real needs of the community must be materialized according to age, education level, and even gender of the participants by instructors prepared to teach people of special cultural and educationally disadvantaged groups. Women's associations or channels that interact with their way of living must be the informants for the benefits of the information society. Reducing the digital inequality must be an on-going process of education and support with a concrete target. Their literacy may be achieved through digital literacy. Helping them acquire this skill may enable them to avoid unemployment and poverty, which is their common fate.

1.3 Further Research

When the researcher started planning the study, taking into consideration all the above, she began searching the connection to ICTs of minority women, of Pontian immigrants from former Soviet Union and of Roma women, all living in the area of Thrace as this was described above (Georgiadou et al., 2006, 2007a, 2007b, 2007c, 2007 f., 2008a, 2010). Then she tried to figure out the ICTs implication on the construction of Pontian immigrants' identity as ICTs helped them keep connected with their relatives in Russia and received information from the area they had left (Georgiadou et al., 2007d, 2007e).

After studying the participation of Roma women in a computer training seminar, the experiences she received from this study led her to investigate the non formal education training programs experienced by Roma women living in Thrace and after that she proposed a better planning for these programs. She also outlined what impact the computer training seminars had on Roma women, and what aims they had after they had finished these programs (Georgiadou et al, 2008b, 2008e, and 2009a).

In addition, she searched out Muslim minority women's views on computer educators as she wanted to find out what qualifications and skills an educator should be qualified with in a class with minority women in order to make the program or the seminar more adaptable and easier to understand (Georgiadou et al, 2009b). As the subject of the thesis involved ICTs and empowerment of Muslim minority women, she had to search this subject in general for the Muslim women in different places of the world (Georgiadou et al, 2008d, 2008 f.) to support the literature review.

Due to lack of statistics concerning Muslim minority in Greece and more specifically concerning women of this community, she tried to find statistics on ICT connection of the Muslim women at Rodopi prefecture (Georgiadou, 2008c). While searching the literature on this topic, she came across with Dr. Farida Umrani, a post doctoral fellow at the Department of Computer Science and Engineering of the Indian Institute of Technology in Bombay, whose research interests were similar as she was targeting women of the Muslim minority at Bombay. Consequently, this collaboration led to working together on a paper entitled "Muslim minority women in India and Greece: Comparing psychological factors that affect their computer use" (Georgiadou et al. 2009c).

1.4 Purpose and Need of Study

Moving a step forward from the above research, our next focus was to penetrate substantially in a population who has been double and triple excluded and isolated as a social entity in the area of Thrace all the past years. We thought that hearing the stories of minority women would be of worth as these seem to be very rare in the bibliography. Due to social conditions formed in a globalized, continuously changing environment a need for educators to understand what conditions can support and promote Muslim minority women's social empowerment and the involvement and how computers can contribute to this. Understanding this is imperative if we expect women of the minority to integrate in a continuously changing, demanding society, mainly West-oriented, to become flexible, and to achieve in participation and in transformation using computer technology.

This study will contribute to an understanding why some women of the minority seem prepared for changes, seem prepared to play a new role in their family and by extension in their community, leaving in the past the roles they were imposed to adopt consciously or unconsciously. In addition, the contribution of members of the minority on this matter, who influence with their political status minority's function and act as stake holders, the key informants of this study, needs to be delineated.

The women who participated in this study recounted stories regarding their engagement in using computers; therefore this data must be analyzed. By looking at behaviour intention-factors, thought to be related to women's successful engagement with computers, we may better understand how to help more women become personal and professional integrated as this seems in these days a permanent, desperate need for the community of the minority, especially urgent these days due to economic reasons.

1.5 Problem Statement

It is usually observed that minority women often find themselves marginalized and excluded within their own communities and in the wider society alike. Hence, despite the changes that ICTs bring to the society, their marginalization and exclusion is not avoided. In the field of educational research, there is a gap in the literature regarding the domain specific to Muslim minority women and their social empowerment through ICT use. Most of the researches on the subject of the Muslim minority in Thrace refer to the education of the minority's children, identity of the minority, or history of the minority, European policies on minorities; and a few refer to adult education and women of this community.

Thus, our research is oriented to this specific subject, never discussed before, and connected to the fact that the Muslim minority in Thrace has been a restricted area for social research until recently because of the disturbed Greek–Turkish relationships. It is evident that through the past years the increasing nationalism on both sides, Greek and Turkish, has undermined the human relationships among the two communities living in the area.

1.6 Statement of Purpose and Research Questions

Hopefully, this study could be a unique opportunity to understand another aspect of Muslim minority's life in Thrace as it is being formed recently. This could also add another more modern option to beliefs regarding activities of the minority women which have been perceived in the past in prejudiced stereotypic ways dominated by a radically simplified type of thinking that may still be called Orientalist (Said, 1997:4).

In summary, this study aims to be of significance for academics and researchers in human and social sciences, policy makers, as well as civil society actors, NGOs and professionals with research interests in gender and minority issues, feminism, multiculturalism, race, class and culture. It is expected that the key contribution will arise from a better understanding of the role of the ICTs in the socio-economic development of minority women who live in a European territory but on the other hand in the margins of the society.

Research questions

To summarize the above discussion and shed light on the problem the following research questions are addressed.

Question 1

- In which way does computer education and digital literacy contribute to Muslim minority women's empowerment and social participation (personal and professional integration, citizen evolution, action and participation, cognitive experience, identity handling, motives for self-cultivation, studies, professional settlement, etc)?

Question 2

- Which are the behavioural intentions factors influencing Muslim minority women's computer usage?

Question 3

- In which ways do stake-holders of the Muslim minority contribute to Muslim minority women's digital literacy?

1.7 Research Approach

The researcher studied the experiences of 28 Muslim minority women living in Thrace, the views and perceptions of 30 key informants and the selected questionnaires from 137 women providing information on their behavioural intention to use computers. This investigation was succeeded through qualitative and quantitative methods for selecting data. Structured interviews were the primary method of data collection. This was completed with the fill in questionnaires. The process began with 30 pilot fill in questionnaires, pilot interviews with seven key informants and with five women. The obtained information formed the basis for the overall findings of the study. Each interviewee was identified by a pseudonym and all the interviews were tape recorded and transcribed.

1.8 Rationale and Significance

The researcher has noticed a gap in the Greek literature on gender and ICTs. The rationale of the study aims to contribute to fulfil this gap, extending the research to the Muslim minority women living in Thrace.

Seen in this context, the basic function of the research, which is the pursuit and the publication of valid data, obtains a political dimension which controls the evident truth and the interests that preserve a cloudy image for the minority. Perhaps the political dimension created the gap of data and the absence of valid information concerning statistics of minority population, of education of minority's children, of information about women, of different kinds of indexes that describe minority's everyday life.

This bibliographical destitution and stagnation of social research seems to raise both practical and theoretical difficulties. It seems that the practice of securing problems caused of the existence of a minority by its nature self-restricted in a putative homogeneous country is the reason for transforming a social problem to a political. Thus, the procedure of approaching the dimensions of these problems becomes difficult.

1.9 Study Structure

The thesis consists of six chapters. Chapter 1 presents the layout of the study, the starting point and the goals of the research, the nature of the research, the reasons for undertaking this research, the research questions, the need for the study, the purpose of the study that derives from the lack of similar subjects from the existing literature about the Muslim minority women in Greek Thrace and finally the research approach and the researcher's contribution.

In keeping with the above concerns, Chapter 2 presents the social profile and formation of the Muslim minority in Greek Thrace, the status of the women in this community and the researches that took place in the past on Muslim minority women. Chapter II is also concerned about empowerment of women through ICTs and its dimensions, computer education and its impact on someone's social participation and finally it concludes with examples of women's empowerment through ICTs in Muslim societies.

As for Chapter 3, it outlines the methodology of the study, the operational definitions of the variables, research model and design; the pilot study; the hypotheses; sample, tools, procedure, coding of variables and statistical analysis of data and finally a review of literature on the Technology Acceptance Model (TAM) and its constituents, the Theory of Planned Behaviour (TPB) model and its constituents.

In Chapter 4, the results of the three procedures, 1)TAM-TPB questionnaires-quantitative analysis, 2) women's interviews-qualitative analysis and 3) key-informant's interviews-qualitative analysis will be provided compared to the initial questions and hypotheses. Chapter 5 is the discussion chapter and consequently findings from Chapter 4 will be further discussed in Chapter 6 with conclusions, the implications and contribution of the study complemented by suggestions for further research.

Chapter 2: Review of Literature

2. Introduction

In the light of its aims, this study will briefly cover the historical and political context in the life of the Muslim minority women in Greek Thrace. The lack of statistics concerning Muslim minority in Greece will be briefly covered by presenting some statistics concerning the choices of Muslim women students. Then a brief review of the literature concerning researchers made in the past targeting Muslim minority women will be presented. Thus, the contribution of this research will become more obvious. Furthermore, some parameters of social empowerment will be discussed and specified by examples of women's social empowerment through ICTs in the Muslim world.

2.1 Muslim Minority in Thrace

The area of the research is Thrace, which occupies the north eastern corner of Greece, bordering Bulgaria to the north, Turkey to the east, and its southern shores on the Sea of Thrace, consisting of three administrative areas: those of Xanthi, Rodopi and Evros.

Figure 2.1: The map of Greek Thrace

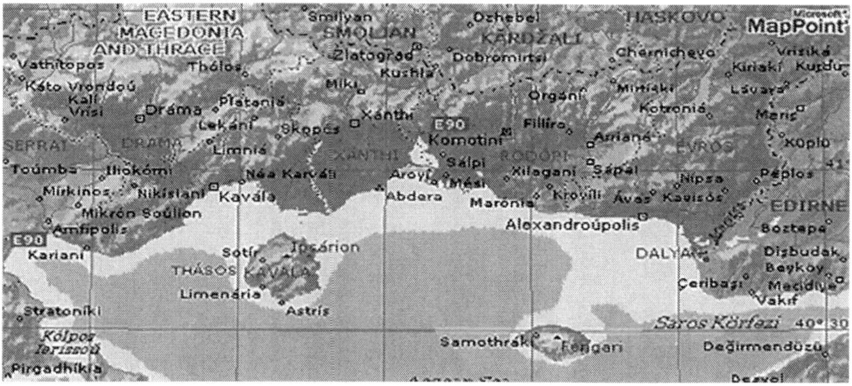

Thrace[3] has been inhabited since around 6.000 B.C.; her history is characterized by colonization, settlements and conquests by several groups of Indo-European tribes inhabiting a large area in southeastern Europe. Thracians inhabited parts of the ancient provinces of Thrace, Moesia, Macedonia, Dacia, ScythiaMinor, Sarmatia, Bithynia, Mysia, Pannonia, and other regions of the Balkans and Anatolia. According to Thucydides there were about 200 Thracian tribes with names as Agrians, Alitous, Astaiaous, Apsinthious, Venous, Vesous, Visaltes, Bistones, Vriantes, Sappaious, Hdones and many others. In the acient world Herodotus called them the second-most numerous people in the part of the world known by him (after the Indians), and potentially the most powerful, if not for their lack of unity. The first Greek colonies in Thrace were founded in the eighth century BC. Raids by Persians, Celts, Huns, Bulgarians, Serbs, Romans and others followed.

The complete conquest of Thrace by the Ottoman Turks took place 100 years before the fall of Constantinople in 1453. The year 1908 marked the beginning of a period of Bulgarian domination in Thrace. With the Balkan wars (1912–1913), the Turks reoccupied the Thracian region, but the Treaties of London (1913) and Bucharest (1913) once again granted Thrace to Bulgaria. At the close of the First World War (1919), the French general Sarpy occupied Western Thrace, while the Greek troops entered Eastern Thrace. In June 1920, the whole of Thrace was occupied by Greek troops. On 24 July 1923, the Treaty of Lausanne granted Western Thrace to Greece and recognised the existence of a Muslim minority in this area. Besides the Muslim community, there have also been living Jewish (exterminated during WW II) and Armenian communities in the area for centuries.

There is a lack of official statistics with respect to the social and professional profile of the minority. Little data is available concerning the Muslim minority's demographical development after 1920. Presently the Muslim minority in Greek Thrace consists of approximately 100.000 individuals (33.14 % of the total population in Thrace, with the Christian population estimated at the level of 226.000 people). The Muslim population is concentrated mainly at the Xanthi and Rodopi provinces whereas at the Evros province the Muslims are only a small part of the total population. In the areas of Rodopi and Xanthi the main part of the population is of Turkish origin. Another part of the population in the area of Xanthi is of Pomak origin, mainly mountain dwellers and a smaller part is of Roma origin, mainly living at the region of Rodopi and Evros (Notaras, 1995; Mavrommatis, 2005). Members of the minority speak the Turkish language, the Pomak language

---

3   Thrace, the land of Orpheus, http://alex.eled.duth.gr, https://en.wikipedia.org/wiki/Thracians

and the Romani dialect. A variety of manners and customs are observed among the populations that compose the minority in Thrace. A major problem Thrace faced through the 20th century was population decline of both major communities; Christians and Muslims.

Ascouni (2006), considering the socio-economic background of the entire minority population, states that the overwhelming majority belongs to the lower social strata. The agricultural sector is especially large, comprising 47.2 % of the total minority population compared with 19 % of the national mean. The agricultural characteristics of the minority consist of small property, traditional family structure and lack of modern infrastructure. Describing their occupational status, it can be said that the participation of Muslim workers outside the public sector is much higher; but on the other hand, inside the public sector it is problematic and limited, regarding the numbers of the minority (Demesticha, 2004). The Muslim minority people in Thrace work mainly as field or construction workers (12 %), as tradesmen (2 %) and as employees in salaried jobs in a quite low participation (5 %) in the public and the private sectors (Imam and Tsakiridi, 2004). Especially the share of Muslim Roma workers engaged in street vending especially with no fixed location is extremely high (Zenginis, 1994).

2.1.1 Education of Minority

A further index of marginalization is the level of the education of the minority members. Almost 80 % of them have completed only six years of primary school although it was 30 years ago that compulsory education was extended to nine years in Greece. High drop-out of school rates is a common phenomenon among minority students. This phenomenon seems to be changing in the period after 2000 as the number of minority students who study at high schools had quadrupled in the period 1991–2006. Children who come from under privileged social strata with parents of low educational level usually exhibit high levels of drop-out. Only 2.6 % of men and 0.2 % of women of the minority hold a university degree (Ascouni, 2006). According to the census of 2001 carried out by the Greek National Statistics Service, 3.6 % of the Greek population is totally illiterate, but the unofficial statistics claims the number to be between 12 % and 13 %.

Furthermore, statistics from the General Secretariat of Adult Education indicates that the highest rate of illiteracy among all regions of Greece is observed in Thrace (15.13 %). The rate of under-educated people in Thrace is 72 %, 15 points above the national average of 57 % (Katsikas, 1997). At the province of Xanthi, 32.84 % have graduated from primary school, 26.4 % have graduated from high school, and only 12.18 % have graduated from university. 13.642 women (34 % of the total feminine population in the Xanthi province) have not received primary education. In the province of Rodopi, 75.8 % of the total population is considered to be under-educated. As Ascouni (2006) claims, at Xanthi the tendency of studying in a state Greek-speaking school is much stronger than the tendency at Rodopi, where there is a strong orientation on minority Turkish-speaking and Greek- speaking elementary schools and a slow penetration to Greek-speaking schools in secondary education.

At the end of the 80s, a tension of urbanization is observed in the minority as people move from their residence on the mountains to urban areas. In the 90s, the rapid and big changes inside the Greek society form a policy towards the minority based on the equality before the law and the state and the equality of rights. In 1995, the Ministry of Education instituted a law, first giving minority students the opportunity to enrol in the secondary schools with no lottery system, as used to be in the past, and then in the Greek universities with a quota system (0.5 % of the total number of students entering the Greek universities each year). Due to the quota system, in order to gain a place in the tertiary education, Muslim students participate in pan-Hellenic exams as a separate group competing among themselves. All these years, after the establishment of the quota system, a yearly increase has been observed in the number of Muslim minority pupils gaining a place in the Greek universities. Hopefully, a better minority education establishes more chances for the minority to quit its isolation, become integrated and not assimilated.

According to Demesticha (2004), in 1996, the first year of the measure, there were only 48 Muslim minority candidates in Thrace. In 1997–98, 334 places were set aside; 114 students out of 120 participating in the exams were accepted in the Greek universities. In 1998–99, seventy-four minority students entered the universities under the quota system, and in 2004 approximately 700 minorities were studying in the Greek universities (data from Human Right Watch Report, Positive Measures). Ascouni (2006) points out the slow trend among the minority towards preferring the state primary school, rather than of their own. So in 2002–03, out of a total of 6887 minority children only 12 % attended mainstream Greek primary schools; in 1996–97 the percentage had been 5 % and, prior to that, practically zero (ibid). While drop-out rates from compulsory education are still very high and problems facing education serious, the trends are promising. Although the girls' drop-out rate is 80 %, the increase in gymnasium attendance over ten years is 76.9 % (compared with 19.6 % for boys).

Nevertheless, a large number of students from the Muslim minority who gain entrance to Greek universities via the quota system still prefer to finish their studies in Turkish universities, where a similar quota system exists from the past for these students. Usually most of the students who study in Turkey used or still use to settle there. Thus, the minority, during the past years, lost the most educated members who could offer a better dynamics in the area.

Figure 2.2: Results of quota system for Muslim minority (1996–2016) (Rodopi Prefecture)

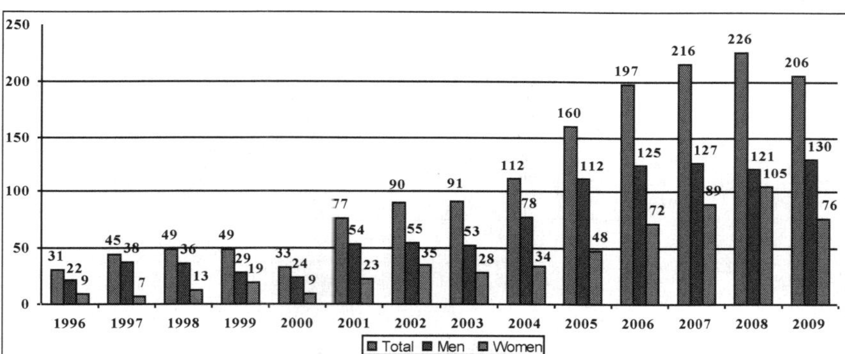

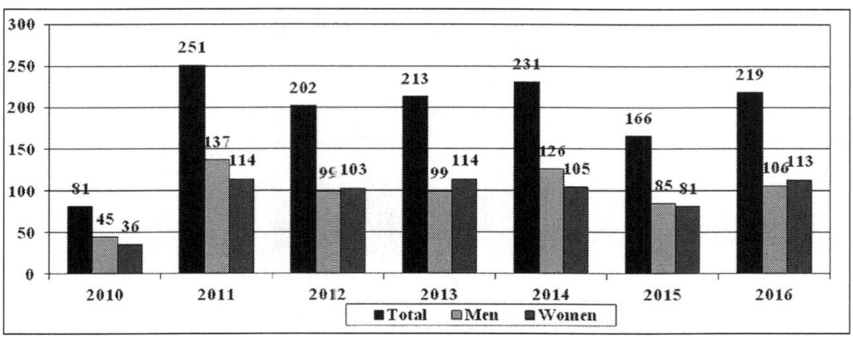

Educated women, who are increasing in recent years, work professionally as doctors, dentists, lawyers, pharmacists, architects, civil engineers and in other professions. Many women are employed by factories in the region. Most of them work in agriculture, some are shopkeepers. Nowadays, some can be found working in the civil services. Data concerning the choices of Muslim minority students at Turkish universities for the years 1998–2008 was collected from the archives of minority members of the Greek Parliament. In these files the researcher selected information for 219 women out of 614 in total living at Rodopi prefecture. The data do not

31

represent all the NARIC (National Academic Recognition Information Centre) data for the years 1998–2008 but constitute a small indicative example as there is probably data for more students connected to these years.

Figure 2.3: Students of Minority who graduated from Turkish Universities

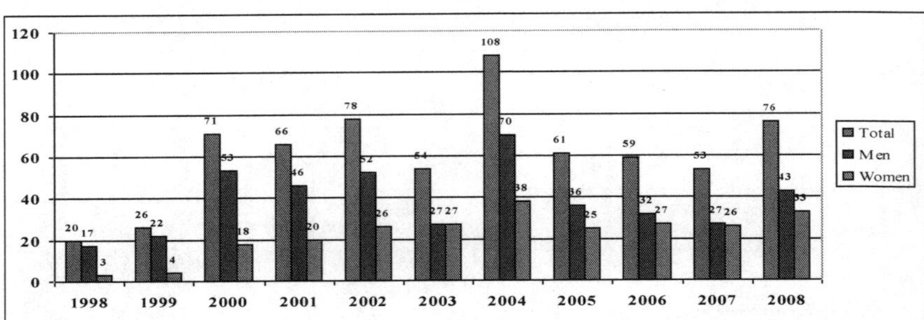

The following detailed table shows the choices the Muslim women made in their studies. Usually medical studies (medicine, pharmacy, nursery, psychology) are the most preferable due to the vocational rehabilitation they provide, followed by educational studies (English and Turkish literature and teacher training).

Table 2.1: Studies of Minority Women in Turkey (1998–2008)

Total:672 / Women:240	
Medicine	25
English literature	21
Pharmacy	19
Nursery	16
Management	15
Turkish Literature	12
Psychology	12
Teacher's Training College	11
Law School	10
Dentistry	10
Architecture	9
Economics	7
Religious Studies	6

Total:672 / Women:240	
Biology	5
Industrial Engineering	5
Information Technology	5
Journalism	4
Pre-school Education	4
Health Management	4
Tourism Management	4
Physiotherapy	3
House Economy	3
International Relations	3
Civil Engineering	3
Mechanical Engineering	2
Mathematics	2
Fine Arts	2
Chemical Engineering	2
Interpretation	2
Sociology	1
Chemistry	1
Social Services	1
Russian Literature	1
History	1
Water Resources Management	1
Archaeology	1

The most significant problem faced by young Muslim people is that of language. Muslim minority members, especially graduates from minority secondary education and Turkish universities, have insufficient knowledge of the Greek language. Nevertheless, there is improvement in this area as the youngsters who graduate from Greek state high schools or Greek universities have a better level of knowledge of the Greek language. Good knowledge and use of languages, computer and other advanced skills, and adaptation to changes brought by new technology and globalization will be demanded of the Muslim minority members as well.

The demands of the market brought by globalization are changing very quickly, and those ready to meet them will take part in this market. Thus, the members of the minority have to adjust to this new reality. The data from the NARIC archives and the results of the Pan-Hellenic exams with the quota system have shown an increasing interest and preference on the part of minority girls for information technology departments. This is obvious in figure 2.4 where elements were collected by going through all the results for both Christian and Muslim women students who succeeded in Greek universities, and then their choices for the departments of computer sciences were evaluated.

Figure 2.4: Number of Women who succeeded in Departments of Computer Sciences in Greek Universities (1996–2016) (Rodopi Prefecture)

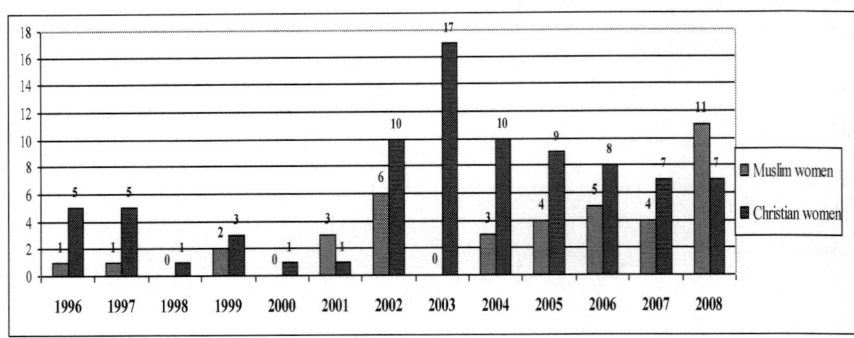

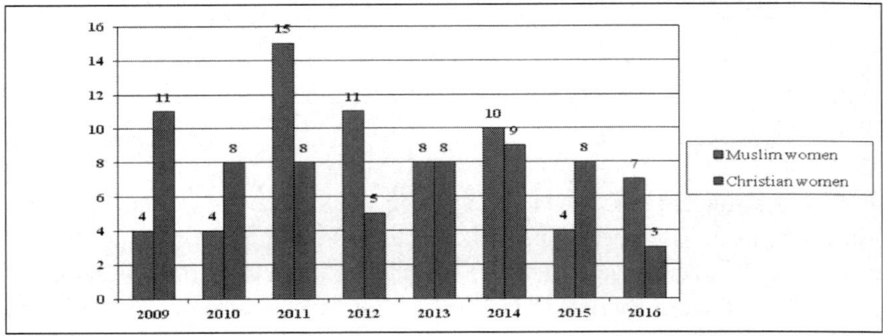

2.1.2 Educational Choices for Muslim Students in Komotini

Figure 2.5 presents the numbers of Muslim students who have studied in sections of computer sciences at the Institute of Occupational Formation at Komotini. Muslim women, during the last years, have shown an increasing interest in receiving knowledge in order to obtain skills and consequently joining in the "exclusively manly professions".

Figure 2.5: Muslim Students in Sections of Computer Science at the IOF

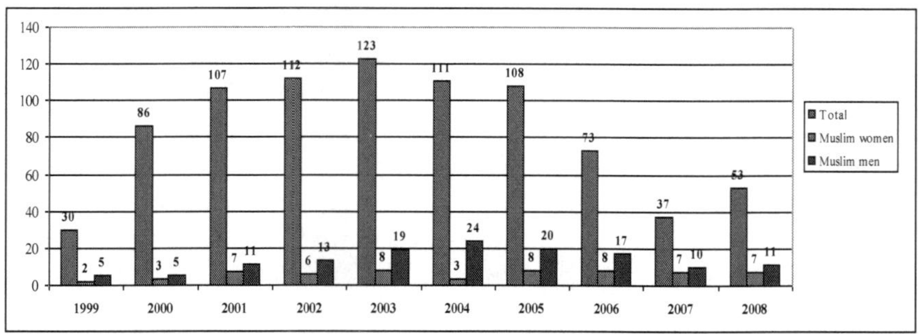

Figure 2.6: provides data for studies specialized on computer science in the 2nd Technical Lyceum at Komotini.

Figure 2.6: Number of Students in Sections of Computer Science (2nd Technical School)

During their interviews, people of the minority who can be considered as key informants due to their high educational, social, and labor status, have highlighted the importance of the fact that women of the minority continue their studies in the Second Chance Schools. Some of the interviewees, due to their positions in civil services, supported and helped women of their community to register at these schools. The nucleus of aspects and thoughts they supported was that women of the minority must have a chance to solve their problems and gain a higher educational and socioeconomic status, become more independent, get out of the fringe that society puts them in, avoid the family oppression, learn the Greek language, improve their personality, obtain skills in order to become more useful to their families and even become identity with the dominant and avant-garde culture.

As it will be observed in Figure 2.7, there is an increasing interest by Muslim minority people in attending the Second Chance School of Komotini. Information (off the record) provided by the headmaster of the school, indicated that for the year 2008 140 students registered

Figure 2.7: Second Chance School of Komotini

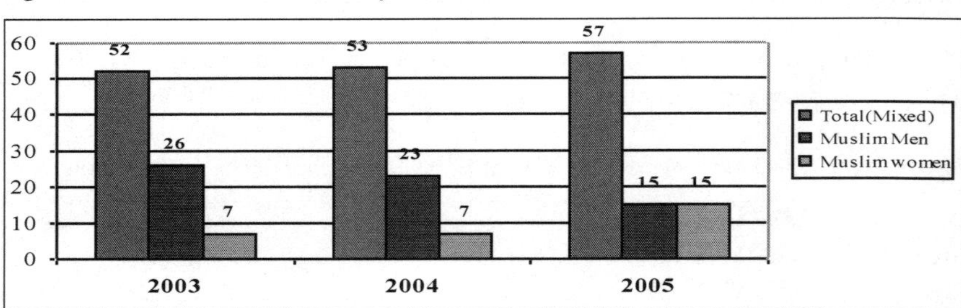

Figure 2.8 shows for the "Evening High School" the participation and the interest of the Muslim working women in continuing their education and increasing their literacy level. The low levels of women participation may be explained by the fact that the students of this high school are working during morning time.

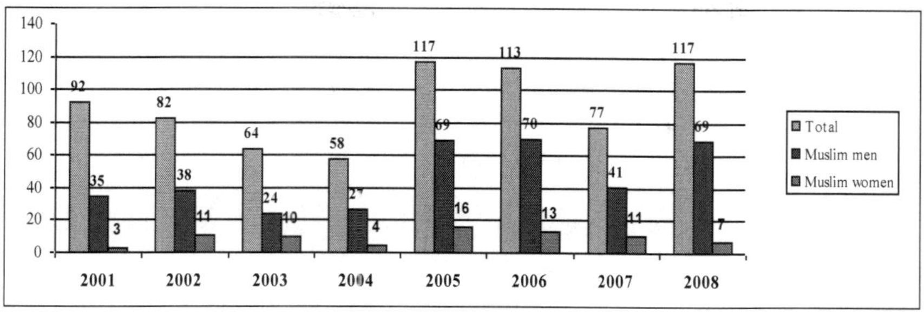

As for Figure 2.9, it shows the number of Muslim students in computer science sections at technical schools or institutes of vocational training who have participated in the EYRIDIKI program. The duration of the program was 2 years, from 2006 to 2008; it was materialized by the Democritus University of Thrace and its aim was to promote and support women to direct their choices to professions usually man occupied. The women were supported for their practices and were provided with scholarships to continue working in these labor fields.

Figure 2.9: Participation of Women Students only in Computer Science Section, program EURIDIKI (Xanthi and Rodopi prefectures)

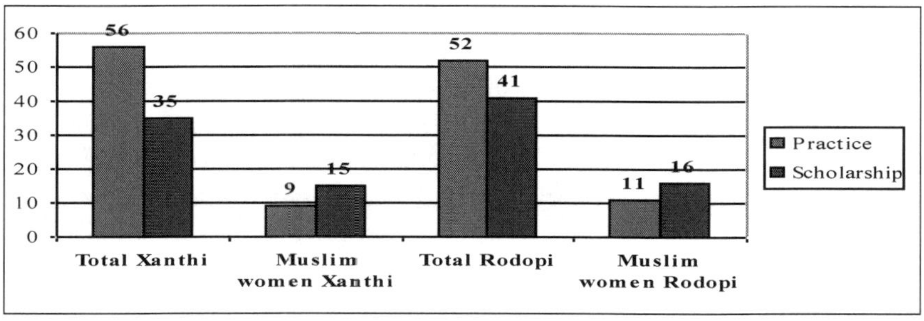

The GMEO (Greek Manpower Employment Organization) secondary education started providing services to students in the town of Komotini in 1984. Until 2004, the participation of the women of the minority was not important as the specialties provided were discouraging for women. After the specialty of tonsorial art became available, the participation of the women of the minority started to increase. In the school year 2007–2008, 19 students were enrolled in the Supporting Systems of Information Technology specialty. Six of them were Muslim men and four were Muslim women. Figure 2.10 provides information on the number of students in the sections of computer science at the Institute of Vocational Training of GMEO. (In figure 2.10 mixed means both Christian and Muslim students)

Figure 2.10: Number of Students in the Departments of Computer Science at the IVT of GMEO

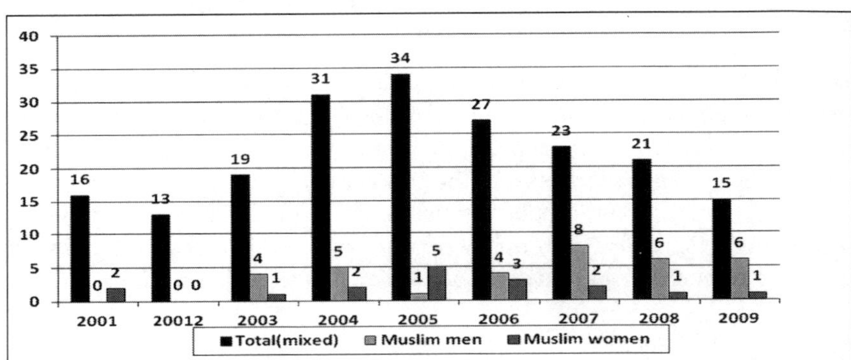

2.2 Muslim Minority Women in Thrace

Esposito and Haddad (1998), mention that *for Islamists the primary threat of the West is cultural rather than political or economic. Women and family have been identified as pivotal in this contest. Women therefore are regarded as the primary culture bearers, as the maintainers of the tradition, relegated to the task of being the last bastion against foreign penetratio, although it can be said that they suffer from centuries of misinterpretation of Islamic tradition.*

On the other hand, in the West, Hazel Blears (Communities Secretary in Britain) comments, "*Public debate about Muslim women too often reverts to stereotypes and preconceptions. We pay too much attention to Muslim women's appearance -with the perennial debate about headscarves and veils- and too little to what they say and do.*" Muslims in the New World Order are confronted as the *new enemy,* which, according to Poole (2001), has resulted in religious identifications on the basis of world-wide inequalities. Islam is generally viewed through Western eyes as static, traditional, anti-modern, and misogynistic and Muslim women are obscured by stereotyped representations (Fereshteh, 2005).

In Thrace, Muslim minority women are distinguished from the way they are dressed: with "feretze" (black gowns) for the old ones, the grandmothers, with scarves and gabardines for the modern mothers or just colourful scarves; the Middle East look a combination of modern clothes and a scarf, or no cover for the young girls. The above differences in their appearance depend on the place they live, on their educational level, marital status, employment status and cultural level.

Tsibiridou (1997) states that in the face of the Muslim woman, as always happens with women, a lot of things are being negotiated, such as national identities, national consciousness and traditional values. Muslim women in Thrace, due to high lack of opportunities for occupation in the area, are usually pushed to retrogress to traditional values and nowadays to the traditional Islamic ethics. This retrogression comes to confirm Esposito's and Haddad's (1998: xvi) statement mentioned above at the beginning of the paragraph. Thus, minority women's Islamic dress code is a primary culture bearer, a maintainer of their tradition and their social values to the West oriented models, and an indication of their existence as a minority.

In the area of Thrace, the Muslim family structure mainly oppresses women and relegates them to a low-level of educational achievement and to confinement to home sphere. The rate of employment for women is rather low. The factors which exclude women from the local labour market are lack of education and training, traditional structures of their society, male status quo, insufficient knowledge of the Greek language and sometimes discriminations towards Muslims. Although in Greece nine years of education is compulsory, Muslim minority families are reluctant to send their daughters to school, especially in rural areas and in lower middle class urban neighbourhoods where the status of women living in these areas is different as they seem to be doubly discriminated against and excluded (Kanakidou, 1994, 1996; Tressou, 1997; Askouni, 2002; Imam & Tsakiridi, 2004). Ascouni (2006:282) claims that one out of five minority women has not received primary education and only 1.6 % of the minority women have entered secondary education.

In the last years, the change of policy of the Greek Ministy of Education to minority's education has contributed to the increasing of the number of members of the minority who become lawyers, dentists, doctors, pharmacists, engineers, archtects. A number of university graduates have started to take positions in the town councils and prefectures. Moreover, the number of educated minority women has been increasing during the last years. Thus, the job opportunities for the women of Thrace have gradually increased. This important change, not only for the Muslim minority women themselves but also for the economic, social and cultural development of Thrace's growth, has resulted from the 0.5 % quota system for entering Greek universities, the establishment of Second Chance schools, the IEK (Centre for Professional Training) and the new EU-supported programs, aiming to incorporate both the Muslim minority and the Orthodox majority into the Greek economic life.

Another important issue regarding minority women's status quo in Thrace is the function of the Sharia Law, an anachronistic law that was put into effect in 1913 during historically and politically transitional and fluid periods, which removes rights and discriminates against Greek Muslim women, thus deviating from the constitutional right for equality between the sexes and the fundamental principle that all citizens should be equal before the law.

2.3 Overview of Literature for Minority Women

The following literature review includes books and articles which refer mainly to subjects connected to Muslim minority women living in Thrace, and contain descriptions of their living status, the structure of the minority family, and their efforts to integrate in the new world.

Kanakidou (1996) analyzes the data in her social-psychological theoretical leveled study about the personality and participation in the traditional structure of training and education of the Muslim woman in Western Thrace. She concludes that the contact of two cultures is not an essential condition for the formation of the Muslim woman's marginal position but an efficient condition on which modernization and tradition are related in different phases. The marginal personality formed in this case leads to traditional behavior as soon as the woman is exposed to the contradictory relation between family and school.

In addition to the above, Malkidis (2005) refers to the status of the minority woman inside the structure of the Muslim family. Although this status is influenced by the Western life style, it still reflexes images from Turkey. Minority women are usually suppressed inside their marriages due to the constructed relations through years and extension of these relations in Muslim minority society. Akritidou (2002) describes the status of the women in the social synthesis of the minority according to their descent (Turkish origin, Pomaks, Gupsy). She provides information on the levels of education, professional status, family status, dressing codes, living status, relations with family and religious influences. Plexousaki (2003), in her ethnographical research, aims to detect the cultural approaches of minority women and their perception and practices associated to education. Ribas Mateus (2000) claims that the Muslim community is defined by relegating the female public presence as a typical feature of Muslim dominated societies with a family structure which mainly oppresses women and relegates them to a low-level of educational achievement and to confinement to the home sphere.

Furthermore, at the level of formation of a new female identity for the women inside the minority, Zaimakis and Kaprani (2005) state that new challenges meet with the traditional perceptions and the power of the customs. In a complementary way, Demetriou (2002), in her study about minority identities among Turkish speakers in Komotini, mentions that the restrictions placed by the rhetorical tradition on gender roles seem to be emphasizing a local *Trakyali* identity over a national Turkish. Tradition becomes a wholly positive trait of *Trakyali* identity, which in turn unites it as a mixture of traditional, modern, and political identities in a different type of Turkishness. Tsimbiridou (1997) describes the feretze or the scarf or the practice of covering as the symbol of conducting the minority stigma. Muslim minority women are the basic victims of the distinction among the two worlds. Simultaneously they suffer a big amount of internal orientalism. The literally and the symbolic closing of the minority women in the urban areas and their exclusion from the different outside world seems to be the price they pay with their psychological disturbance and their recourse to psycho-medicines in high rates. Giannakouli (2005) states the importance of discrimination between sexes that seems more profound inside the Muslim minority family in Thrace. Women in the area are socialized and judged every day under the Muslim ethics, which is male dominated and restrictive for them.

In general terms, in her research Demesticha (2004) argues that many women of the minority during the last years are employed by factories of the region and participate in educational structures, such as centers for professional training and the Open University, aiming at improving their fluency in Greek and their professional skills. In a more complementary way, Triantafillidou (2007) claims that the past two decades have seen the large scale entry of minority women into the labour market of the region, primarily as workers in the textiles and tobacco processing factories of the region. Women's entry into Thrace's labour market in general accounts for the increase in the size of the economically active population despite the overall demographic decline the region has witnessed over the past twenty years. In the case of the minority, women's undertaking paid employment has been one way for families to deal with reduced income from agriculture, on which Muslims extensively depend as levels of agricultural subsidies provided by the EU Common Agricultural Policy (CAP) have been declining.

Furthermore, Askouni (2006:338), in her book about minority education in Thrace, gives in detail, using numbers and statistics, the changes that have taken place in the education of minority children in the last decades. More specifically, she explains that the number of educated minority women has been increasing during the last years; but on the other hand, the status of women living in the rural areas and in the mountains still remains unchanged as they seem to be doubly discriminated against and excluded.

As for Hatzikosta (2008), her research aim is the registration of participating educational techniques, especially those of conversation and group work, used in adult education classes. Women participating in adult education seminars were thrilled with this procedure and seemed happy attending such programs that gave them the chance to expand their sentimental and cognitive fields. Panousi (2007) focuses on a program materialized in a center of educational training at Komotini to learn the Greek language with the participation of Muslim minority adults (men and women) from 23 to 40 years old. To be more specific, she tries to investigate those factors that contribute to marking obstacles on the learning procedure and the correct learning of the Greek language. She aims at matching the results which are connected with the participation of the Muslim adults and which follow the trainees in their effort to acquire the Greek language with complex images of serious problems: linguistic, social, religious, family, economic, political in order to substantiate the view that life long learning is an institution which can contribute to confrontation of social exclusion.

Finally, Navrozidou (2008) presents the results of a research among Muslim minority women who participated in adult education seminars. The deriving factor is that in the case of the Muslim minority women, the basic function of adult education is the effort to avoid woman's social downgrading by providing the necessary knowledge and the skills in order to achieve minority women's empowerment and development of a discerning mind.

2.4 Gender and ICTs

2.4.1 Information Society

A century after the industrial revolution, we live the transition from the industrial society to the information society, the knowledge society to the learning society of the 21st century. We are in the process of another big change in the human civilization, this of the revolution of the information which has given birth to the information society. The world's history is influenced by knowledge and technology. The digital revolution changes the world in social, economical, cultural and political ways. As people participate in the information society, they have the chance to live great changes in the way they organize their lives.

The ICTs, especially the Internet which according to Turkle (1995:17) is the material expression of the philosophy of postmodernism, are the gates in this new age. Vitsilaki and Eythimiou (2007) explain that the term ICT concerns the integration of the classic services, foremost stable and mobile phone, access to the Internet, and the services that provide, electronic mail, electronic commerce, video games, TV, radio broadcasting and generally transmission of content like movies, news, etc. plus the development of new services that cannot have been materialized without this convergence.

According to Marcelle (2000a), ICTs comprise a complex and heterogeneous set of goods, applications and services used to produce, distribute process and transform information. ICT and Internet reach many people, have a wide geographical coverage and are efficient in terms of time and cost. They facilitate access to markets, commercial information, new processing technologies and knowledge. The defining characteristic of the ICT is the capacity to harness access and apply information and diffuse knowledge at electronic speed to all types of human activity, thereby giving rise to contemporary knowledge-based economies and societies. Internet is emerging as a source of considerable potential for individuals, businesses and countries. The rhythm of growth for ICT and the speed of their spread in almost all human activities have taken impressive dimensions in our days.

As Makrakis (2000:18) states, technology is something more than a tool. It is the means that influences the progress of our thought and interaction with others, with machines as well as our conscience, our visions and our expectations. The interaction between technology and society is so huge that their implications on the environment, the society and the person are expanded beyond the direct aims of the technological innovations and their implementations. While considerable optimism is vested in the promise of information and communication technologies for human progress, it is also true that the information age is not all optimistic; the benefits of this new age have not yet reached all of humanity and all its outcomes are not necessarily positive.

2.4.2 Digital Divide

The digital divide refers to the differences in resources and capabilities to access and effectively utilize ICTs for the development that exist within and between countries, regions, sectors, and socio-economic groups (Marcelle, 2000a). When describing the term "digital divide", which according to Hafkin (2002) is actually several gaps in one, these characteristics have to be considered: gender, age, race, ethnicity, education, income, unemployment, geographic location, English language ability, wage and labour discrimination, cultural stereotypes and physical and cognitive disability, have to be considered (NTIA, 1995; Hafkin and Huyer, 2006).

According to Latimer (2001), social gaps in society cause the digital divide; but the digital divide in turn may intensify existing social gaps and create new ones. Because members of minority groups and people from lower socioeconomic groups have less access to technology they are likely to be even further disadvantaged from attaining some of the higher positions in tomorrow's economy, thus widening the economic divisions that already exist. Furthermore, when women are excluded from learning, health care, and public sphere, the world looses the creativity and productivity of half its population (Sharma, 2003).

The nature of digital divide can be defined by three broad perspectives: the Information Technology Access Gap, the gap that represents the divide between those who have physical access to the computer (at home, school, work place or cyber cafes) and those who do not; the Information Technology Application Gap, the gap which separates those who know how to apply existing information technology to create wealth and those who do not (Cooper &Weaver, 2003:3–5); the Information Technology Creation Gap, the gap with three levels which represents the divide between those who conduct fundamental research and development in information technology; those who use and create ICTs products and services with existing technology; and those who are only consumers of the ICTs products and services (UN, 2007).

ICTs have been compared to a double-edged sword: advancing knowledge society on one hand and deepening social divides and gender based on pre-existing social divisions on the other (Melhem and Vivek, 2006). Sharma (2003) claims: *"The impact of information technology on society has not been uniformly beneficial, and the technological divide is being increasingly felt, especially in the developing countries. Serious obstacles still continue in achieving gender equality. Cultural attitudes and gender stereotyping are impediments to education leading to more men than women in scientific and technical careers and in decision-making positions, thus increasing gender inequity. Equal access to science is not only a social and ethical requirement for human development, but also essential for realising the full potential of scientific communities and for orienting scientific programmes towards meeting the needs of humankind."*

As Cooper and Weaver (2003) comment, the digital divide between males and females is very real and very damaging. It is damaging for women who will have to combat more than a few barriers to achieve comfort with information technology. It is damaging for society because half of the potential workforce must fight an uphill battle to contribute to the creative process in information technology.

Some of the main gender issues in ICT that are central to an understanding of the application of IT to society as suggested by Hafkin (2003) are presented below.

Lack of infrastructure

These inequities are more pronounced for women in general, for women from developing countries in particular (Gurumurthy, 2004:11–12) and are commonly found in high rates among women in the Muslim world. Women's access to ICTs is also constrained by socially and culturally constructed gender roles and relationships, the basic factors shaping and limiting the capacity of women and men to participate on equal terms in the information society. To emphasize the above, Ess (2001:9) mentions that historically women and minorities have enjoyed less access to technologies. According to UNDP, in no society do women enjoy the same opportunities as men (UNDP, 1995). The world over, most women are poorer than men, are less educated and with lower levels of illiteracy. They tend to earn less and hold fewer positions of power and decision making in the family, in businesses, and in political and public life. These inequalities affect women's ability to benefit equally from the opportunities offered by information technology and to contribute fully to shaping the developing global knowledge economy and society.

In most countries, the typical Internet surfer used to be male; young (particularly in the developing countries); under the age of 35, well educated and well off, living in urban areas and English speaking. This stereotype is changing in some countries rapidly, in others slowly. In general, the gender digital divide is greater in countries where women have less access to education than men as is the case in many poor countries and in those which for cultural or religious reasons discriminate against women. Women who have less income than men usually cannot afford to buy a computer, for a use at home, or to get connected with Internet.

As a result, many women stay digital illiterate, compared to men who may have access through their jobs or public places such as schools, universities, Internet cafes and community centres. These places are in general less accessible to women who lack basic and higher education and who for cultural and religious reasons have less access to public places. In a more realistic approach to factors that constrain women's use of ICTs, it can be remarked that women are less likely than men to own communication assets like radio, mobile phones, etc; in poor households they do not have the income to use public (ICTs) facilities; information centres maybe located in places that women are not comfortable visiting or have difficulty travelling to.

Cyber cafés, for instance, often have a predominantly male customer base and tend not to provide a separate space for women and may not be open at times convenient for women who have heavy domestic responsibilities. Women usually face lack of training, lack of access, the high costs of equipment and connection as well and software and hardware applications and designs do not normally reflect women's needs (Gurumurthy 2004, Arun and Arun 2002; Hafkin 2000; Mitter 2005; Prasar 2003; Hafkin & Huyer, 2006; Hafkin & Taggart, 2001; Mitter & Sen 2000).

Education and skills

Sophia Huyer (2003), in a few words, includes and describes the main problem women face in the digital age: *"Women and girls are poorly placed to benefit from the knowledge society because they have less access to scientific and technical education specifically, and to education in general."*

Access to education continues to be a greater barrier for women than men. As estimated, two thirds of the world's literate people are women (UNESCO, 2009). Even as computer education promises to alter gender relations, women are concentrated lower rank jobs, like data entry operators while men are placed in jobs of high skill end like networking. This is mainly due to two reasons: 1) Women face greater barriers than men in receiving education and training that equips them with computer literacy, English literacy(the dominating language on the Internet), and business skills (Mitter, 2004); and 2) They often settle for less demanding jobs because of domestic responsibilities (Arun & Arun, 2002). Women are also less likely than men to know the international languages that dominate the web. Given their limited access to schooling, women, especially those in rural areas, are also much less likely than men to have computer skills. There are clear correlations between family income, racial background, educational levels and ICT use. Family income shows an important correlation with ICT use and adoption, but racial background and especially educational attainment are much stronger indicators (Stewart et al, 2004). These problems are particularly acute for women, and when women do have access to ICTs, they can substantially improve their lives and increase their income (Huyer, 2005).

Education in science and technology is considered a male domain in many cultures (OECD, 2009: 44). Training in ICT skills is rarely gender sensitive or tailored to women's needs (Melhem et al., 2009) and is sometimes delivered by a mail trainer who has embedded perceptions about women's capabilities inconsistent with a research-based understanding of women's competencies and contributions in these fields (Kennedy et al, 2003; Spender, 1997; Tannen, 1994; Kramarae and Taylor, 1993).

The rapid changes in ICT sector create a continuous need for upgrading skills; but women are at a disadvantaged position to follow this procedure given their multiple roles in work, family and community and the cultural bias that tends to value an investment in men's education before women's (Melhem et al., 2009; Gurumurthy, 2004; Tandon, 2008).

Social and Cultural Issues

Silvera (2000) verifies that many researches document the fact that parents who present for a child the point of contact with the world on the base of traditional gender stereotypes and perceptions make sure of the familiarization with new technological products for boys but not for girls, by spending double amounts of money for boys than girls on computers. Part of the reason girls may not have access to a computer at home is because the computer is typically placed in the boy's bedroom instead of being placed in an open family area (Verbick, 2002; Margolis and Fischer, 2003:22).

Other researches in the school area show that teachers' and even boys' attitudes in the classroom tend directly and indirectly to exclude girls from equal access to computers and consequently to undermine girl's access to opportunities in the emerging knowledge and information society and also diminish the potential of ICTs to be an effective tool for the promotion of gender equality (Hartman, 1986, 1987). When a woman reaches the psychological stage of gender constancy, she will incorporate society's ideas of computers as boy-toys, not girl-toys, into her own self concept of what it means for her to be a girl (Cooper and Weaver, 2003). Margolis and Fisher (2003:80) claim that lack of exposure to information technology at a young age can lead to an erosion of confidence, which in turn leads to an increased attrition rate among young women in the ICTs field.

Computers and Internet skills have the potential of creating an impact on the women; but they are faced with barriers that need to be negotiated. The experience of the e-Homemakers portal in Malaysia has exhibited that lack of finances; knowledge and social support prevent women from using ICT in becoming home-based entrepreneurs for economic self-reliance (Krishnan & Puvaneswary, 2005). On the other hand tele working erases cultural issues as women who work isolated at home are excluded from selected career trajectories where "in office" time is critical or mobility is essential (Melhem et al., 2009).

Another aspect that Cooper and Weaver (2003) put forth for discussion is the situation of being a member of a minority. The two writers explain that wealth and socioeconomic status have frequently made education and employment opportunities more accessible to some than others. Unequal distribution of wealth, even in the public sector, has created schools that are unequal in facilities, staff and, in the end, academic performance of their students. The unbalanced relationship between race and socioeconomic status bears prime responsibility for the lower academic performance of traditionally under presented minorities. The cycle perpetuates itself as under presented minorities are in a disadvantaged position to compete for the higher paying technology jobs of today's and tomorrow's workplaces. The same writers mention the reality of stereotype threat. Stereotype threat is not unique to computer skills. It exists any time there is a negative stereotype threat about a group, and a group member has the expectation of being judged by that stereotype. This threat is more commonly encountered among members of a minority who usually exhibit multiple identities.

Financial resources

Almost all communication facilities cost money. Generally in developing countries and commonly in traditional societies, men manage the money of the family income, decide how the income is spent and women who may contribute materially to the household lack of money usually or depend on their husbands. Thus, women living in an environment under these structures cannot afford to own radios and televisions or to access them when they want to, in the case of household possession of the technology. Lack of money and social also constrain women visiting cybercafés, especially in rural areas

Content on the Internet

Much of the content on the Internet has not been developed to address the needs of women and girls in developing and developed countries nor is it available in the language they speak. Lack of useful content for and by women is a major barrier to use information technology. Digital technology has also been used for harassment and sexual exploitation of women and girls in the form of pornography, trafficking and predatory e-mail (Melhem et al, 2009). Regrettably, increasing graphic pornography is easily available to all who seek it and even to those who do not.

As Hafkin (2003b) explains, little Internet content is available that meets the information needs of women in developing countries in a form they can use. The amount of content in local languages, which women tend to use exclusively more than men, is miniscule. As Arend (2002) comments, technology, like science, is seen as deeply implicated in the masculine project of the domination and control of women and nature.

Industry and Labour

Patterns of work in the ICT industry are highly gendered. Women are found in disproportionately high numbers in lowest paid and least secure jobs. Few are found at higher levels, particularly in hardware and software engineering and at management levels. Men continue to crowd out women in training required for high skilled work (Hafkin, 2003a). Wajcman (1991:20) points out that women's alienation from technology is accounted for in terms of the historical and cultural construction of technology as masculine. Thus, technology from its origins reflects male power as well as capitalist domination.

Lack of statistics

Huyer and Mitter (2003) explain that good global figures on women's use of the Internet do not exist. Most government statistics agencies do not provide a breakdown by gender; so globally comparable and consistent data are not yet available. Furthermore, Michael Minges (2003), an expert on gender and ICT data, claims that traditional ICT statistics are either provided by telecommunication organizations (i.e. telephone companies), or estimates are based on shipment of, for example, personal computers. He also explains that lack of disaggregated data is a result of the failure of many government organizations to collect national ICT statistics.

However, we do know that women's access to and use of ICTs is much lower than men's around the world; several recent project reviews indicate that women continue to benefit less than men from the implementation of ICTs (Thioune, 2003; Rathegeber, 2002; and Hafkin and Huyer, 2003). Much like the digital divide, a statistical divide exists where the need is greatest; that is in developing nations (Huyer et al., 2005). Collection of sex-disaggregated statistics is more developed in rich countries than in poor countries. Critical areas for the collection of sex-disaggregated statistics and development of gender-specific indicators are access data, content of sites they use on the Internet, employment, education, gender issue in ICT policy, participation in telecommunications and ICT decision making, impact of ICT projects on women (Hafkin, 2006:49).

Power and decision making

Women are underrepresented in virtually all ICT decision making structures, including policy and regulatory institutions, ministries responsible for ICT, board and senior management of ICT companies. ICT decision making is generally treated as a purely technical area, where civil society viewpoints are given little or no space (Hafkin, 2003b). Even if women do have access to basic education, few women pursue careers in ICTs professions, a phenomenon probably based on employers' sexist stereotypical prejudices, i.e. women are incapable of managing or of rational thought or even on economical business criteria, i.e. women leaving for pregnancy (Vitsilaki, 2004).

Ramilo, Hafkin, and Jorge (2005) note that in developing countries fewer women have information technology skills than men and the number decreases as the skills level rises; women have less access to the technology itself and fewer opportunities to learn how to use it; women receive far fewer of the business benefits of the technology as they are generally distributed without equal opportunity policies; women are absent from the decision making positions in fields of information technology in developing countries.

In short, women's lower socio economic status, lack of technical skills training, literacy, autonomy, low levels of employment, all have added to the digital divide for women.

2.5 Empowerment of Women

Empowerment is a notoriously contentious concept. According to the Oxford English Dictionary, the English term "empowerment" originated in the second half of the 17th century; but it only gained wide spread currency in the 1960s, linked to North American Black radicalism. In the 1980s the term was adopted by Non Governmental Oranizations in both the South and the North to signify an alternative development agenda for poverty alleviation based on principles of participation and self-help. In the 1980s neo-liberal politicians also adopted the term empowerment to underline a commitment to increasing individual choice and self-help on the context of market reform (Mayoux, 2005).

Empowerment is fundamentally a motivational process of an individual's experience of feeling enabled (Corsun & Enz, 1999). It refers to enabling people to take charge of their own lives. Women's empowerment is defined as a multidimensional process of civil, political, social, economic, and cultural participation and rights. Women's empowerment is conceptualised in terms of the achievement of basic capabilities, of legal rights, and of participation in key social, economic, and political domains (Moghadam and Senftova 2005). For women, empowerment emphasizes the importance of increasing their power and taking control over decisions and issues that shape their lives, including in relation to access to resources, participation in decision making and control over distribution of benefits (UN, 2005). Women's empowerment addresses power and relationships in society intertwined with gender, class, race, ethnicity, age, culture and history. Power is identified with equity and equality for women and men in access to resources, participation in decision making and control over distribution of resources and benefits. Gender equality is the condition of *fairness and equality of opportunity* whereby gender is no longer a basis for discrimination and inequality among people. The Gender Empowerment Measure (GEM) is even more specific and ranks countries by women's access to political power and economic resources through measures such as the female share of parliamentary seats, women's share of managerial and administrative jobs, the female share of professional and technical workers, and women's GDP per capita, or share of earned income (Lister 1997, Moghadam 2003).

Access to resources refers to both the means and the right to obtain services, products or commodities. Gender gaps in access to resources and services are a major obstacle in women's development. The process of empowerment includes mobilizing women to eliminate these gaps, the process through which women who are currently most discriminated against achieve gender equity. This will include support for men to change aspects of their behavior, roles and privileges which currently discriminate against women. The extent of current disadvantage and inequality means that women's empowerment may require support from development agencies at household, community and macro levels (Mayoux, 2005).

Mayoux (2005), in her article "Gender and Empowerment Concepts", describes the term empowerment with several frameworks. Under the Longwe (1989, 1991) in Mayoux (2005) framework, there are five levels which as a circular progression make women achieve increased control, lead them to better access to resources, and therefore improved socio-economic status. Women's empowerment is a progression through 1) welfare: the level of material welfare of women, relative to men in such matters as food supply, income and medical care; 2) access: women's access to the factors of production as land, labour, credit, training, marketing facilities and all publicly available services and benefits on an equal basis with men; 3) conscientisation: the understanding of differences between sex roles and gender roles, and that the latter are cultural and can be changed; 4) participation: women's equal participation in the decision-making process, policymaking, planning and administration; 5) equality of control: over the factors of production and the distribution of benefits so that neither men nor women are in a position of dominance.

Rowlands (1995) in Mayoux (2005), puts in the framework of empowerment four dimensions: 1) power from within: individual changes in confidence and consciousness; 2) power to: increase in skills, abilities including earning an income, access to markets and networks; 3) power over: changes in power relations within households, communities and at macro-level; 4) power with: organisation of the powerless to enhance individual abilities and\or ability to challenge and change power relations.

Kabeer (2003) in Mayoux (2005), describes empowerment with two concepts 1) dimensions: resources (conditions), agency (process), achievements (outcomes); 2) levels: deeper levels-structural relations of class/caste/gender, intermediate levels-institutional rules and resources, immediate levels- individual resources, agency and achievements.

Schuler, Hashemi and Riley (1997) use eight indicators, each including a variety of specific actions or items: freedom of mobility, ability of making small purchases, ability of making larger purchases, involvement in major household decisions, relative freedom from domination by the family, political and legal awareness involvement in political campaigning and protests, economic security and contribution to family support.

Chen's (1997), in Mayoux (2005), empowerment framework includes 1) material change (income, resources, basic needs, earning capacity); 2) perceptual change (self-esteem, self-confidence, vision of future, visibility and respect); 3) relational change (decision-making, bargaining power, participation, self-reliance, organisational strength).

Malhotra, Schuler and Boender (2002) remark that they hold several concepts in common: options, choice, control and power. These pertain to women's ability to make decisions and affect events and circumstances around them; benefit from resources and opportunities; change from a condition of disempowerment; exercise control over decision making, all with the result of increasing or achieving autonomy and improving health and well-being.

In her article "Understanding gender equality and women's empowerment in the Knowledge Society", Huyer (2006), in answer to the question how we know when empowerment is achieved and how we measure or assess it, states that main targets or indicators are generally used (Malhotra, Schuler and Boender 2002; Lopez- Claros and Zahidi, 2005). These targets or indicators are presented under two main categories: 1)Socio economic empowerment (economic empowerment, socio-cultural empowerment, familial/personal empowerment, psychological empowerment, education) 2)political empowerment.

2.6 Empowerment of Women and ICT

We are in the beginning of the twenty-first century and this moment mirrors new faces for women: promotion of their empowerment through ICTs for a more gendered world and active participation in the knowledge society.

The potential of ICT as a tool for widening access to information is well recognized (Huyer & Carr, 2002). The research has clarified its impact on enhancing individual's capacities in the area of education, income generation, health care delivery, distance education, improving rural productivity through access to market information and access to finance, promoting empowerment and participation in national and international policy processes, improving service delivery by governments, improving environmental monitoring and response systems, and facilitating environmental activism (Hafkin, 2002; Mitter, 2003; Huyer and Mitter, 2003). Still others have highlighted personal (self confidence) and social gains (status, increased connectivity) that come from ICT; according to United Nations, ICTs are ranked as the third-most important issue facing women after poverty and violence (Hafkin & Taggart, 2001; Umrani & Ghadially, 2003).

Information and communication technologies hold great potential for economic, political and social empowerment of women, and promotion of gender equality; but that potential will only be realised if the gender dimensions of the information society. Unless gender issues are straightened out into technology analyses, policy development and programme design, can women and men equally benefit from ICTs and their applications (GEM project).

Bhatnagar (2006) presents ICTs as the new options in education: e-learning, distance learning, learner-centeredness, peer to peer exchanges, etc. E-learning enables those who have access to the equipment to obtain global culture and education by overcoming the separation between educators and learners. ICTs can function as portals for life long learning, providing chances to obtain new skills and new possibilities of work. As individuals have more freedom and greater possibilities for self-realization, it paves the way for their empowerment.

Nath (2001) believes that distance education through internet and television broadcasts opens up avenues for women to continue with their education at their own pace and from the confines of their homes even after having discontinued it due to family or social responsibilities. Learning and training continues throughout women's lives as new skills and competencies gain value, and this ensures that avenues for women to expand their roles from household economy to a wider market economy remain open.

The Internet is abolishing race, class, gender and even age, which have been factors through centuries for oppression. The invisibility of the physical characteristics of the person who participates in cyberspace groups, such as women and minorities, can be secured as they can cross the barriers that they usually confront (Leggon, 2006). Due to the unsuitable environment and patriarch structures of their societies, many Muslim women have a restricted life. Usually girls are prohibited to enter universities although they secure high marks. Even talented and educated Muslim women lack opportunities. The net is providing a non-corporate, gender-neutral environment that is a big lure, especially in cultures where women have education but lack opportunity. The net has also opened up new avenues for higher education. There are virtual universities offering courses at both graduate and postgraduate levels. Recent statistics show that typical online learners are between the ages of 17 and 57. Approximately 52 per cent of these students are females.

Muslim women through Internet search and find well qualified and experienced female doctors. Muslim women in particular are coming together on the Internet and creating a cyber-sisterhood unimaginable some years ago. Many of these women need a neutral place to go for support and basic information. Women from all over the world are able through Internet to provide one another with encouragement and resources in areas as diverse as infertility, wearing the face veil with confidence and finding the best Islamic websites for children. It can be said that cyberspace is a zone where there is no distinction between the veiled and the unveiled since the computer itself acts as a form of veil. The cyber veil is a reality that stands as a step for them to act as cyber feminists giving them the chances lost for the old generations, to gain their emancipation, psychological uplift and personal content.

In this vein, we will present several examples of the Muslim world that concern options of empowerment of Muslim women through ICT education as these women are doubly disadvantaged facing an additional gender barrier (Hasan and Menon, 2004 in Khan and Ghadially, 2010).

2.7 Muslim Women's Empowerment through ICTs

2.7.1 Economic Empowerment

In **Malaysia,** the e-Homemakers portal, (APC News a), a web-site programme is set up attempting to provide management skills to run a home business. It contains valuable information as to how to come up with a business plan or registration requirements with the government; it features ICTs tips and home-based profiles of the 400 home-based businesses that work in fields as diverse as landscaping, accounting, translation cooking, ICTs training, research and advocacy. A marketing website called Just Marketing is developed to promote the services and products these women generate.

Putting ICTs in the Hands of the Poor project (APC News a) is developed by the Seelampur Community ICTs Centre in **India**, the Datamation Foundation

Charitable Trust and the UNESCO inside the Babul-Uloom-Madrasa, an Orthodox Muslim religious school, with the help of a prominent "Ulema", religious leader, for the women of the Muslim minority of Seelampur who live in extreme poverty, rarely venture out of their homes, and wear the burqa. It is designed to encourage livelihood skills among women through vocational CDs, providing computer skills training and developing linkages for marketing women's traditional arts and crafts products.

The International Labour Organisation in **Pakistan** identified that most females (50 % of Pakistan's total population while female labour participation rate is only 16 %) have no access to information of incentives and initiatives introduced by private sector or government bodies for business development, nor have any proper knowledge regarding the roles of various organizations. To bridge this information gap through ready access to information, export markets and increased networking opportunities, the small and medium enterprise development authority launched Pakistan's first exclusive women entrepreneurs web portal (www.win. org.pk) improving the bargaining power of women.

In **Mubai, India,** the city of 15.000.000 inhabitants, which generates the 40 % of India's GNP, four of the five National Councils for Promotion of Urdu Language (NCPUL) centres are located in Muslim concentrated areas. Half of their students are girls, a fact that challenges society's stereotype of Muslim women. Young women in Mubai are eager to become computer skilled, pushed by their mothers whose work aspiration for their daughters is computer related. In the centres, the one-year course Diploma in Computer Applications and Multilingual DTP is designed to promote computer education at the grass root level of the Urdu speaking population; the Arabic-Urdu Calligraphy Training Scheme provides knowledge of the Urdu language giving them the chance to work on Urdu software (Ghadially and Umrani, 2004).

Rural women agricultural producers in **Senegal** were provided cell phones with Web Access Protocol, thereby extending their access to the Internet. This technology helped women obtain information about market prices of the inputs for their food processing activities and for the sale of their produce. Women in the project appreciated the economic benefits of the technology (UN, 2005b).

In two villages of **Morocco**, rural women, mostly illiterate, sell rugs and other textiles they weave on the Internet, and this provides a solution to the perennial problem of marketing their products. In addition, it allows them to keep a larger share of the final profit, which often instead goes to middle women/men. Selling textiles online (www.marrakeshexpress.org) gives these Moroccan women more control, influence, ownership over some areas of their lives, profit and even the ability to buy exactly what they want, and also make their own decisions in a group without their husbands' interference (Schaefer, 2004:53).

In **Bangladesh** the Pallitathya Help-Line project is based on an original communication system adapted to the needs of rural populations with scarce access to information about health, education, legal procedures or administrative hassles. Mobile Operator Ladies regularly visit remote villages and gather questions that villagers formulate. After finding the information, they return to the communities for another round of consultations. The women who use the Help-Line gain tremendously from the experience since they increase their self-esteem by using this service and eventually even increase their authority over spending decisions (APC News b).

2.7.2 Socio-Cultural Empowerment

As Wheeler (2006a) describes, in **Egypt** Internet users celebrate the ICTs tools ability to improve their English. Having knowledge of English and computer use promotes job placement and job status. Consequently, they are using the technology to network for better jobs. The Bayt.com and the CareerEgypt.com websites give them opportunities to improve their job prospects.

Besides the benefits women get by increasing their income, commendably is what Loh-Ludher (2007) states as *"Many of e-homemakers in **Malaysia** use part of their earning to beautify themselves and dress up for their husband, as their religion provokes an inner fear and a sense of insecurity from the fact that Islam allows a husband to have four wives"*.

The programme "Mothers for Mothers-(M4M)" in *Malaysia* is a network of single mothers from multi-ethnic communities in Malaysia involved in women's networking activities to promote the concept of working from home. The objective of the evaluation is to explore how women's family lives and home situations affect tele working. The M4M hopes to use the results of the evaluation to promote tele commuting to the Malaysian government as well as to convince companies to consider tele working and create virtual office environments for their employees (GEM project).

Niknejad (2005) argues that for young **Iranians** the Internet is the ultimate veil. The web sites www.HotIranians.com and www. Iranianpersonals.com, are dating portals where members post pictures of themselves and have site visitors rate them to set up dates. Postings originate even from the holy city of Mashhad, from near the Iraqi border in Ahwaz, or from the south-eastern province of Kerman, among other locations. Some of the women are tightly veiled, yet fishing for a compliment. The web sites www.Muslima.com or www.Qiran.com

are Muslim marriage and Muslim matrimonial sites that assist people to find a Muslim partner for friendship or marriage. In Iran the Iranian blog community, known as Weblogistan, was started by three young educated women in late 2001. *"Cyberspace is our social space of freedom. Here is a free city where we can express ourselves freely, and we can write whatever we like"* explains one of the women-bloggers. Estimates for 2006 rank Iran ninth in the world for the number of web logs; the Persian Web log Service Provider (WSP) reports hosting over 180.000 registered web logs, and the WSP Blogfa records traffic of over two million visitors a day (Hendelman-Baavur, 2007). The government of Iran tries to block web logs or servers by arresting some bloggers and on-line journalists. Fereshteg Ghazi, a young on-line journalist, who was held for over forty days in solitary confinement, later wrote on her blog, *"Our first sin was to open the window, the other to destroy the wall"* (Fereshteh, 2005).

The **Jordanian** experiment "Netcorp Jordan" helped build an ICT skilled workforce. As women constituted more than 60 % of the participants in Netcorp Jordan, they finally found themselves empowered by the program. Jordan has one of the lowest figures of women in the work force (21 %) in the Arab World. The program managed to encourage entrepreneurship, voluntarism and benefit of life skills in order to shape a better future for the participants. Especially, women demonstrated skill in training others in ICTs. The Net Corps Jordan program has repeatedly demonstrated that if one person is trained, this one person will educate many (Wheeler, 2006b).

2.7.3 Political Empowerment

VFH (The Voice for Humanity) distributed 41,000 solar-powered digital audio players, called Sada, half pink coloured to women and half silver coloured to men. The Sada content, produced in **Afghanistan** by Afghans, consisted of 15 hours of civics education material that promoted peace, national unity, democracy, civic engagement in the parliamentary election, human and women's rights and related rural development and health issues. Some of the results of the project were that women voted in the elections, women joined the work force (e.g. tailoring), women decided to educate their children, especially girls, they increased their decision making regarding marriage for girls (Sengupta et al., 2007).

When women students in **Bangladesh** faced administrative inaction in response to increasing instances of campus rape, they publicized their situation on the Internet. The resulting international and national response pressured the university administration to conduct an inquiry (Alauddin et al., 2006; Ahmed et al, 2006). At **Kuwait** a sit-in was organized in late July 2000 by Kuwait University students to protest the new gender law which would divide the campuses along gender lines. One of the leaders of the protest, a young woman, noted that the non-aligned student opposition movement intended to use the Internet to alert the world media and human rights organizations about their protest and about the ways in which the gender law violated women's rights in Kuwait (Wheeler 2001).

2.7.4 Empowerment of Women through Internet

Many of the women Wheeler (2001, 2006a) interviewed at **Kuwait, Jordan and Egypt** stated that surfing on the Internet gave them the opportunity to talk with members of the opposite sex because they did not generally have first-hand knowledge of how men think. That could improve communication and understanding between the sexes in marriage and the family. Internet has promoted open and free discussions and interactions with the opposite sex, both within and beyond their home countries.

The Permanent Arab Court to Resist Violence Against Women (Pan-Arab) has used the Internet (www.arabwomencourt.org) to voice women's testimonies on sexual violence from a personal issue into a public concern. Another goal is to exert pressure on the Arab government and NGOs to take measures to protect and support women victims of violence. In **Egypt** Arab Women's Solidarity Association (AWASA, www.awsa.net/profile.htm) participates in campaigns against honour killings. The Center for Egyptian Women's Legal Assistance (CELAW, www.cewla.org/en/index.htm) offers Egyptian women legal support and assistance regarding their rights under the Egyptian Constitution. One of its most important accomplishments has been to initiate legal help so that Egyptian women may obtain their legal papers, such as birth certificates, divorce or marriage papers and so on (Tadros, 2005).

The FATIMA Women's Network (www.fatima-network.com) in **UK** has improved the ability of Muslim women groups to enter and have a say on local issues affecting them. Training is provided in policy development, financial management and funding to equip women with the skills they need to influence decision making and public policy. Through the Internet Muslim women search and find well qualified and experienced female doctors. By access to medical information on the Internet and by posting their problem on the online community of doctors, they can complete their treatments with the assistance of their local female doctor.

The Muslim Women's National Network in **Australia** (www.mwnna.org.au) presents the views of Muslim women to Federal, State and Local Governments and to government agencies throughout Australia, holds information on workshops and seminars to inform Muslims and non-Muslims of religious and cultural issues; which affect Muslim women in Australia, sponsors English language classes for Muslim women and provides information on domestic violence against women. KARAMAH (www.karamah.org), in **USA**, is a charitable, educational, Muslim women lawyer organization that focuses on the domestic and global issues of human rights for Muslim women. The site provides information on the subject of domestic violence.

The Women's Net pilot training project in **Limpopo Province of South Africa** is an initial attempt at community-targeted ICT training with focus on gender awareness and empowerment of women through development. It is also aimed to foster collaboration between community radio stations, tele centres and women's and gender organisations in the community through training for community members, specifically women from small rural villages, on computer basics, email and internet basics; useful, self-identified skills, such as how to write a CV and how to create a pamphlet; training in starting a small business and training for tele centre staff and teachers in Mohodi on more advanced computer skills (GEM project).

A range of ICT models have been employed to support the empowerment of women all around the world. In Africa, groups like the **Africa Women's Network** of the Association for Progressive Communications (APCa) have conducted training workshops to support electronic networking among group of women. In **Uganda,** the Forum for Women in Democracy uses the Internet and the email to research issues for the country's women MPs, and Women's Net is a similar initiative in South Africa (World Bank, 2000). Knowledge networking catalyses the process of women's empowerment, through approaches elucidated in the subsequent paragraphs.

In **Bangladesh**, the Internet became a principal tool for advocacy and garnering support when women students from a university began a campaign against campus rape. Pressure that was exerted internationally and nationwide added to the massive physical protests by the students, forcing the establishment to conduct an enquiry (Alam et al, 2000). These processes open up a range of options for women to deviate from the conventional media for information transfer to those which offer a greater control over the information that they wish to broadcast to the global civil network in the least possible time. Women for the first time have realized that they may be isolated or barred from participation in processes within their immediate community; but that does not prevent them from communicating to the outside world (Nath, 2001).

Chapter 3: Methodology

3. Introduction and Overview

The purpose of this multi-case study is to explore the impact of technology adoption on the empowerment of Muslim minority women in Thrace. The study is carried out under three parts; each with a different set of objectives since the best way to understand what is going on in a community is to collect information using a variety of methods. The initial part is aimed at testing the Technology Acceptance Model and the Theory of Planned Behaviour to detect the psychological factors that contribute to women's behavioural intention to use the computer. The following part seeks to study empowerment flowing from computer access and use. The final part explores the view of key informants, distinguished members of the minority, on the subject of the research. The researcher realized that a better understanding of this phenomenon would allow the indication of fruitful choices and suggestions for the improvement of the status of these women with a justification of the fact that resilient communities can only exist where women are playing a full and active part. In pursuit of this phenomenon, the study addresses three research questions:

1. In which level does computer education and digital literacy contribute to Muslim minority women's empowerment and social participation?
2. Which are the behavioural intention-factors influencing Muslim minority women's computer usage?
3. In which ways do stake holders of the Muslim minority contribute to Muslim minority women's digital literacy?

3.1 Methodology and Discussions

This chapter describes the research methodology of the study and includes discussions with regard to the following areas culminating with a brief concluding summary:

- rationale for the quantitative, structured interview, questionnaire approach and the qualitative, semi-structured, face-to-face, interview approach
- description of the research sample
- overview of information needed
- overview of research design methods of data collection
- definition of variables

- hypotheses
- tools used for collecting data
- the pilot study
- coding data
- analysis and synthesis of data
- ethical considerations
- issues of trustworthiness
- limitations of the study.

3.2 Rationale for Quantitative and Qualitative Research Designs

The initial data detecting whether Muslim minority women in Thrace used the computer was collected from 32 women of the minority for the study presented in Chapter I. While considering and designing our next step, trying to find out whether Muslim minority women would achieve their social empowerment through computer education, we thought that we should first detect what factors could influence these women to learn how to use the computers.

Hence, a quantitative method (questionnaire) is adopted in this initial part as this research strategy entails a deductive approach to the relationship between theory and research in which stress is placed on testing theories; incorporates practices and norms of natural scientific models, positivism in particular; and embodies a view of social reality as an external, objective reality (Bryman, 2004).

In the succeeding parts of the study, a qualitative method (structured, face-to-face, in-depth phenomenological interviewing) is adopted as in this phase of the research extraction of rich data becomes necessary to address the proposed research purposes. The qualitative method suits this study with regard to the following reasons: 1) It understands the processes by which events and actions take place, 2) It develops contextual understanding, 3) It facilitates interactivity between researcher and participants, 4) it adopts an interpretive stance, 5) It maintains the flexibility of the design. The purpose of phenomenological research is to investigate the meaning of the lived experience of people to identify the core essence of human experience as described by research participants (Bloomberg and Volpe, 2008:11).

3.3 Sample

As for sampling in this study a non probability sampling procedure is employed. The sample size at each part of the study is varied. The description of the sample characteristics is arranged in terms of the part depending on the study. Although the non probability sampling is not recommended for quantitative analysis, the fact that the population targeted for the research was not over used for such procedures made the collection of data valuable. Some of the special social characteristics of the population in research were also the determining factors for the sampling employed.

3.3.1 Women in Quantitative Research

The group of research population in Thrace is composed approximately of 25.000–30.000 adult women. The sample size of the first group population was drawn from the sample size estimation formula of Yamane (1973), which compromises the sample size for over 100.000 population to be 400 samples. Paraskevopoulos (1993:49) in addition states that in researches where Pearson's correlation coefficients are detected, means and percentages are compared, x^2-tests and t-tests are calculated, the number of at least 100 participants is a good starting point. The sampling frame is organized and identified for the purpose of the study according to their residence area and age, which form sampling strata.

In accordance with the above, data was collected from 137 women of the Muslim minority, all Greek nationals, of different ages, living in the prefectures of Rodopi and Xanthi, in the towns of Komotini and Xanthi, in villages, with the criteria of having a computer at home, at work or being familiar with ICTs. To reach as many potential participants as possible, a type of "snowball" sampling technique was also employed after deciding on the categories of people to be interviewed within each category. The sample size was determined finally by the social limits set by the life structure of the Muslim minority, by the will of the women to participate in the research and by the aim to produce a sample that reflects a population in terms of the relative proportions of women in different categories with various social characteristics that shape the image of the minority. After the preparation of the questionnaire and the changes indicated by the pilot study, the initial part was developed from 10 February 2009 to 15 April 2009.

3.3.2 Women in Qualitative Research

A purposeful sampling procedure is used to select the sample of the interviews. As Patton (1987) claims, in qualitative research the selection of the research sample is purposeful; and the logic of this kind of sampling lies in selecting **information-rich cases** with the objective of yielding insight and understanding of the phenomenon under investigation. Information-rich cases are those from which one can learn a great deal about issues of central importance to the purpose of evaluation, thus the term purposeful sampling. Bloomberg and Volpe (2008:69) add to the above that in qualitative research the researcher's intent is to describe a particular context in depth, not to generalize to another context or population. Representative ness in qualitative research is secondary to the participant's ability to provide information about themselves and their setting. The strategy for purposeful sampling is that of criterion sampling.

Furthermore, Patton (1987) argues that criterion sampling can add an important role to qualitative component, to a management information system or an on going program monitoring system. Criterion sampling can also be applied to identify cases from quantitative questionnaires. Consequently, 28 women out of the 137 who took part in the quantitative part of the research were chosen to be interviewed as they gave indications for prosperous interviews. Of the 28 women interview participants, 15 live at the Rodopi administration, 13 at the Xanthi administration, 13 in villages and 15 in towns. The interviews took place from February to April, 2009.

While interviewing the women we had to face several reactions by their side and as for this, we tried to invent different ways to approach them (Georgiadou and Kekkeris, 2010). Some of the women participants felt better to correspond in a group; any photo of them was denied; and some felt reluctant to speak. Participants said that the occasion of their interview was the first time they were asked to talk about their lives, that they really appreciated being listened to and that the interview procedure was an important experience for them.

3.3.3 Key Informants

The individuals in this part of the research were selected with the contribution of the secretary of one of the minority deputies in the Greek Parliament. Some of the key informants also identified other individuals to be interviewed. Key informants included 30 individuals. The size of the sample was figured out under the anxiety of approaching in a short time a big number of people considered to be in leading positions inside the minority. In order to be as descriptive as possible, we tried to contact a sample that was representative and reflected the wide range in the larger population under study.

Although interviewers who propose to explore their topic by arranging a one-shot meeting with an interviewee whom they have never met tread on thin contextual ice as Locke et al. (2006) claim in Seidman (2006:17–18), we did not attempt to contact a series of three separate interviews with the key informants as this would have been very difficult and disturbing for members of a minority who suffered kinds of discriminations all the past years and lived under a regime of suspiciousness and discredit from members of the majority.

Having gained access to potential participants of the key informants, approached in the way described above, the author called to each key informant and arranged to meet at a place and time that was convenient to them, private, and familiar. The project was initially explained to them in order to build interviewing relationships according to Seidman's (2006:46) suggestion on making contact. The nature of the study was presented as broad in context as possible and what was expected of the participants was also explained to them. The extent to which the researcher might use the material from the interview was clarified to them.

The key informants' interviews for our study were conducted from August 2008 through December 2008, with individuals who had leadership and eminent roles inside the life of the minority in Thrace and were the key stakeholders for changes and innovations that could be implemented. Their perspectives are important as they act as filters of the minority to the policies implemented by the Greek government. Three of the interviews took place in cafés where it seemed convenient; but the noise and the lack of privacy heard in the tape recorder undermined the effectiveness of such a place for interviews; one in the clubhouse of their Youth association; all the others in the informants' work areas, offices or homes, which obviously assisted in our understanding of their thoughts relative to the subject of our thesis. Duration of the interviews ranged to an average of 45 minutes and all were conducted by the author face-to-face.

3.4 Overview of Information Needed

This study focused on 137 women for filling questionnaires, 28 women for interviews and 30 key informants for in depth interviews. To understand how computer education would contribute to Muslim minority women's empowerment three research questions were set up to gather information needed. To answer the following questions the conceptual framework determined for this fell into three categories: 1) demographic, 2) perceptual and 3) theoretical. This information included the following points:

- Information for participants' demographics on their age, gender, residence area, studies, use of languages, profession,
- Perceptions of women and key informants regarding the connection of ICTs to the social empowerment of women and their contribution to this,
- Review of the literature providing the theoretical grounding of the study.

3.5 Research Design Overview

The followings summarize the steps used to carry out this research.

1. A selected review of literature was contacted to study the contributions of other researchers and writers on the subject of women's empowerment through computer education
2. A "gate keeper" of the minority had to be approached to start the survey for receiving an approval for the questions to be asked. After three pilot studies for the three parts of the survey respectively, changes were made to the initially designed questionnaires and interviews
3. Potential research participants were approached by telephone or face to face conversation or with the snowballing method and appointments were made with those who agreed to participate
4. Semi structured, in depth-interviews were conducted with 28 women and 30 key informants in the Prefectures of Rodopi and Xanthi, and 137 question-naires were filled by women of the minority
5. Data gathered was finally analyzed.

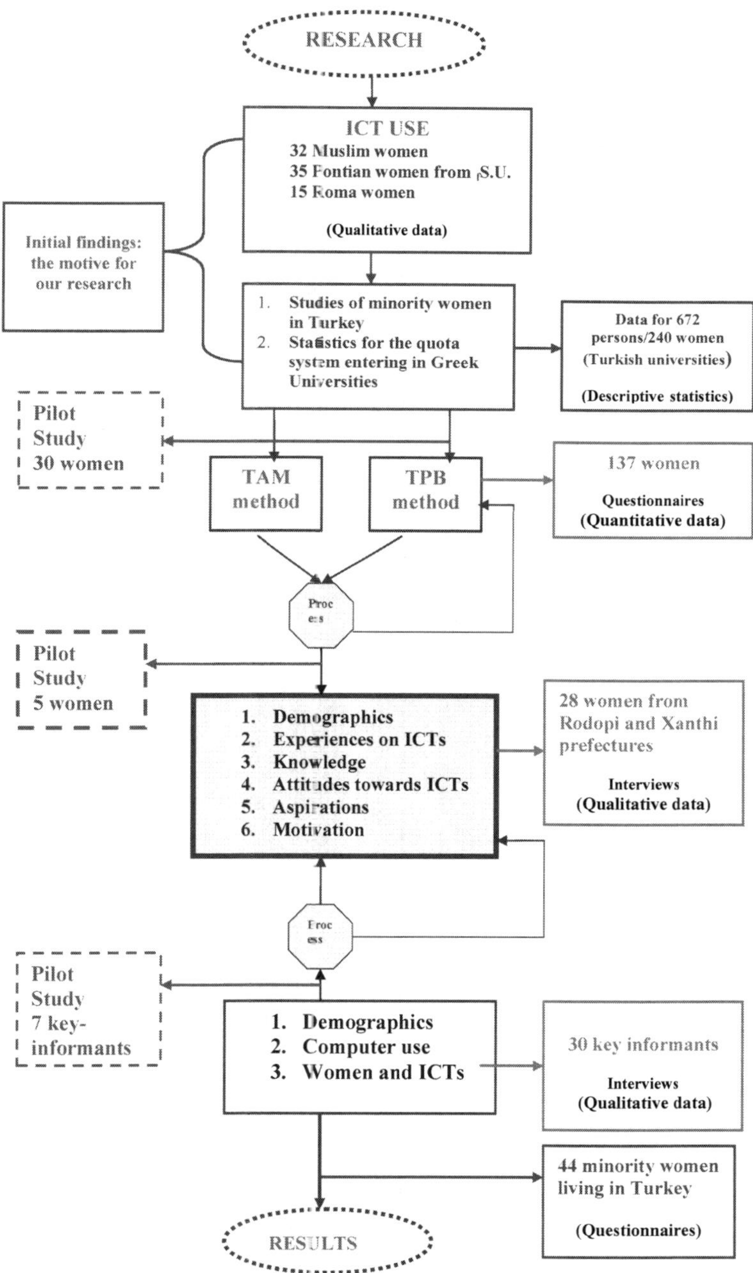

RESEARCH
ICT USE
32 Muslim women
35 Pontian women from S.U.
15 Roma women
(Qualitative data)
Initial findings: the motive for our research
1. Studies of minority women in Turkey
2. Statistics for the quota system entering in Greek Universities
Data for 672 persons/240 women (Turkish universities)
(Descriptive statistics)
Pilot Study 30 women
TAM method
TPB method
137 women
Questionnaires
(Quantitative data)
Process
Pilot Study 5 women
1. Demographics
2. Experiences on ICTs
3. Knowledge
4. Attitudes towards ICTs
5. Aspirations
6. Motivation
28 women from Rodopi and Xanthi prefectures
Interviews
(Qualitative data)
Process
Pilot Study 7 key-informants
1. Demographics
2. Computer use
3. Women and ICTs
30 key informants
Interviews
(Qualitative data)
44 minority women living in Turkey
(Questionnaires)
RESULTS

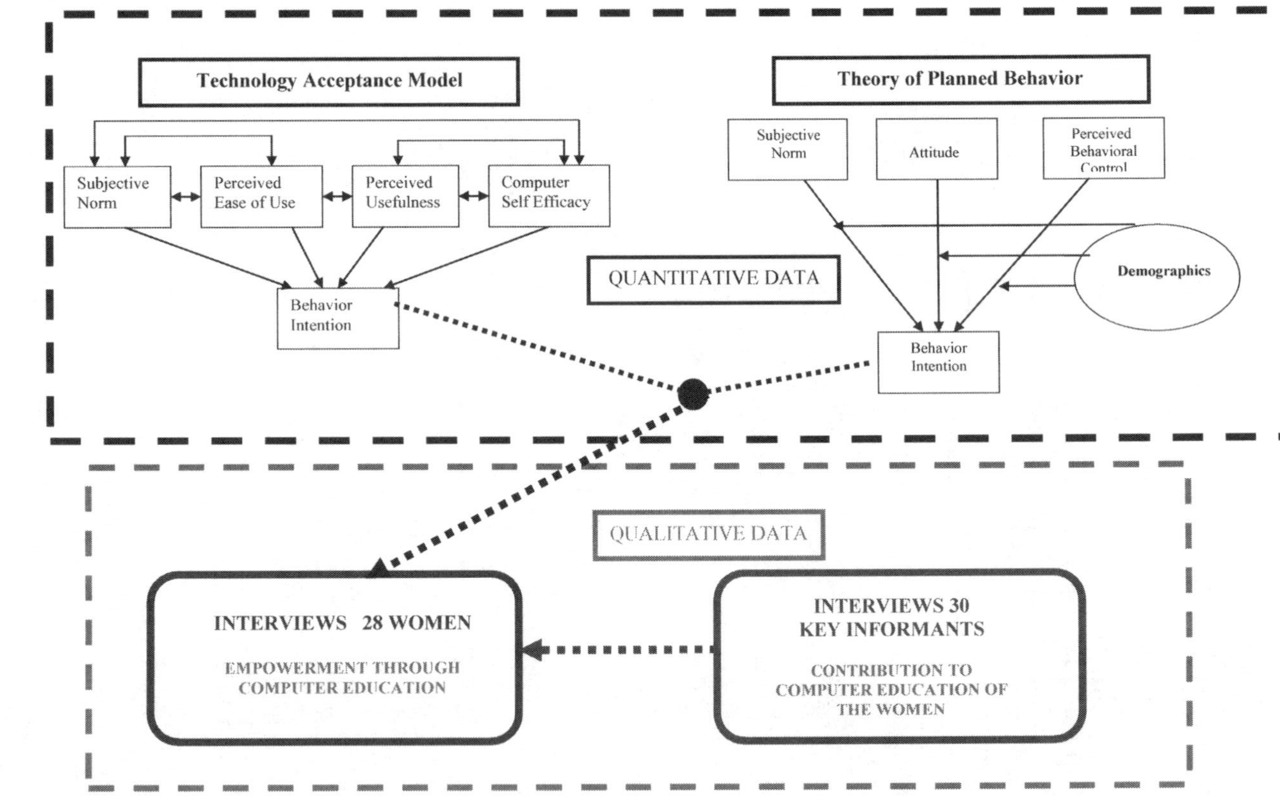

Technology Acceptance Model
Subjective Norm
Perceived Ease of Use
Perceived Usefulness
Computer Self Efficacy
Behavior Intention
Theory of Planned Behavior
Subjective Norm
Attitude
Perceived Behavioral Control
Demographics
Behavior Intention
QUANTITATIVE DATA
QUALITATIVE DATA
INTERVIEWS 28 WOMEN
EMPOWERMENT THROUGH COMPUTER EDUCATION
INTERVIEWS 30 KEY INFORMANTS
CONTRIBUTION TO COMPUTER EDUCATION OF THE WOMEN

3.6 Data Collection Methods

3.6.1 Models Measuring Behaviour

Researchers and practitioners have studied for many years determinants of technology acceptance and adoption (Pfeffer, 1982; Chaffe, 1985; King, 1990; Keil, 1991; Slappendel, 1996).

The **Theory of Reasoned Action** (TRA) (Fig. 3.1) is initially developed to measure attitudes in determining behaviour. It is a widely studied model from social psychology, proposed by Fishbein and Ajzen (1975) which elaborates on the determinants of consciously intended behaviours that are under volitional control of the individual. The two basic determinants identified by the theory are attitude and subjective norm (Fishbein & Ajzen, 1975, 1977 cited by Malhotra and Galetta, 1999). According to TRA, a person's performance of a specified behaviour is determined by his or her behavioural intention (BI) to perform the behaviour. The beliefs someone has about an object lead to attitudes towards it and that, in turn, leads to behavioural intentions regarding the object. Behavioural intention (BI) is jointly determined by the person's attitude (AT) and subjective norm (SN) (Umrani, 2003).

Figure 3.1: Theory of Reasoned Action (TRA) (Fishbein and Ajzen, 1975)

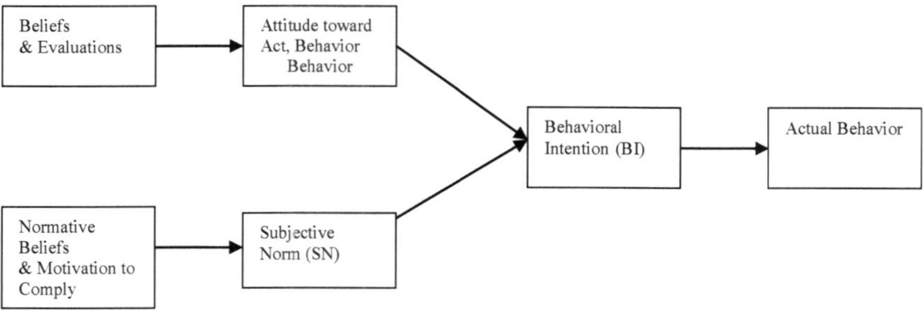

The **Theory of Planned Behaviour** (Ajzen, 1985) (Fig 3.2) is a modified version of **TRA** and designed to predict behaviours in which individuals have incomplete volitional control. The **Theory of Planned Behaviour** (TPB) includes an additional concept of perceived behavioural control; a function of two factors, namely, control beliefs and perceived facilitation. According to the theory, human behaviour is guided by three kinds of considerations: beliefs about the likely outcomes of the behaviour and the evaluations of these outcomes (behavioural beliefs); beliefs about the normative expectations of others and motivations to comply with these which impede performance of the behaviour; (normative beliefs) and the beliefs about the perceived power of these factors (control beliefs). Behavioural beliefs produce a favourable or unfavourable attitude toward the behaviour; normative beliefs result in perceived social pressure or subjective norm; and control beliefs give rise to perceived behavioural control. In combination, attitude toward behaviour, subjective norm, and perception of behavioural control lead to the formation of a behavioural intention (Ajzen, 2006). **TPB** asserts that behaviour, in this case technology usage is a direct function of intention to use that technology, and that the intention to use the technology is jointly influenced by one's attitude, subjective norm, and perceived behavioural control. Recent meta-analyses suggest that **TPB** explains about 41–50 percent of variance in intention, and 28–34 percent of the variance in behaviour with non-IT applications (Baker, 2007).

Figure 3.2: Theory of Planned Behaviour (TPB) (Ajzen, 1985)

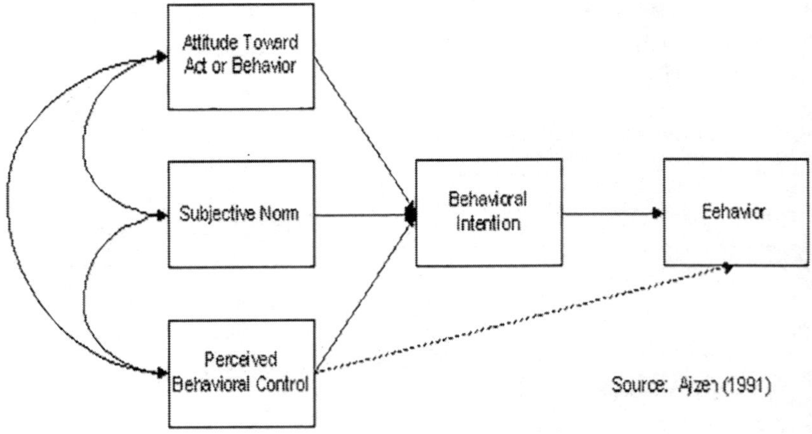

The **Technology Acceptance Model (TAM)** (Fig.3.3) is developed by Davis (1989) to explain the user's acceptance of information systems and the computer-usage behaviour. The goal of **TAM** is to provide an explanation of the determinants of computer acceptance that in general being capable of explaining user behaviour across a broad range of end-user computing technologies and user populations while at the same time being both parsimonious and theoretically justified (Davis et al, 1989). **TAM** uses TRA as a theoretical basis for specifying causal linkages between two key sets of constructs: (1) perceived usefulness (PU) and perceived ease of use (PEOU), and (2) user's attitude (AT), behavioural intentions (BI), and actual computer usage behaviour (ACU) (Malhotra and Galetta, 1999). As demonstrated in the **Theory of Reasoned Action**, the **Technology Acceptance Model** postulates that the use of an information system is determined by the behavioural intention; but on the other hand, it asserts that the behavioural intention is determined by the person's attitude towards the use of the system and also by his perception of its utility.

Davis claims that the attitude of an individual is not the only factor that determines his use of a system but is also based on the impact which it may have on his performance. Therefore, even if an employee does not welcome an information system, the probability that he will use it is high if he perceives that the system will improve his performance at work. Besides, the **Technology Acceptance Model** hypothesizes a direct link between perceived usefulness and perceived ease of use. With the two systems offering the same features, a user will find more useful the one that he finds easier to use.

Figure 3.3: Technology Acceptance Model (TAM) (Davis, 1986, 1989)

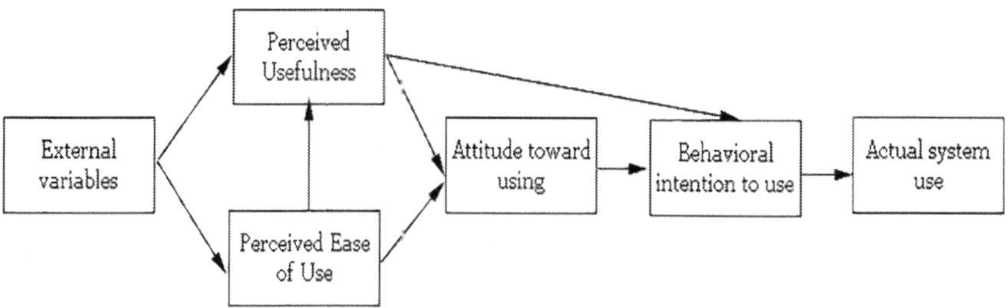

Another **TAM** method, **TAM II**, introduced by Venkatesh and Davis (2000) (Fig 3.4) and Venkatesh (2000), synthesizes the previous efforts and reflects the previous requests for the elaboration of the model. It clearly defines the external variables of PU(Perceived Usefulness) and PEOU (Perceived Ease of Use) and provides a concrete means to advance the multi-level model.

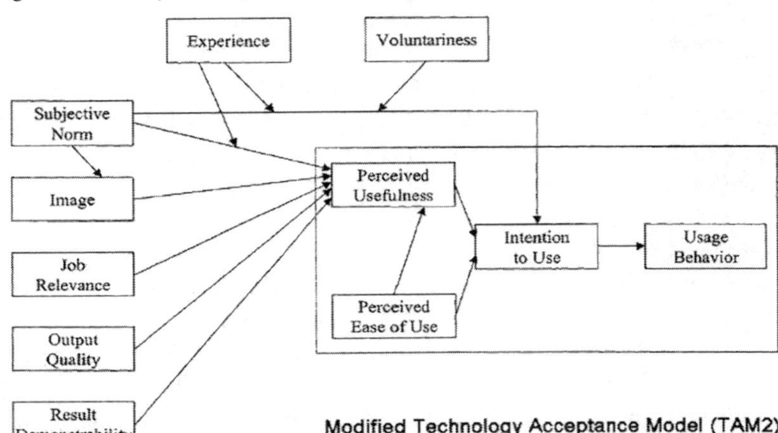

Venkatesh and Davis (2000), for instance, define the external variables of PU, such as social influence (subjective norms) and cognitive instruments (job relevance, image, quality, and result demonstrability). Venkatesh (2000) provides the external variables of PEOU, such as anchor (computer self-efficacy, perceptions of external control, computer anxiety, and computer playfulness) and adjustments (perceived enjoyment and objective usability). Experience and voluntariness are included as moderating factors of subjective norm.

The **Unified Theory of Acceptance and Use of Technology (UTAUT)** proposed by Venkatesh et al. (2003) extends TAM to take into account several new constructs (Performance Expectancy, Effort Expectancy, Social Influence and Facilitating conditions) that bear significant influence on behavioural intention and ultimately usage of technologies. Gender, age, experience and voluntariness of use are posited to mediate the impact of the four key constructs on usage intention and behaviour (Venkatesh et. al., 2003). As Uzoka et al. (2007) describe, **UTAUT** attempts to improve the predictive ability of other individual models by identifying communalities and capitalizing on the best aspects of each model. The theory is developed through a review and consolidation of the constructs of eight models employed in earlier research to explain IS usage behaviour (Theory of Reasoned Action, Technology Acceptance Model, Motivational Model, Theory of Planned Behaviour, a combined theory of planned behaviour/technology acceptance model, model of PC utilization, innovation diffusion theory, and social cognitive theory). Subsequent validation of UTAUT in a longitudinal study has found it to account for 70 % of the variance in usage intention (Venkatesh et. al., 2003).

Figure 3.5: The Unified Theory of Acceptance and Use of Technology (Venkatesh et al. 2003)

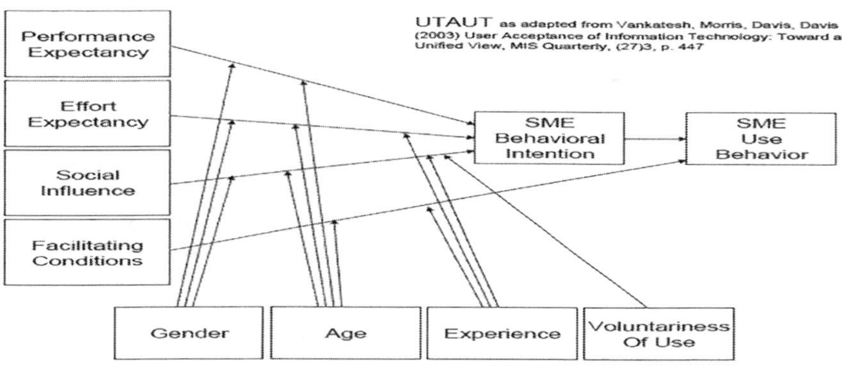

3.6.2 TPB Method Adopted in Research

There have been a number of studies investigating the adoption and use of technology through the application of TPB, which is successfully applied to the understanding of individual acceptance and usage of many different technologies (Mathieson, 1991; Taylor and Todd, 1995; Harrison et al., 1997; Markauskaite, L., 2006; Koutroumanos, 2006; Al-Gahtani, 2006; Baker et al., 2007; Alexopoulos et al., 2008; Agbonlahor, 2008). The research model in this study, shown in Figure 3.5, adopts the TPB method in investigating the behavioural intention factors influencing computer usage. The components of TPB are attitude, subjective norm and perceived behavioural control. This research model excludes computer usage, focusing on intention to use the computer as the dependent variable.

Our focus is to investigate how well attitude, subjective norm, and perceived behavioural control predict intention to use technology in the future. Furthermore, our aim is primarily to aggregate and determine the factors which influence Muslim minority women in Thrace to adopt the computer technology and secondly to answer the research questions stated below to explore the behaviours:

1. What are the current state of beliefs and attitudes toward computer technology of Muslim minority women in Thrace?

2. How do the beliefs and attitudes influence the computer technology adoption of these women?

In this research model, (Fig 3.6) the constructs for attitude, subjective norm and perceived behavioural control are also displayed, as moderated by age, level of education, residence area (town-village/ prefecture), marital, economic and professional statuses, assessing the effect of each one of the interactions on behavioural intention as similarly studied by Morris et al. (2005) and Baker et al (2007).

Behavioural Intention to use computer, according to TPB, can be employed to directly predict behavioural achievement or actual behaviour. When the person has complete control over the behaviour in question, that is, when the behaviour is completely voluntary, intentions alone should adequately predict behaviour (Ajzen and Fishbein, 1980). In these cases, it is the existing behavioural intention to perform the behaviour that can significantly predict actual future behaviour. Behavioural intention has long been recognized as an important mediator in the relationship between behaviour and other factors, such as attitude, subjective norm, and perceived behavioural control (Ajzen, 1991; Ajzen and Fishbein, 1980).

Subjective Norm is defined as the individual's perception of whether the people who are important to him or her think the behaviour should be performed and also as the perceived social pressure to perform or not to perform the behaviour by the individual (Ajzen, 1991). It refers to an individual's estimation of how others feel about one's use of computers and motivation to comply with their feelings. Motivation to comply is the extent to which the person wants to share the wishes of the other party (Mathieson, 1991). Studies have found subjective norm to be an important determinant of behavioural intention to use ICT (Hartwick and Barki, 1994; Moore and Benbasat, 1991 both cited in Baker et al, 2007).

Attitude toward the behaviour is defined as the individual's positive or negative feelings about performing the behaviour, as a consequence, the degree to which performance of the behaviour is positively or negatively valued. It is determined through an assessment of a person's beliefs regarding the consequences arising from behaviour and an evaluation of the desirability of these attributes.

Perceived Behavioral Control is defined as the perceived ease or difficulty of performing behaviour (Eagly and Chaiken, 1993 in Umrani, 2003). In terms of TPB, it is the perception of behavioural control as opposed to the degree of actual behavioural control that directly impacts the intentions to perform behaviour and the actual performance of that behaviour as well.

Figure 3.6: Research Model Adopted for TPB Method

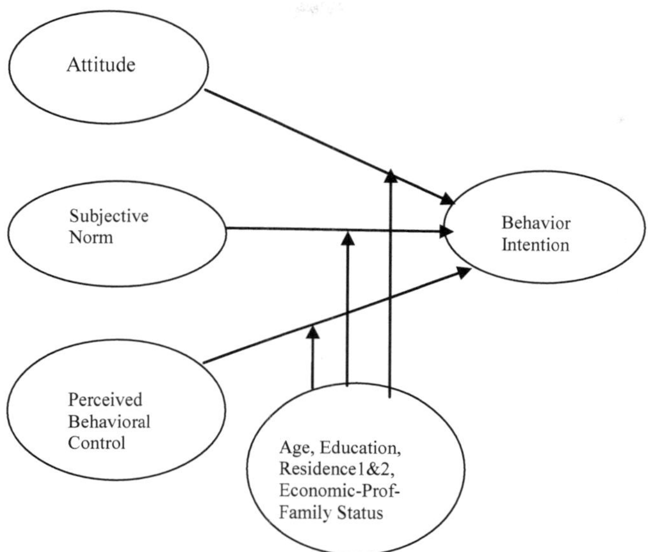

3.6.3 TAM Method Adopted in Research

Among the many adoption models, TAM has been claimed to be the most influential and the most employed to predict the acceptance and use of various technologies due to its strength in theoretical basis and empirical support (Saga and Zmud, 1994). Therefore, the Technology Acceptance Model (TAM), which has been widely used in technology adoption studies, is employed with minor modifications to provide the theoretical foundation to study the behaviour of Muslim minority women in Greek Thrace towards computer use. TAM's constituents in this survey are as follows:

Behavioural Intention to Use Technology: In terms of TAM, behavioural intention can be used to directly predict behavioural achievement or actual behaviour. When the person has complete control over the behaviour in question, that is, when the behaviour is completely voluntary, intentions alone will adequately predict behaviour (Fishbein, 1980). In these cases, it is the existing behavioural intention to perform the behaviour that can significantly predict the actual future behaviour. Behavioural intention has long been recognized as an important mediator in the relationship between behaviour and other factors, such as attitude, subjective norm, and perceived behavioural control (Ajzen, 1991; Ajzen and Fishbein, 1980).

Perceived Usefulness refers to a person's belief that the use of the computer will result in the achievement of personally relevant goals. It is defined as being the degree up to which a person believes that the use of a system will improve his performance (Davis, 1989).

Perceived Ease of Use refers to a person's belief that using computers will be free of cognitive effort (Umrani and Ghadially, 2003). Davis (1986) advances that perceived ease of use also influences in a significant way the attitude of an individual through two main mechanisms: self-efficacy and instrumentality. Self-efficacy is a concept developed by Bandura (1982), which points out that the more a system is easy to use, the greater should be the user's sense of efficacy. Moreover, a tool easy to use will make the user feel that he has a control over what he is doing (Lepper, 1985). Efficacy is one of the main factors underlying intrinsic motivation (Bandura, 1982; Lepper, 1985) and it is what illustrates here the direct link between perceived ease of use and attitude.

Computer Self-Efficacy refers to the individual's subjective evaluation of efficacious ability in dealing with computers. Previous experiences the individual carries on to technology use can be a function of the accumulated technical knowledge and the augmented working relationships with technology suppliers.

Subjective Norm refers to an individual's estimation of how others feel about one's use of computers and motivation to comply with their feelings. Motivation to comply is the extent to which the person wants to share the wishes of the other party (Mathieson, 1991). Subjective norm is defined as the perceived social pressure to perform or not to perform the behaviour by the individual (Ajzen, 1991). Studies have found subjective norm to be an important determinant of behavioural intention to use ICT (Hartwick and Barki, 1994; Moore and Benbasat, 1993 both cited in Baker et al, 2007).

Figure 3.7 below depicts the research model employed in this study for the behavioural intention towards computer use. The model is mainly derived from TAM with two additional constructs, namely "Subjective Norm" and "Computer Self Efficacy". These two constructs are shown in italics in Figure 3.7. Ten relationships between the constructs in Figure 3.7 are hypothesized and discussed below.

Figure 3.7: The TAM for Behavioural Intention to Adopt Computers

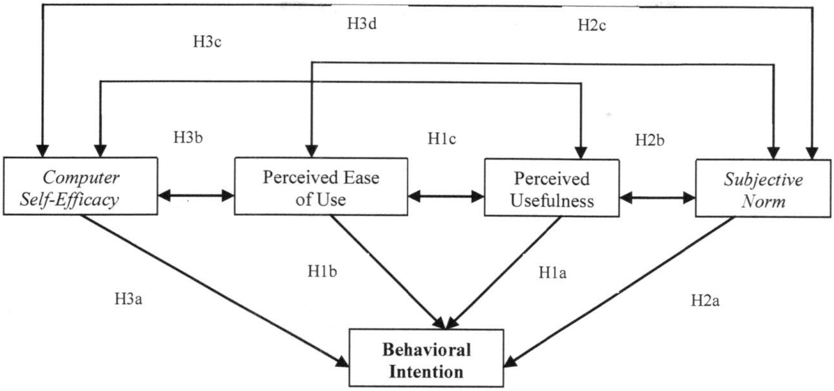

Mathieson (1991:185,187), comparing the TAM and the TPB methods, concludes that TAM is easier to apply, less expensive but supplies only very general information on user's opinions about ease of use and usefulness of an information system. TPB is designed topredict behaviour across many settings and can be applied to information system use. TPB delivers more specific information measuring the performance of the system on various outcomes, and identifies factors that respondents feel might be barriers to system use. TAM explains attitude towards using an information system much better than TPB and may be the model of choice when this variable is of particular interest. Both models can be used together very effectively.

Suppose a system was built to serve users in several different functional areas. An analyst could use TAM to identify dissatisfied users and discover the general nature of their complaints. TAM is ideally suited to this purpose since (1) it is inexpensive to apply and (2) TAM's general constructs (usefulness and ease of use) are probably meaningful to most people, no matter what their functional area. Once a group of particularly dissatisfied users is identified, TPB can provide more detailed information specific to the group. In other words, the general and inexpensive information TAM provides can identify areas where it will be desirable to have more specific and extensive information TPB provides.

3.6.4 Structured Interviewing

Interview is a fundamental tool in qualitative research. The qualitative research interview is described by Kvale (1996) as an *attempt to understand the world from the subject's point of view, to unfold the meaning of people's experiences, to uncover their lived world*. The researcher's logic for using this data collection method is that a legitimate way to generate data is to interact with people (i.e. talk to and listen to them), thereby capturing the meaning of their experiences in their own words (Bloomberg and Volpe, 2008:82).

After examining what the informants said and taking into consideration what affects an interview might have on women living in villages, in remote areas on the mountains, being covered with a scarf or living behind tall walls, it was decided that the interview should have a structured character. The reason for this choice can be supported by the fact that structured interview, sometimes called a standardized interview, entails the administration of an interview schedule by an interviewer. Bryman (2004:119) suggests that the aim of all interviewees is to be given exactly the same context of questioning and exactly the same interview stimulus. Moreover, Bryman (2004:110) comments:

> *"The goal of this style of interviewing is to ensure that interviewees' replies can be aggregated and this can be achieved reliably only if those replies are in response to identical cues. Interviewees are supposed to read out the questions as exactly and in the same order as they are printed on the schedule. Questions are usually very specific and very often offer the interviewee a fixed range of answers. This type of questioning is often called closed, closed ended, pre-coded or fixed choice."*

The process of the interview is strictly structured in order to ensure the validity and the reliability of the measurement; the initial planning remains constant; an inflexible process is kept; the answers are coded in an easy and fast way and an interview usually with each individual takes place.

As Bryman (2004:161) claims:

> *"While constructing the questionnaire, the researcher should consider using questions that have been employed by other researchers for at least part of the under construction questionnaire. In this way employing existing questions allows the use of questions that have in a sense been piloted. If any reliability and validity testing has taken place, the measurement qualities of the existing questions in use will be known. A further advantage of using existing questions is that they allow comparisons with other research. This might allow to indicate whether change has occurred or whether place makes a difference to findings. At the very least, examining questions used by others might give some ideas about how best to approach the researcher's own questions."*

3.6.5 Key Informant Technique

The aim of the final part of the study is to interview key people acting, and interacting with the profession in order to describe their views on the subject of the research. As Marshall (1996) says, a key informant is an expert source of information. The key informant technique is an ethnographic research method, which was originally used in the field of cultural anthropology and then more widely in other branches of social science investigation. Key informants, in a "statistical sense", need to be representative of the population from which they are drawn; rather, they are selected based on the insights they are capable of providing as a foundation for future research. Key informants are selected on the basis of standard protocols for a qualitative research setting:

1. Key informants should occupy roles in the community that make them knowledgeable by absorbing the information meaningfully and should be exposed to the kind of information being sought by the researcher.
2. Key informant should also be able and willing to communicate their knowledge in a manner that is intelligible to the interviewer and to cooperate as fully as possible.
3. Key informants should be objective and unbiased.

Any relevant biases should be known to the interviewer (George and Reve, 1982 in Marshall, 1996). Key informants, as a result of their personal skills or position within a society, are able to provide more information and deeper insight into what is going on around them and in-depth information about causes of the research problem. Interviews can be further combined with other techniques. Information can be received from many different people, including minority or silent majority viewpoints. They provide the opportunity to establish rapport and trust, and get the insider's views.

3.7 Definition of Variables

Variables used in this study compose of three types:

1) **Dependent Variable**: Behaviour intention to use computer technology by Muslim minority women in Thrace is defined as dependent variable composed of influencing levels of factors, barriers, incentives toward the adoption. Social empowerment is concerned with increased status.
2) **Independent Variables**: There are six main independent variables defined in the study: attitude, subjective norm and perceived behavioural control, computer self-efficacy, perceived ease of use, perceived usefulness.
3) **Moderating Variables**: In addition, the moderation of age, level of education, residence area (town-village/ Rodopi-Xanthi), marital, economic and professional statuses to attitude, subjective norm and perceived behaviour control are modelled by assessing the effect of each one of the interactions on behavioural intention.

3.8 Hypotheses

The hypotheses and research questions of the study will be given according to the three-phase project designed for this research.

After reading the already existing literature on Muslim minority women in Thrace and taking in consideration their socioeconomic status, the following hypotheses are taken into consideration:

3.8.1 Hypotheses on Demographics

H1: A significant difference in computer ownership is expected between prefectures of Rodopi and Xanth and between town and village dwellers.

H2: A high correlation is expected between computer ownership and professional status, family status, educational level of the interviewees.

H3: A significant difference is expected in the preference of the gender of the trainer, connected to the family status of the women or connected to their residence area.

3.8.2 Hypotheses for TPB Method

Based on the framework, the following hypotheses are proposed and empirically tested:

H4: Attitude, Subjective Norm, and Perceived Behavioural Control will have a positive influence on Behavioural Intention.

Within the framework of the descriptions quoted above, which refer to Muslim minority women's way of living, we conclude that most of the minority women who are educated, work and contribute to the family budget are expected to be young ones, especially town-dwellers. Gradually, more and more Muslim minority women achieve higher levels of education. The rapid increase in the number of students of the Muslim minority who complete programs of higher education has lead to the formation of a new order inside the minority, in which women have an important role to play. The ascertainment above makes us propose the following hypotheses:

H5: The moderation of Attitude, Subjective Norm, and Perceived Behavioural Control is expected to be significant with age, level of education, residence area, marital, economical and professional status upon the Intention to use computer technology.

3.8.3 Hypotheses for TAM Method

The TAM method proposes that Perceived Usefulness (PU) and Perceived Ease of Use (PEOU) largely determine whether or not a technological innovation will be employed. PU is defined as the degree to which a person believes that using a particular system will enhance his or her job performance while PEOU refers to the degree to which a person believes that using a particular system will be free of effort (Davis, 1989). Based on this, we have constructed the following hypotheses in relation to Behavioural Intention to computer use:

H6: There will be a positive relationship between Perceived Usefulness, Perceived Ease of Use and Behavioural Intention to use computers.

Moreover, the improved technology acceptance model (Davis, 1993) proposes that Perceived Usefulness is influenced by Perceived Ease of Use, not vice versa. This relationship has been confirmed in a number of other studies (Davis et al., 1989; Davis, 1993; Taylor and Todd, 1995; Chau, 1996). Therefore, it is hypothesized that if consumers find computer easy to use, then they will also find it useful.

H7: There will be a positive relationship between Perceived Ease of Use and Perceived Usefulness to computer use.

In regard to the Theory of Reasoned Action (Ajzen and Fishbein, 1975), a person's Behavioural Intention (BI) is also affected by Subjective Norm (SN). Subjective Norm is the social pressure exerted on the person to perform the behaviour. We reason that if friends, relatives, colleagues believe that computer use is beneficial, then a person may agree and accept their belief and in turn establish an intention to use it.

H8: There will be a positive relationship between Subjective Norm and Behavioural Intention, Perceived Usefulness, Perceived Ease of Use towards using computers.

Finally, as aforementioned, Computer Self-Efficacy refers to the individual's subjective evaluation of efficacious ability in dealing with computers. A person's Behavioural Intention (BI) is also affected by his Computer Self-Efficacy (CSE). Therefore, it is hypothesized that if consumers feel self-efficient to use the computer, then they will also have the intention to use it.

H9: There will be a positive relationship between Computer Self-Efficacy and Behavioural Intention, Perceived Ease of Use, Perceived Usefulness, Subjective Norm towards using computers.

3.8.4 Questions for the Qualitative Research

Creswell (2009:129) states that in a qualitative study inquirers state research questions not objectives or hypotheses. Consequently, for the qualitative research of the study, we state the following central questions:

Women, Empowerment and Computer Education: *How is social empowerment achieved through computer education of Muslim minority women in Thrace?*

Key Informants: *What is key informants' impact on computer education of Muslim minority women in Thrace?*

3.9 Tools

3.9.1 Questionnaire Used for TPB Method

Our questionnaire items, comprising the constructs of Perceived Behavioural Control, Attitude toward Using Technology, Subjective Norm and Behavioural Intention to use technology, were developed based on the existing, well-established questionnaire used in the Baker's et al. research (2007) in Saudi-Arabia among 1088 knowledge workers within 56 private and public sector organizations, including banking, merchandising, manufacturing, and petroleum industries engaged in the use of desktop computers for the purpose of their work. The questionnaire used for the Baker's research, was adopted with some minor modifications to suit this particular case. The wording of the question was modified slightly before the final format was accepted, based on remarks and suggestions made by the pilot study participants in order content validity to be (Zikmund, 2003 in Chatzoglou et al., 2010).

All survey items, originally published in English, were adapted for this study in Turkish using back translation method. The items were translated back and forth between English and Turkish (Brislin, 1986). Different translators were used in these two stages. When a major inconsistency occurred in the translation, a discussion between two translators was conducted to reconcile the differences. The process was repeated until both versions converged. The questionnaire was translated into Turkish being the mother tongue of the Muslim minority in Thrace.

The questionnaire consisted of two parts. The first part of the questionnaire measured eleven variables identified as being relevant to TPB. To achieve consistency, all instruments were adapted to the theory of TPB, and respectively, standardized tests were used to assess the psychological variables on a five-point Likert-type scale. Following Baker's questionnaire for our research, Behavioural Intention (BI), Perceived Behavioural Control (PBC) and Subjective Norm (SN) were assessed by a three-item scale (BI1, BI2, BI3/ PBC1, PBC2, PBC3/ SN1, SN2, SN3), ranging respectively from totally disagree to totally agree. The Attitude (ATT) was assessed with a five-item scale (ATT1, ATT2, ATT3, ATT4, ATT5), ranging respectively for each question from totally bad to totally good, from totally foolish to totally wise, from totally unfavourable to totally favourable, from totally harmful to totally beneficial and from totally negative to totally positive.

The second part captured the sample characteristics, such as age measured with a five category ordinal scale: 1) 20–30 years, 2) 31–40 years, 3) 41–50 years, 4) over 50 years; level of education measured using also a five category ordinal scale: 1) less than high school (primary school), 2) high school, 3) lyceum, 4) university 5) IPT (institute of professional training) 6) master, and residence area measured by two categories: 1) town-village and 2) Rodopi-Xanthi prefectures. Some supportive data was also collected on the subjects' marital status, economic level, and professional status.

3.9.2 Questionnaire Used for TAM Method

Our questionnaire items, comprising the constructs of Perceived Usefulness, Perceived Ease of Use, Computer Self-Efficacy, Subjective Norm and Behavioural Intention to use technology, were developed based on the existing, well-established questionnaire used at the Umrani's research (2003) in Mumbai-India among 100 women trainees at a premier private computer-training institute. The questionnaire used for the Umrani's research was adopted with some minor modifications to suit this particular case. Standardized tests were used to assess the psychological variables on a 5-point Likert-type scale. All survey items, originally published in English, were adapted for this study in Turkish using back translation method. The items were translated back and forth between English and Turkish (Brislin, 1986). The questionnaire was translated into Turkish, since it is the mother tongue of the Muslim minority in Thrace.

Following Umrani's (2003) questionnaire for our research, Behavioural Intention to use computers was indicated on a two-item scale ranging from definitely no to definitely yes. Perceived Usefulness was assessed first with a 20-item checklist of benefits (grouped in four categories: job/career, personal/family gain, entertainment, and information), rating the extent of usefulness. Then the subjects were asked to write eight benefits in the order of importance to them that would result from learning of computer use (Hill et al., 1987 in Baker et al., 2007). Perceived Ease of Use and Subjective Norm were assessed by a seven-item scale and by a two-item scale respectively, asking subjects to evaluate the extent to which the statements held true for them (Mathieson, 2001). For Computer Self-Efficacy, a four-item scale was employed to assess it from totally disagree to totally agree.

3.9.3 Women's Interviews

The six primary stages of these interviews were:

1) To gather information concerning the demographics of the women interviewees
2) To look for information on their experiences on ICTs
3) To detect their knowledge on computer use
4) To outline their attitudes towards ICTs
5) To search for their aspirations through ICT use and finally
6) To detect their motivations in general for ICT use.

After a study of the relevant bibliography and the definition of the aims, the objectives and the methodology of the research were designed as well as the format of the questionnaire.

With videoconferencing guidance through Skype from Prof Mary Kalantzis, the researcher used the research questions study as the framework to develop the interview questions. Two doctoral colleagues were then asked to review and provide feedback to the researcher. Their comments were incorporated and the researcher resubmitted the schedule of questions to Prof. Kalantzis. With the advisor's approval, five pilot interviews were carried out (see 3.10). Many of the questions were chosen from questionnaires used in past researches concerning the Greek computer user (AGB, Observatory for the Greek Information Society), research among Mumbai Muslim minority women in India (Umrani, 2003), research among Muslim minority women in Thrace (Georgiadou et al., 2007), Greek scale of self-sufficiency on computer use (Kasotaki and Roussos, 2006).

The researcher developed a series of structured interview schedules which included a combination of mixed questions, descriptive questions for selecting demographic data, both open and closed-ended questions and scale items for collecting data relevant to the research questions. The structured interview procedure was built around a core of structured questions providing a general framework in which the respondents could elaborate or lead themselves onto other issues relevant to ICT or their communication and learning needs. The open-ended questions were included to enable respondents to express their individual assessments, facilitating an in-depth account of their views within a frame of reference. The closed-ended questions and scale items of the schedules were included for quantification where important comparisons could be obtained.

The researcher's objective was to reduce the possibility of variability in the recording of answers in the structured interviewing and provide the interviewees the ability to answer unselfconsciously. Such communities' reliance and trust takes effort and time to build, which is easily destroyed by a small mistake. The questions were posed by the researcher in a way so as not to offend, embarrass or insult anybody, or provoke criticism by the local Muslim community. The interview consisted of 49 questions. In social research the fundamental base for the conclusions and generalizations is the empirical data, is the information the researcher gathers. The size of the sample is connected to the information that is ensured by the participants. Consequently, the more information gathered, the smaller the sample (Paraskevopoulos, 1993:49).

Only three of the interviews and only at the administration of Rodopi were carried out in the women's houses. Most of the interviews were made in their work place, or in private areas. The reason for choosing places appointed by the interviewees was that the researcher wanted for them to feel more comfortable in their environment so that the interview would proceed in a friendlier and quieter way, augmenting in this way the chances for a more productive procedure. The researcher did not stint time, money and effort to approach women interviewees even if they were living on remote villages on the mountains.

An identical warning for identical reasons can be registered in connection with the recording of answers by interviewers, who should write down respondents' replies as exactly as possible. This method as recommended by Creswell (2009:181) was followed during the research where the answers were written down exactly as given and also tape recorded during the whole procedure in case the recording equipment failed. The researcher used an interview protocol for asking questions as Creswell (2009:183) suggested. A heading containing the date, the place, and the interviewee was put in the beginning. Some instructions were given to the participants so that standard procedures would be maintained from one interview to another. Demographics were asked in the beginning although some researchers suggested asking them in the end of the interviewers as ice-breaker questions *"Who should I continue my interviews with? Do you have anyone to suggest?"* was posed. Space was left between the questions on the paper in order to make hand-written notes. Each interviewee was specially thanked for her contribution to the research.

3.9.4 Key Informants' Interviews

The three primary stages of the interviews which consisted of 29 questions were: 1) To gather information concerning the demographics of the key-informants,

2) To look for information on their what and how relative to ICTs, 3) To search for their thoughts and beliefs on the subject of women, empowerment and ICTs.

The researcher developed a series of structured interview schedules which included a combination of mixed questions, descriptive questions for selecting demographic data, both open and closed-ended questions and scale items for collecting data relevant to the research questions. The structured interview procedure was built around a core of structured questions providing a general framework in which the respondents could elaborate or lead themselves onto other issues relevant to ICT or search for key informants' thoughts and beliefs on the subject of the research. The open-ended questions were included to enable respondents to express their individual assessments, facilitating an in-depth account of their views within a frame of reference. The closed-ended questions and scale items of the schedules were included for quantification where important comparisons could be sustained. Some were yes/no questions, not resulting from lazy thinking and preparation, but rather with consideration of the kind of subjects to be interviewed and also in an effort to help these women by clarifying the meaning of the questions.

3.10 Pilot Study

3.10.1 Psychological Variables of TAM and TPB Method

The researcher first conducted a pilot study from December 1, 2008 to December 20, 2008 for the questionnaires schedule of the TPB and the TAM methods in order to measure psychological variables that affect women's intention to use computers. Of the two survey adopted, the initial questionnaires used the one for the TAM method at Umrani's research (2003) in Mumbai, and the other for the TPB method at Baker's research (2007) in Saudi Arabia.

The questionnaires originally published in English, were adapted for this study in Turkish using back translation method. The items were translated back and forth between English and Turkish (Brislin, 1986 in Baker et al., 2007). The process was repeated until both versions converged. The questionnaire was translated into Turkish; it being the mother tongue of the Muslim minority in Thrace. The Turkish translation helped provide easy reference for clarification and facilitated understanding scale items. The scales, to be administered in person by the researcher were felt to be important, providing step by step instruction and clarification when and where required by the subject. The pilot study took place mainly to test the reliability of the questionnaires, to determine whether the questions were comprehesible and was interpreted by the respondents as intended.

Foddy (1993:185) comments that interviewer's impressions are an indirect source of information about how the respondents "see" questions and researchers are content to instruct interviewers to note those questions that respondents have difficulty with, that is: "hesitate over", "laugh at", "ask for clarification", etc.

Thirty women of the minority who were familiar with computers participated in a pilot instrument of the survey. The mean age of the sample was 27.2; the median was the range of 20–30 years; 19(63 %) of the women were Rodopi-dwellers and 11(34 %) of them were Xanthi-dwellers. Of the women, 13(43 %) were university graduates, 5(16 %) primary school graduates, 7(23 %) high school graduates, 4(13 %) lyceum graduates and 1(3 %) held a master's degree.

Of the respondents, 4(13 %) belonged to the low-income, 24(80 %) to the middle-income group; 2(7 %) came from the upper-income group. Considering their professional status, 16(53 %) of the women were working, 6(20 %) were students, 8(27 %) were housewives. Reliability results from testing the measurement model were calculated using Chronbach's alpha. The data indicated that the measures were robust in terms of their internal consistency reliabilities as indexed by their Chronbach's alpha results, based on the average inter-item correlation. The reliability of the five different measures in the model ranged over 0.70, which exceeded the recommendation of Fornell and Larcker (1981).

The author observed the pilot subjects as they completed the survey. Potentially important items that had been overlooked were included in the final questionnaire. Feedback from the subjects, observations by the author and copious notes in the margins of the questionnaires taken during piloting the questionnaires resulted in some changes in the survey instructions; changes in the order of selected items, reformation of the initial structure of the questionnaire, refinement of the wording of several items in order to be easily comprehended; and finally adaptation of the questionnaire to Muslim minority women's social limits. In addition, based upon the results of the pilot study, adjustments were made to the methodology for this study, which included: 1) Not filming the women while they were completing the questionnaire as this was not beneficial to the study, 2) Asking women to complete the questionnaire as a group rather than individually, especially in remote villages where women were more reluctant to participate in the research, 3) Putting signs and colours on the questionnaire in order to make them more comprehensible, 4) Enlarging the letters of the instructions.

For the TPB method, standardized tests were used to assess the psychological variables on a 7-point Likert-type scale and the questionnaire elicited information to support related variables. Although on top of each group of the questions there was a clarification as to what had to be done, we had to explain the reference of the numbers (1–7) we put next to each item of the questionnaire in order to measure their intention of agreement or disagreement.

Some reluctance and hesitation to answer the questions was observed as the women could not understand the slight difference between "quite" and "to a certain extent". Upon that, the tests used to assess the psychological variables for the TPB method on a 5-point Likert-type scale were eliminated which would have been more convenient for the women to answer as we wanted to help them give answers and overcome their hesitations to participate in the research. The two questionnaires were separated by questions receiving information on the demographics of the women. That was adopted in order to make them feel more comfortable answering the two separate questionnaires, giving them the time to answer something that was easier to understand.

In Thrace, people of the minority in official or administrative positions were approached and contacted as channels to arrange appointments to meet the women. Especially in remote villages on the mountains, this interaction was the only way to meet women in groups inside their "cutting and sewing" clubs. Of the 137 women 28 of them who considered to be of more interest due to the reasons of computer use were targeted to give more detailed interviews.

TPB Questionnaire

Attitude: Participants of the pilot research had difficulties in answering the question "*All things considered, my using computers is*" as they could not easily figure out the "*all things*" in the question. Therefore, it had to be explained several times since the answer required several adjectives with slight differences.

Subjective Norm: Participants of the research could not understand in the question "*Most people who are important to me think I should use computers*", what was meant by "*most people who are important to me*". To this the interviewer replied that they were expected to respond according to their estimation of what others who are important must be thinking.

Perceived Behavioural Control: The following clause "*Given the resources, the opportunities and the knowledge to use the computer, it would be easier for me to choose computers rather than any other means available*" was difficult to answer as the words were complicated especially for the woman village dwellers. The interviewer clarified the meaning by explaining it.

Perceived Usefulness: The 20 items comprising this part of the questionnaire seemed to be strenuous as women had to be encouraged to reply to all of them.

As for the other psychological variables, such as Perceived Ease of Use, Computer Self-Efficacy, Subjective Norm and Behavioural Intention, participants did not raise any questions about the items in the scale adopted for the research.

3.10.2 Women Interviews

The researcher conducted a pilot study from December 1, 2008 to December 10, 2008 in the prefectures of Xanthi and Rodopi. The pilot interview study provided valuable insights into the research process. It first helped the researcher to critically think about the boundaries of the thesis. Commencement of the interviewing was preceded by five pilot interviews in order to check how clear and comprehensible the questions were for the interviewees. Other determinant factors were:

1) Whether the questions were linked to each other in order to develop an argument in the thesis?
2) If the questions were being answered in a similar way and not forming variable or confused positioning in the interview?

It was checked how well the questions flowed and whether it was necessary to reorder some of them. The comments of the five interviewees were taken into consideration when reshaping the final questionnaire. Pilot interviews provided the interviewer with some experience in using the questionnaire although it was not the first time she conducted an interview; this infused her with a greater sense of confidence.

By way of explanation is Bryman's (2004:159) statement worth mentioning:

"It is always desirable, if at all possible, to conduct before administering a self-completion questionnaire or structured interview schedule to the sample. In fact, the desirability of piloting such instruments is not solely to do with trying to ensure that survey questions operate well; also, with interviews, persistent problems may emerge after a few interviews have been carried out and these can be then addressed. It may be possible to identify questions that make respondents feel uncomfortable and to detect any tendency for respondents interest to be lost at certain junctures. The pilot should not be carried out on people who might have been members of the sample that would be employed in the full study in order not to affect any of the representative nesses of any subsequent sample."[4]

---

4   Bryman, A. (2004). *Social Research Methods*. Second Edition, Oxford, p. 160

The complexity of narrowing the pilot interview questions down to more specific issues was confronted. Some research questions had to be revised and others had to be avoided for being incomprehensible or repeatious. When the researcher heard the tape of the first interview, she realized that she was prompting the interviewee with clues and answers. She learned that in an interview such as this, the role of the researcher is to facilitate the interview and let interviewees produce their own answers. It was realized that both audio taping as suggested by Fowler and Mangione (1990:93) and notes taking by the researcher would be wiser in order to avoid loss of information since many times during the interviews women did not want some of their answers to be recorded. The researcher had to be patient and understood the necessity for neutrality concerning the issues being investigated. As part of the data collection stage, the researcher prepared a research protocol. After conducting the first interview, the researcher revised this protocol and added some more questions for the benefits of potential solutions to overcome issues that arose.

The researcher felt that in order to detect the ways ICTs could help minority women improve their social participation, it was important to include key stakeholders as the unit of analysis but additionally to ask women participants how they would expect the stake holders to help them with ICTs. The views and opinions of the most influential stakeholders would help form a better image of the Muslim minority society.

3.10.3 Key Informants

The researcher conducted a pilot study from July 2, 2008 to July 30, 2008 for the interview schedule to be followed. The researcher had to figure out the data indicators and the problems in collecting and analyzing meaningful data that would answer the research questions.

Questionnaire for the key informant was pilot tested on 7 subjects from amongst the participant pool of the key informants. The subjects were asked questions about their demographics, their use of computers, and their opinions on the use of computer by minority women. At the beginning, the subjects made some comments on the structure of the questionnaire and they were asked whether they could understand the meaning of all the questions. In accordance with their comments, the order of some questions was changed; some initial questions were omitted as they did not contribute to the research. It was realized that except the audio taping of the interview it would be better for the researcher to keep notes in order to avoid loss of information about the way the interviewees reacted and how the interview was conducted. The pilot survey enabled the researcher to understand that during the interviews the subjects must feel free to talk about the issues of the research and also about the problems that concerned the minority in general and were connected to the subjects of the research. The researcher sensed that when fixing the appointments for the interview, she should brief the participant about the objectives of the research so that the interviewee would not feel reluctant to participate in the research.

3.11 Data Coding

When analyzing the results of the women's interviews, the demographic data is coded in nominal scale. Age use is coded as 1(18–20), 2(21–30), 3(31–40), 4(41–50), 5(>50). Education is coded as 1(primary education), 2(high school), 3(lyceum), 4 (university), 5(master), 6(IOT). Residence area is coded for resid1 as 1(Rodopi), 2(Xanthi) and for resid2 as 1(Town), 2(Village). Subject of specialization is coded as 1(housewife), 2(student), 3(working). Economic situation is coded as 1(low income), 2(medium income), 3(high income). Computer ownership at home is coded as 1(yes), 2(no). Points of access is coded as 0(home), 1(cyber café), 2(relative's/friend's/ neighbour's house), 3(workplace) 4(other). Family members who are computer literate are coded for father (0(no) 1(yes)), mother(0(no) 1(yes)), brother (0(no) 1(yes)), sister(0(no) 1(yes)), (husband (0(no) 1(yes)), son(0(no) 1(yes)), daughter(0(no) 1(yes)). Gender for computer's teacher is coded as 1(man), 2 (woman), 3(neutral). Scales assessing TAM variables had a Likert-type rating; they were coded as 1 to 5.

3.12 Data Analysis and Synthesis

To test the hypotheses, we surveyed the Muslim minority women's perceptions of computer use in Thrace. The data collected for the demographics of the 137 women was analyzed quantitatively, using Statistical Package for Social Sciences (SPSS, Version 14); application and appropriate statistical techniques were employed to process the data from the collected questionnaires.

Statistical techniques included frequency distribution, percentage, arithmetic mean, chi-square, Mann-Whitney U test, multiple regression analysis, and Partial Least Squares (PLS). The predictors of Behavioural Intention to adopt computers (the psychological variables of Perceived Usefulness, Perceived Ease of Use, Computer Self-Efficacy, and Subjective Norm) were analyzed using SPSS, Version 14. The predictors of Behavioural Intention to adopt computers (the psychological variables of Perceived Behavioral Control, Attitude toward Using Technology and Subjective Norm) were analyzed using Smart PLS. Smart PLS is a software application for the design of structural equation models (SEM) on a graphical user interface (GUI). These models can be measured with the method of partial least squares (PLS) analysis. Hence, it becomes possible to import data of manifest (indicator) variables in the model. This software was created in a project at the Institute of Operations Management and Organizations, School of Busines, University of Hamburg, Germany.

For the qualitative data, we followed Vygotsky's (1987) idea that *"each word a participant speaks reflects his or her consciousness."* Tapes were transcribed to text and then translated from Greek into English. Care was taken not to loose the richness of the data while translating; and when it was required, the researcher went back to the original text and recording to obtain more clarity. In order to keep confidentiality, the audiotapes and the interview data are kept in a secure place to guard against the names of participants being accidentally revealed.

Silverman (1984, 1985 in Bryman, 2004) has argued that some quantification of findings from qualitative research can often help to uncover the generality of the phenomena being described. Descriptive statistics was adopted to present most of the data collected from the interviews 28 women had given as the questions used to absorb the information were closed-ended with multiple choices. Statistical techniques included frequency distribution, percentage, arithmetic mean, chi-square. Ten of the 49 questions were open-ended and provided data analyzed using the method of *content analysis*. Even though the answers given were not rich in words, but the fact of receiving answers with a lot of meanings from such a sample of women deserves praise. The answers can be described brief but very honest and powerful.

Presenting data from 30 key informants' interviews can be challenging. The data the key informants provided was very rich and thick of ideas, beliefs and findings. The quality of ideas and the richness of information varied among informants and were related largely to their background; some gave a feministic perspective, others a social one, some emphasized on relations between men and women forming under new conditions and especially by access to computer use, and others offered a religious view point. As Bryman (2004:533) suggests, the requirement of not including all the results but only those findings that relate to the research questions of the study so that the thread of the argument is not lost, was a rather painful process. The *open coding technique*, which breaks data apart and delineates concepts to stand for blocks of raw data, was used to code data. Next to it stood the technique of axial coding to relate concepts/categories to each other.

Capabilities approach was employed as the evaluative framework of social policies since it provides an appropriate tool to measure people's well being. According to Amartya Sen's evaluation, equality among people does not identify with equality of primary goods they enjoy. Sen (2000) has treated the matter of social exclusion with capabilities approach explaining them as opportunities which have been successfully converted into particular forms of action. In the same vein, we classified the factors that obstruct opportunities conversion into real capabilities into five different levels: (1) knowledge/awareness (knowing the existence of specific opportunities), (2) means (absence of realized capabilities), (3) external factors (conditions that constrain a person's development), (4) aims of action (previous circumstances that make a person reject new choices), (5) education as capability of development (Baros, 2009). The five levels which were used as codes for identifying similar concepts contain also several sub-codes for grouping and sub-grouping the information.

Before cutting and pasting all data into the codes, the researcher evaluated samples of three coded interviews with a scholar. Under every sub-code chosen, the researcher prepared 17 memos, which according to Strauss (1987) is the written version of an internal dialogue going on during the research.

Each of the interviews was analyzed in accordance with the data the answers provided; some of the questions were analyzed with MAXQDA, a professional tool for qualitative analysis that helps researchers systematically evaluate and interpret qualitative texts, and some of the questions were analyzed with the Statistical Package for Social Sciences (SPSS, Version 14) and the data was presented in a quantified way as explained above.

3.13 Ethical Considerations

In view of Bloomberg and Volpe (2008:85), ethical issues can indeed arise in all phases of the research process: data collection, data analysis and interpretation, dissemination of research findings. Mostly, issues of ethics focus on establishing safeguards that will protect the rights of the participants and include their informed consent, protecting them from harm, and raise confidentiality.

Prior to the pilot interviews and to the actual interviews, the interview questions were presented to a specific person's judgment who is considered to be the başcı (leader-gatekeeper). This protocol ensured that the questions of the interviews would not provoke any inconvenience to the participants. It was also explained to him how the material of the interviews would be used and it was made clear that participants could go off the record if they so wished. Seidman (2006:43) states that usually in small groups, there is at least one person with no formal authority who nevertheless holds moral suasion. If that person participates in a project, then it must be okay; if not, then the group feels there must be a good reason not to do so. To the extent that interviewers can identify informal gatekeepers, not using them in order to seek access to others but gaining their participation in the project as a sign of respect of the effort, access to others in the group may be facilitated.

It has been observed that people of the minority usually need a guarantee or a feeling of safety with an interviewer in order to express their opinions due to reasons which derive from the social status of the minority. Before starting the research, people of the minority in official or administrative positions were approached and interacted as channels to arrange appointments to meet women. Especially in remote villages on the mountains, this interaction was the only way to meet women in groups, only inside their cutting and sewing clubs, with the presence of the woman who is in charge of these clubs.

Pilot studies were conducted to establish trust and respect with the participants and to detect any marginalization before the study began. In the beginning of each interview after the normal introductions and establishment of a warm rapport, we had a brief negotiation about how we would proceed, including the use of the tape recorder. The interviews were tape recorded only with the permission of the interviewees. The majority did not express hesitation about the tape recording and agreed to go ahead; only two denied being tape recorded and this right was respected. The guidelines for research ethics had to be followed. An information letter was handed to all participants of the research before the interview (Appendix A), followed by a conversation to clarify any questions they might have.

Especially in in-depth interviews and in intensive qualitative research, confidentiality plays an important role in developing steady relations between the researcher and the participants' environment to draw rich data and information (Iosifidis, 2003).

Confidentiality can be a difficult issue for key informant interviews, especially in small communities. In this research, participants were guaranteed of confidentiality and were assured of the use of pseudonyms to protect their identity while presenting the selected data. Holloway and Jefferson (2005) claim that confidentiality can be one of the least problematic of ethical issues. If information is treated and used in such a way as to be secure and to ensure the anonymity of participants, ethical responsibility usually ends there. This should be the case whether or not an explicit pledge of confidentiality has been established.

Honesty and trustworthiness are points which must be kept in mind by the researcher during the interviews. Seidman (2006:70) states that the participant has the right to privacy and the right to request that his/her identity remain confidential, allowing time at the end for the respondent to add any information he/she wishes to convey further ideas and opinions on the content of the research.

Sometimes in this research, during the interviews, the researcher's intervention was needed just to give the interviewees a consciousness of conversation rather than an interview in order to extract more data. Cautionary measures were taken to secure the storage of research related records and data; nobody other than the principal researcher and the supervisor of the thesis would have access to the written and taped material.

Informed consent is the most important matter of ethics in a research procedure. The researcher did not use a written consent although prepared from the beginning of the research (Appendix B), as the procedure in this research could provoke sentiments of denial from the potential participants. The researcher's final aim was to develop a trust with the participants in informal ways. If they were asked to put their signatures on any paper, this would be hazardous to the ways relationships were established, especially among grass-roots in the area. More specifically in Greece, sustaining the rules of methodology is problematic due to existing limitations of financing the research, time-consuming bureaucracy, total lack of social support for the research; reluctance for cooperation, indifference for completion of forms. Kvale (2007:7) claims that interviewing, in qualitative research, is increasingly interpreted as a moral inquiry. As such, he adds that interviewers need to consider how an interview will improve the human situation, how a sensitive interaction may be stressful for the participants, whether participants have a say in how their statements are interpreted, how critically the interviewees might be questioned and what the consequences of the interview might be for the interviewees and the groups to which they belong.

Rubin & Rubin (2005:95) come to conclude that the researcher has to consider that those people who are providing data for the research are people who deserve respect and concern; they are not objects or impersonal entities. Due to the above, the researcher decided to create an investigator's verification of explanation and sign it in front of each participant (Appendix C). Fifty eight verifications are kept confidential.

One of the issues taken into serious consideration in this study was the use of language or words that were not biased against people with a minority social status. The words used in the questionnaires or during the interviews were stripped of racial and ethnic prejudice as the researcher avoided raising such issues. When these issues were put on the table of the conversation by the participants, they did not ensure any continuity. The researcher had to be careful not to hurt any participant and as a consequence of this to provoke the closure of the research field for future researchers. Considering the interview technique adopted to approach women from a feminist angle, it can be stated that a female interviewer on this occasion would have been better off to get women to talk concretely in a less defensive way about their experiences on ICT use (Hollway and Jefferson, 2005:90).

3.14 Issues of Trustworthiness

The research model in this study adopts both the TPB method and the TAM method in investigating the behavioural intention factors influencing computer usage. The TPB method plus the equivalent questionnaire plus the TAM method and the equivalent questionnaire were both examined for their reliability.

For the TAM method used in the research, the inter-item internal consistency reliabilities for each multi-item instrument were calculated using Chronbach's alpha. As recommended by Fornell and Larcker (1981), internal consistency reliabilities must be higher than 0.7. Inter-item reliabilities for each multi-item instrument used in the TPB questionnaire were calculated using Composite reliability and AVE (average variance extracted/explained). Composite reliabilities of different measures in the model range must exceed the recommended threshold value of 0.70 (Nunnally, 1978). Furthermore, consistent with the recommendation of Fornell and Larcker (1981), average variance extracted (AVE) for each measure must exceed 0.50. Convergent validity is tested with PLS-Graph by extracting the factor loadings (and cross loadings) of all indicator items to their respective latent constructs.

According to Creswell (2009:190), validity does not carry the same connotations in qualitative research as it does in quantitative research, nor is it a companion of validity (degree to which something measures what it purports to measure), reliability (examining stability or consistency of response over time) or generalizability (external validity of applying results to new settings, people or samples).

We read in Creswell (2009:190) that Gibbs (2007) suggests several procedures for reliability which he describes as the researcher's consistent approach across different researches and different projects; some of his suggestions were tested during this research in order to check research reliability. First of all, the transcripts were checked several times just to make sure that they contained no mistakes (during transcription). Data was constantly compared with the codes to prevent a shift in the meaning of the codes. Raw data was provided for an independent external editor to cross-check the codes that were decided to be used. The new researcher suggested the use of similar codes with slight modifications to the initial concept of the codes. After that, the researcher reviewed the data in the light of those guidelines made what revisions were called for and reconciled the differences in interpretations that arouse. Some of changes were substantial. In other subject areas, fewer updates were needed.

Bloomberg and Volpe (2008:86) suggest that validity involves asking how well matched is the logic of the method to the kinds of research questions that are being posed and the kind of explanation that the researcher is attempting to develop. Creswell (2009:191) recommends eight primary validity strategies to check the accuracy of the findings during a research. Some of them were adopted during the research in order to ensure validity. To support the methodological validity of the study, the researcher triangulated data sources as well as data collection methods. She collected data from both women interviews and key informants interviews asking similar questions in order to compare their answers and thus to derive further conclusions. Gathering data from multiple sources provides a richer and more satisfying image of the phenomenon under research. Moreover, the researcher collected data through a questionnaire addressed to 137 women using quantitative methods of analysis. This data enriched the study by describing the feelings of women on their behavioural intention to use the computer. This seems logical to start with when the researcher wants to finally outline minority women's social empowerment through computer use.

Member checking proposed by Lincoln and Guba (2000) or member validation in Bryman's (2004:274) words was adopted by the researcher in order to detect the accuracy of the qualitative findings by taking the final report back to some of the participants. Their comments were meaningful and valuable and added more to the analysis of the total data.The researcher uses a rich description to unfold the findings just to achieve more realistic results. Consequently, during the analysis data derived from the ideas and thoughts the key informants have on subjects that concern the minority but are not connected to research's subject, will be presented.

In Chapter 1 the researcher described the reasons that made her detect answers to the questions which resulted from her initial researches among socially excluded groups of women living in the area of Thrace but also due the prolonged time she co-exists in the area together with Muslim minority women. This time has given her the opportunity to develop an in-depth understanding of the situations minority women live in. This experience is valuable for the researcher and can ascribe more validity to her views.

On the other hand, the researcher as a native in the area of Thrace is a member of a Christian community. This can result in prejudice and bias that may influence the way the researcher explains and analyzes the answers the women and the key informants have given. Comments by the researcher about how she will interpret the findings will be included. The researcher trades on the fact that her being a woman makes the situation of a woman interviewing women much easier. She also trades on the fact that she has worked for two years in a Muslim minority parliamenter's office and that has made her a familiar image inside the minority. Furthermore, contradictory information whenever found is presented.

As we can read in Bryman (2004:273), Guba and Lincoln (2000) suggest another criteria for evaluating qualitative research; that of authenticity. In the specific study, the researcher acted as an impetus to key informants to engage in action to change the way they reacted to women's empowerment through ICTs. This is described as the catalytic authenticity.

3.15 Limitations of Study

The study contains certain limitation, some due to the common aspects of quantitative and qualitative research methodology. Therefore, an overriding concern is that of researcher bias, framing assumptions, ideas, and perceptions regarding the researcher's origin as a member of the majority in the area of Thrace. Although many steps are taken on behalf of the Greek state over the last twenty years to improve the living conditions of the members of the minority, the area in spite of these efforts is an example of co-existence of multi-cultural populations under social polarization (Troubeta, 2000:246). To reduce the potential bias during data analysis, the researcher removed names of all the participants and coded all the interview transcripts blindly so as not to associate any material of data with any particular individual.

Sometimes during the research, some of the interviewees were observed to give answers under a feeling of cooperation with the researcher, which they perceived might be convenient to her. When this was diagnosed during the interview, the questions were posed in another way or were checked by similar following questions. Furthermore, the researcher deliberately made an attempt to create an environment during the interviews which gave the participants a feeling of honesty and reliance. Difficult and abstract words were both avoided. Difficult words that had to be used were defined before in order not to insult the intelligence of participants as their knowledge of the Greek language was in some cases in dispute. The researcher tried the overriding principles of brevity, simplicity and concreteness as suggested by Foddy (1993:185) to form the basis of the interview questionnaire.

The researcher also took care of her dress code when visiting the houses of the participants. She was usually dressed up with long black clothes, wearing many gold bracelets on her arm in order to adopt the traditional dress code of the Muslim minority women. While entering the participant's house, she followed their habits, i.e. leaving shoes outside the door. The researcher wanted to raise in the participant a feeling of meeting someone familiar at the interview, not a foreign figure. As research participants were of a different traditional background, in order to achieve her goal the researcher had to demonstrate respect, thoughtfulness and interest in every participant.

A further major limitation of this study in addition to the above was the restriction of the research sample. Nevertheless, the aim of the research was rich description and detailed information regarding the connection of minority women to computer use and their social empowerment as this information is rare in the literature.

An important issue in this research that has to be highlighted is the linguistic difference between the researcher and the research participants. Although the research took place in Greece, a few interviews had to be carried out in the Turkish language. The fact that the researcher spoke Turkish and was therefore more familiar with this culture was important to understand what was said more authentically, reflecting the participants' thinking. On the other hand, the questionnaire used in the Baker's et al. research (2007) in Saudi-Arabia among 1088 knowledge workers was adapted with some minor modifications to suit this particular case. All survey items, as mentioned above, originally published in English, were adapted for this study in Turkish using back translation method. The items were translated back and forth between English and Turkish. The researcher believed that since the words used in the questionnaire were difficult to comprehend, they had to be explained in the mother tongue of the participants. Furthermore, women did not want any photos of them to be taken.

Seidman (2006:41) points out the imbalances occurring in the relationship between researcher and participants, one of the most difficult to negotiate occurs when researchers try to use an in-depth interviewing approach with people in positions of power. In this study, though the researcher did not face problems of access with the key informants in positions of power, but she had problems in carrying out her interviewing plan. Most of the key informants would have very busy schedules and would give the researcher a shorter amount of time or would receive telephone calls during the interviews. Most of them followed the programme of the interviews and others tried to take charge of the interviews; but they were allowed consciously to do so as data of this kind was very scarce in the literature and this would probably give them a chance to feel free to speak up and describe things that happened in their community unknown to those outside of it.

With regard to the research on the Muslim minority women in Thrace, we have to mention the following aspects:

- Lack of detailed literature on the Muslim minority women in Thrace; lack of valid and recent statistics referring to the Muslim minority as a group, and invalidation of many data from past researches due to changes which have occurred in the minority during the recent years.
- Old traditions and culture of a Muslim minority trying to keep its identity inside a Christian society. This phenomenon puts minority women in the front line for maintaining minority features. The researcher has been aware of this idiosyncrasy while contacting these women, collecting and analyzing data.

Taking into consideration the ethics and the limitations of the study described above, the data collected for this research confirms that when the researcher gains confidence, then the result is positive and women become flexible to describe their ideas, emotions and perspectives. The efforts made for an objective research coordinated with the prevailing ethics and the existing limitations seem to be rewarded with the upcoming results, unveiling a new way of thinking and function for the women of the minority beyond prejudice, propaganda and stereotypes promoted by the mass media and entangled institutions.

Chapter 4: Findings

4. Introduction

The purpose of this multi-case study was to explore the Muslim minority women's perceptions of how the computer education could lead them to pathways for their social participation and moreover the contribution of members of their community, in administrative positions, to this effort. The study was carried out in three parts:

The initial part was devoted to empirically validate the Technology Acceptance Model (TAM) and the Theory of Planned Behaviour (TPB) and analyze how it varies across computer attitude. The data collected from a sample of 137 women was analyzed quantitatively, using Statistical Package for Social Sciences (SPSS, Version 14); application and appropriate statistical techniques were employed to process the data from the collected questionnaires. The predictors of Behavioural Intention to adopt computers (the psychological variables of Perceived Usefulness, Perceived Ease of Use, Computer Self-Efficacy, and Subjective Norm) were analyzed using SPSS, Version 14 The predictors of Behavioural Intention to adopt computers (the psychological variables of Perceived Behavioural Control, Attitude toward Using Technology and Subjective Norm) were analyzed using Smart PLS.

The succeeding part assessed the benefits of computer education, in terms of the nature and extent of empowerment experienced by 28 women of the minority. The six primary stages of these interviews were:

- to gather information concerning the demographics of the women interviewees
- to look for information on their experiences on ICTs
- to detect their knowledge on computer use
- to outline their attitudes towards ICTs
- to search for their aspirations through ICT use
- to detect their motivations in general for ICT use

The final part explored through 30 interviews the thoughts and the aspects of key informants about the potential of social participation of minority women through computer education. The three primary stages of these interviews were:

- to gather information concerning the demographics of the key informants
- to look for information on their what and how relative to ICTs
- to search for their thoughts and beliefs on the subject of women, empowerment and ICTs

Descriptive statistics was adopted to present most of the data collected from the interviews held with 28 women and 30 key informants. The method of structured interview, due to reasons explained in Chapter III, was adopted for the large part of the interviews, and the questions used were mostly closed-ended with multiple choice answers. Capabilities approach was used as the evaluative framework of social policies since it provided the appropriate tool for measuring people's well being. Each of the interviews was analyzed according to the data the answers provided; some of the questions with MAXQDA, and some of the questions were analyzed with the Statistical Package for Social Sciences (SPSS, Version 14).

4.1 Problems during the Research

The motive of this research was an internal need of the researcher to detect whether the women of the Muslim minority in Thrace are integrated in the information society. The researcher believes it will be good for the reader of this study before going through the data selected from the questionnaires and the interviews to have in his/her mind some of the difficulties she has faced during this research.

The researcher felt like she had to function as a channel to transfer data from one society to another. And this channel had to function with no bias and prejudice. Initially she had to overcome her own ways of thinking and expressing her thoughts about Muslim minority people, then identify the inter-bias that exists in the Muslim society, and to forward the findings in a negotiable way to members of the majority population. Some members of the majority community were hostile when they realized that someone who belonged to them would be interested in the other part, the Muslim minority women. *"What do you think you are doing? Are you going to solve the minority issue?"* was a question someone made with a suspicious and ironic way. *"Why we have to search things for them, or for the Roma? We don't have other populations to take care off here?"* was one of the remarks that a member of the majority, a woman and gynaecologist, made having an expression of reject on her face for the whole project. Another question expressing feelings of agony and doubt when they were reaching remote villages on the mountains of Xanthi for the first time in their lives was asked by the researcher's mother: *"Are you sure that these women who live on the mountains will have a computer here? They are so isolated."* Her already existing biased knowledge was shaping the results of the research while she was accompanying her daughter on their way to mountain villages to meet with women of the minority. The researcher informed majority women members of a Christian Association about Muslim minority women and their connection to ICTs. Some of the majority women's reaction was to start learning how to use the computer as they could not deal with the fact that some of the ones considered as inferiors to them were more skilled. Another unfortunate event took place when the researcher dared to mumble that she found a woman of the minority at the age of 50s living in a village and that she was using the Skype to communicate with her daughters in Turkey. The reaction was: *"What are you talking about now? "Gulden" is an exception due to her husband. All the women of the minority are not like this."* The intension for generalization of the woman who made this remarks emanated from her bias and her real thoughts regarding this part of the population.

During the interviews women hesitated to answer as a consequence of fear mainly and respect less when they were asked questions about some members of the minority who formulate policies inside the minority; the key informants of this research. On the other hand, there were other women who gave bold answers describing these people with no real interest in the problems that concern women. This reaction figured a new identity for the women of the minority: that of a quiet critical power. This attitude acted for the researcher as a motive for a more careful study. After transcribing the data herself in order to know the data intimately and listening to it as she read the transcriptions, the researcher realized that she was talking too much during the interviews. That was a result of her intention to make the participants be more descriptive and to provide "thicker" information as it is rare to find this combination of people of the minority to speak up and explain things. Women on the mountains were afraid to speak when they were first approached. They were negative to answer and take part in the conversation. They would feel more comfortable to speak all together in the same area so that the identity of their speech would be lost in the verbalism of a group.

During the interviews, the concept of "a minority inside the minority as an internal gap" came up several times. This controversy about the image of the minority raised new challenges in the research. That was a sign of the existence of agitations inside the minority, which can be recognized as a vital transmuting organism. The continuous juxtaposition between the East and the West culture for the minority might be considered as the source of such conflicts and bias. We tried to select data from people who have different demographic characteristics and people who live in different parts of Thrace just to manage obtaining pluralistic and more valid data.

4.2 Places of Research

Data for the three parts of the study was collected from members of the Muslim minority, women and men, of different ages, with the criteria of having a computer at home, or at work or being familiar with ICTs or having leadership and eminent role in the social life of the minority. All these people are living in the prefectures of Rodopi and Xanthi, in the towns of Komotini and Xanthi and in villages. In the prefecture of Rodopi, the sample was chosen from the town of Komotini and from 18 other villages, where the main part of the Muslim population lived there. The villages are mainly on the central plain of the area, some of them totally inhabited by Muslim populations and some by both Christian and Muslim populations, where people are mainly occupied in agriculture. These 18 villages are Itea, Amaranta, Thamna, Polianthos, Vragia, Kikidio, Galini, Aratos, Filira, Iasmos, Dokos, Mishos, Amvrosia, Sapes, Megalo Pisto, Omiriko, Arriana, and Likio. In the prefecture of Xanthi the sample was chosen from the town of Xanthi and nine villages, mainly on the mountains of Xanthi in the North part of the prefecture. The villages are Pelekiti, Sounio, Simandra, Oraio, Kentavros, Miki, Dourgouti, Selero, Sartri. The Muslim populations in these villages are mainly of Pomak origin.

In the following Figure 4.1 the places where the research took place are marked on the map of Thrace with yellow circles for Rodopi administration and orange circles for Xanthi administation.

Figure 4.1: Research Area

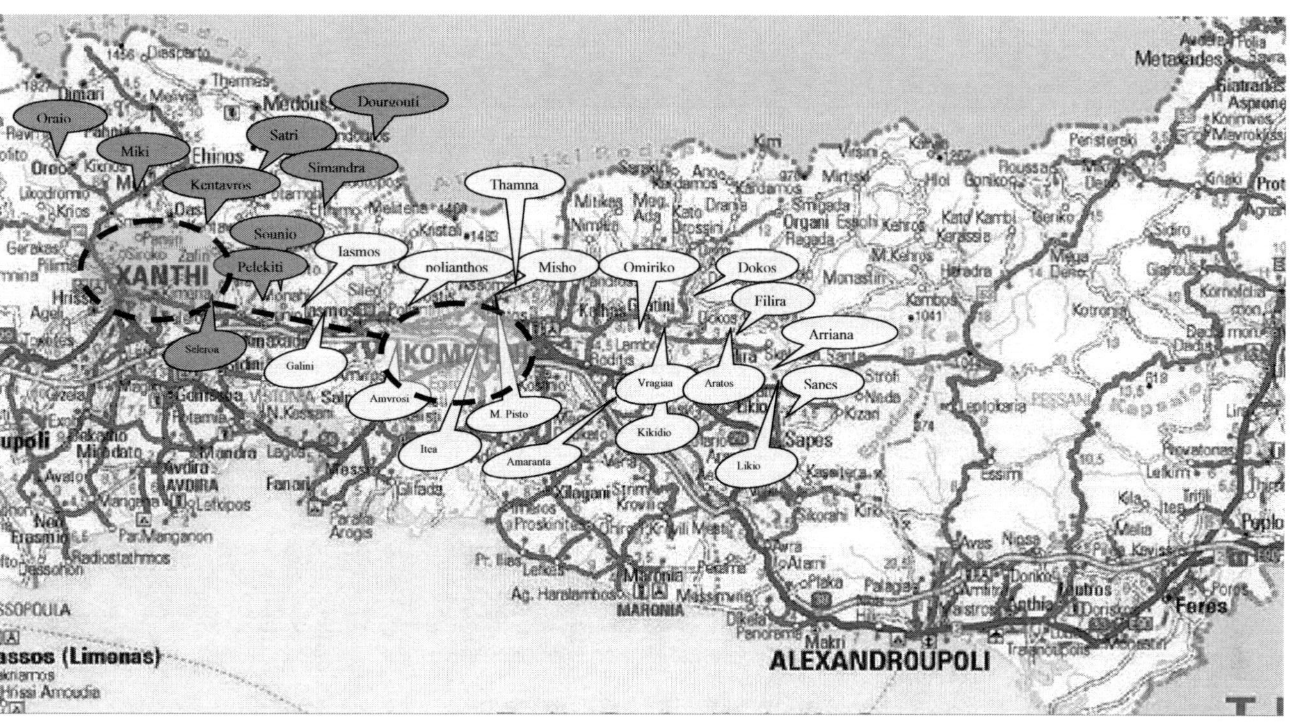

105

4.3 Quantitative Research

4.3.1 Demographics of Women

Out of the 137 participants, 57.7 % live in the towns of Komotini and Xanthi and 42.3 % live in villages.

Figure 4.2: Residence Area

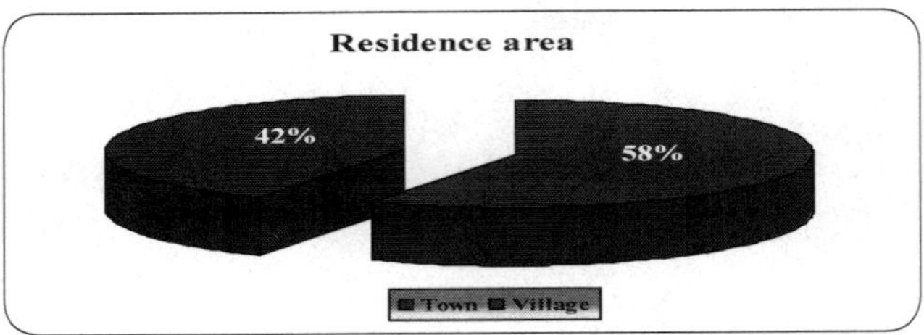

The mean age of the sample is 32.5; the median of the age is the range of 31–40. The percentages of each age range are illustrated in Figure 4.3.

Figure 4.3: Age of Women

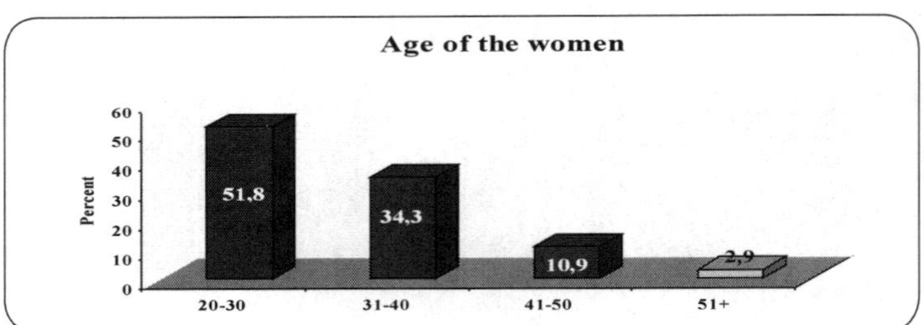

As for their educational level, the highest percentage range corresponds with the university graduates.

Figure 4.4: Education of Women

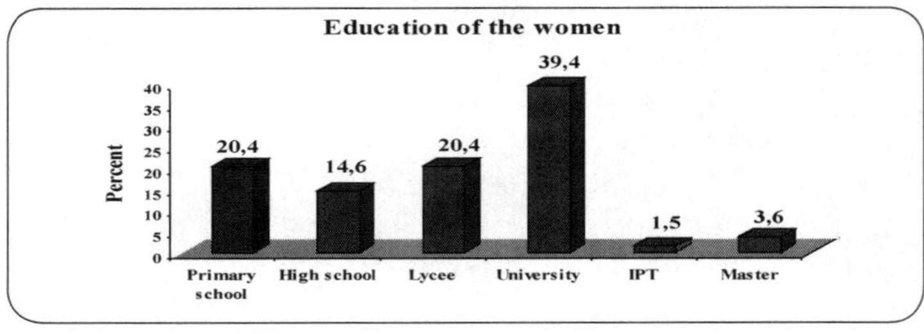

In the following figure the marital status of the participants is presented. Most of them are married.

Figure 4.5: Marital Status

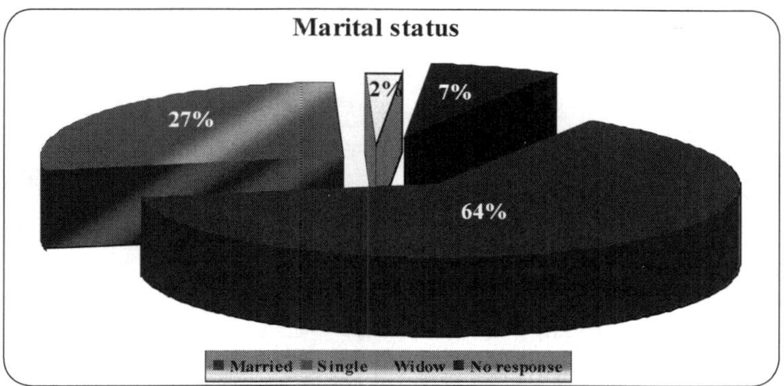

While detecting their economical status, we have found out that the highest rate of the participants' family belongs to the middle income group. Findings are illustrated in Figure 4.6.

Figure 4.6: Income of Women

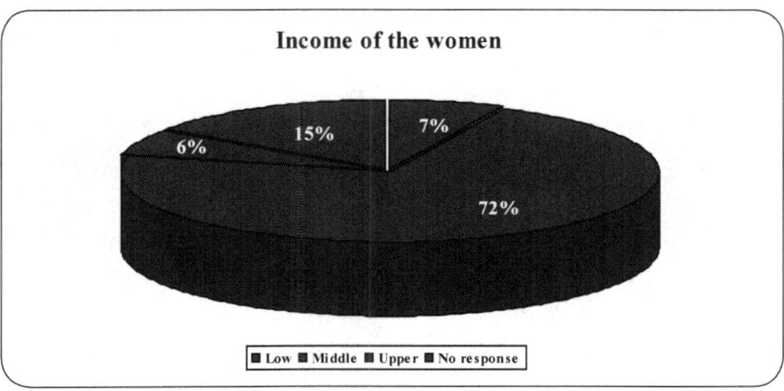

Private family income of 6.120 euros or less is classified as low income group; between 6,120 and 12.130 euros as low middle income group, and from 12.130 to 30.000 euros as middle income group; and income above 30.000 euros is classified as upper income group.

Regarding their professional status, 52.6 % of them are employed; of the respondents, three women (2.19 %) have an engineering background.

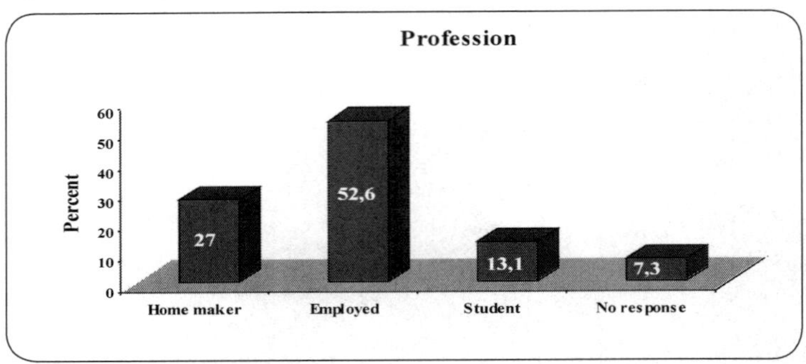

They all speak Turkish and more than two-thirds speak Greek. Mountain village dwellers on the mountains of Xanthi have as a mother tongue the Pomak language, but they also speak Greek and Turkish.

Hypothesis 1: *A significant difference in computer ownership is expected between the prefectures of Rodopi and Xanthi and between town and village dwellers.*

The analysis of the collected data revealed that 13.9 percent of the women did not own computers whereas 86.1 percent did (x^2=71.54, df = 1, p<0.001). The difference is significant, showing a big rate of computer ownership and simultaneously subjects' ability to practice or use the computers. By the way, in Greece the national figure for ownership is 44 %. According to Eurostat (2008) 73 % of Greek citizens have never used the Internet, only 22 % of them have access to it, 62.8 % do not know the computer use, more than 80 % own a mobile-phone and half of them speak only their mother tongue. At present, there is no data on the penetration of computer education among Muslim minority people living in Thrace (Hellenic Observatory for Information Society, 2008). Thus, comparatively, the size of computer ownership found in this research is extremely high but this due to the characteristics of the sample as was collected from the beginning.

A Mann-Whitney U test has indicated that there is a significant difference in computer ownership between the prefectures of Rodopi and Xanthi (U=1841, z=-3.123, p=0.002<0.05). The proportion of computer owners in the Rodopi prefecture is higher than that in Xanthi. The same criteria have revealed that women of the two towns have statistically significant high levels of computer ownership compared to those living in villages (U=2020, z=-1.972, p=0.049). The proportion of computer owners in towns is higher than that in villages.

Hence, hypothesis 1 that a significant difference in computer ownership is expected between prefectures of Rodopi and Xanthi and between town and village dwellers is accepted.

Hypothesis 2: *A high correlation is expected between computer ownership and professional status, family status, educational level of the interviewees.*

There is a small correlation between computer ownership and professional status (student, housewife, working) with an increase of the ownership for working women (Cramer's V=0.247, p=0.024). A Mann-Whitney U test reveals in addition that there is a statistically significant difference in computer ownership between women students and working women (U= 477, z=-2.334, p=0.020) and between students and domestic housewives (U=2020, z=-1.972, p=0.049) as the women of the sample who are students indicate lower proportions of computer ownership. On the other hand, there is not a statistically significant difference in computer ownership among working women and domestic housewives (U=1176, z=-0.462, p=0.644).

A chi-square test for independence has shown that there is a small negative correlation between computer ownership and family status with a decrease of ownership from married to single women x^2(1, 125)=5.50, Phi=-0.238, p=0.008.

The Cross tabulation between computer ownership and educational level (primary, secondary, tertiary) has also revealed a significant percentage of computer ownership for the women of primary education (82.1 %) while for those of secondary, 80 % and for those of tertiary, 93.2 %. Nevertheless, no correlations and no statistically significant differences between the two variables can be maintained. A Mann-Whitney U test has shown that there is a statistically significant difference in computer ownership between women with secondary education and those with tertiary education (U= 1280, z=-2.046, p=0.041). The latter records higher levels of computer ownership.

Hence, hypothesis 2 that a high correlation is expected between computer ownership and professional status, family status, educational level of the interviewees is rejected.

Regarding the place where women use the computer, it is observed that 71.5 % of them have access to a family computer and 8.8 % at friends' or relatives' houses, followed by Internet cafes (8.8 %), working places (6.6 %) (x^2=228.92, df = 4, p<0.01). Only 15.3 % of the women use their computer out of house in general. The data analysis shows that single women tend to use the computer outside their homes, but this is not statistically significant (Phi=0.158, p=0.074). A cross-tabs test indicated that the highest percentage of the women using the computer out of their houses was women at the age under 30s. The cross-tabs test among the variables of educational status of the women (a new variable for the education consisted only of primary, secondary and tertiary level) and places where they used the computers indicated that the highest percentage of the women visiting Internet cafes were women who received secondary education (52.4 % of the 22 women who used the computer outside their house).

Of the women, 93.4 percent had one or more computer literate family member while only a small percentage (9 percent) had no such member. The chi-square test revealed that this proportion is statistically significant (x^2=103.365, df =1, p<0.001). Due to the great percentage of the computer literates, the results of the chi-square are extremely high, showing the differences between the two groups. The frequency order of the literate members is siblings (n=67; sister, n=31, brother, n=36); children (n=57; daughter=29, son=28); husband (n=66); parents (n=16; mother=4, father=12). The background of these women is characterized by at least one computer literate family member who contributes to the computer literacy of the others and plays the role model that can be observed or imitated.

***Hypothesis 3**: A significant difference is expected in the preference of the gender of the trainer, connected to the family status of the women or connected to their residence area.*

While answering the question about the gender preference of the trainer, 78.8 percent of the women which is significant, expressed no gender preference while 21.2 percent had a preference (x^2=45.55, df = 1, p<0.001). In general, those who claimed for a preference for the gender of the trainer mostly preferred the female choice (x^2=9, df = 1, p<0.003). 16.8 percent of the women preferred a woman trainer; 5.1 percent opted for a man trainer and 70.1 percent were neutral. In this study, the gender of the trainer is found not to be important. A Mann-Whitney U test has revealed that there is not a significant difference in the preference of the gender of the trainer connected to the family status of the women (U=1559, Z= -0.547, p=0.584). A cross-tabs test between the preference of the gender of the trainer and the family status of the women revealed that the married women who claimed for a preference for the gender of the trainer preferred mostly the female choice (x^2=8.895, df = 1, p<0.003). The same test showed that there was not a significant difference in the preference of the gender of the trainer between town and village dwellers (U= 5333, z= -0.727, p= 0.468) and between Xanthi and Rodopi dwellers (U= 1984, z= -1.757, p= 0.079).

Hence, hypothesis 3 that a significant difference is expected in the preference of the gender of the trainer connected to the family status of the women or connected to their residence area is rejected.

110

4.3.2 Results of TPB Method

Measurement model

Reliability results from testing the measurement model are reported in Table 4.1, where inter-item reliabilities for each multi-item instrument are calculated using composite reliability and AVE (average variance extracted/explained). The data indicates that the measures are robust in terms of their internal consistency reliabilities as indexed by their composite reliabilities and by their AVE.

Table 4.1: Reliability Assessment of Measurement Model

Variable constructs	Composite reliability	AVE
Attitude (ATT)	0.85	0.53
Behavioural intention (BI)	0.87	0.69
Perceived Behavioural Control (PBC)	0.80	0.57
Subjective Norm (SN)	0.89	0.74

The composite reliabilities of different measures in the model range from 0.80 to 0.89, which exceed the recommended threshold value of 0.70 (Nunnally, 1978 as we read in Baker et al., 2007). Furthermore, consistent with the recommendation of Fornell and Larcker (1981), the average variance extracted (AVE) for each measure exceeds 0.50.

Table 4.2 reports the results of testing the discriminant validity of the measure scales. The bolded elements in the matrix diagonals, representing the square roots of the AVE, are greater in all cases than the off-diagonal elements in their corresponding row and column, supporting the discriminant validity of the scales.

Table 4.2: Discriminant Validity (inter-correlations) of Variable Constructs

Latent variables	ATT	BI	PBC	SN
ATT	1,00			
BI	0,39	1,00		
PBC	0,45	0,55	1,00	
SN	0,35	0,44	0,40	1,00

We tested convergent validity with PLS-Figure by extracting the factor loadings (and cross loadings) of all indicator items to their respective latent constructs. These results presented in Table 4.3, indicate all the items loaded on their respective construct (i.e. the bolded factor loadings) from a lower bound of 0.53 to an upper bound of 0.92 all of them exceeding the recommended cut-off value of 0.5 suggested by Straub (1989).; and higher on their respective construct than on any other construct (i.e. the non-bolded factor loadings in any one row).

A common rule of thumb to indicate convergent validity is that all items should load greater than 0.7 on their own construct (Yoo and Alavi, 2001 in Baker et al. 2007) and should load more highly on their respective construct than on the other constructs. The factor loading of each item time on its respective construct is rather significant (p<0.05). The loadings presented in Table 4.3 confirm the convergent validity of the measures for these latent constructs.

Table 4.3: Factor Loadings (bold & italicised) and Cross Loadings

	ATT	BI	PBC	SN
ATT1	**0,53**	0,18	0,21	0,15
ATT2	**0,78**	0,32	0,37	0,37
ATT3	**0,76**	0,33	0,34	0,18
ATT4	**0,75**	0,24	0,28	0,27
ATT5	**0,80**	0,32	0,40	0,28
BI1	0,30	**0,77**	0,44	0,24
BI2	0,33	**0,83**	0,45	0,44
BI3	0,34	**0,88**	0,50	0,39
PBC1	0,15	0,31	**0,64**	0,26
PBC2	0,51	0,43	**0,80**	0,35
PBC3	0,32	0,49	**0,81**	0,28
SN1	0,29	0,45	0,40	**0,92**
SN2	0,38	0,41	0,32	**0,89**
SN3	0,15	0,16	0,28	**0,76**

Hypothesis 4: *Attitude, Subjective Norm, and Perceived Behavioural Control will have a positive influence on Behavioural Intention.*

Figure 4.8 presents the results of the structural model where the beta values of the path coefficients indicate the direct influences of the predictor upon the predicted latent constructs. Attitude toward technology exhibits a strong positive influence ($\beta=0.128$, p<0.05) on Behavioural Intention, as does Subjective Norm ($\beta=0.232$, p<0.05) and Perceived Behavioural Control ($\beta=0.404$, p<0.05).

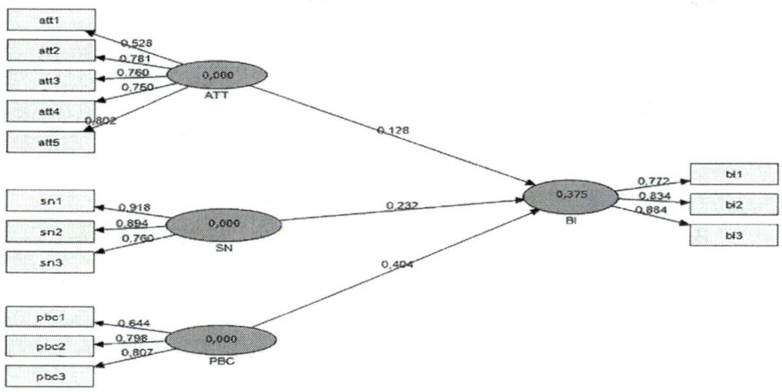

TPB is validated in this study, explaining approximately 37.5 percent of the variance in behavioural intention. The magnitude of this variance is similar to that reported in previous studies of technology adoption modelled by TPB.

Hence, hypothesis 4 that Attitude, Subjective Norm, and Perceived Behavioural Control will have a positive influence on Behavioural Intention is accepted.

Hypothesis 5: *Moderation of Attitude, Subjective Norm, and Perceived Behavioural Control is expected to be significant with age, with level of education, with residence area, with marital, economic and professional status upon Intention to use computer technology.*

For the moderating (interacting) variables, there were no statistically significant interactions for age, professional, marital and economic status, and residence1 (Rodopi-Xanthi) with the exception of the moderation of Subjective Norm on Intention to use technology by level of education and Perceived Behavioural Control on Intention to use technology by level of residence 2 (town-village).

Specifically, as Figure 4.9 presents, higher levels of education has a negative moderating effect (β=-0.863, p<0.05) on the positive influence of Subjective Norm on Intention to use technology. Direct influences of Attitude, Subjective Norm and Perceived Behavioural Control account for approximately 43.6 percent of the variance in Behavioural Intention (R^2= 0.436) (Cohen et al., 2003; Everitt and Dunn, 1991; Loehlin, 1991 in Baker et al., 2007).

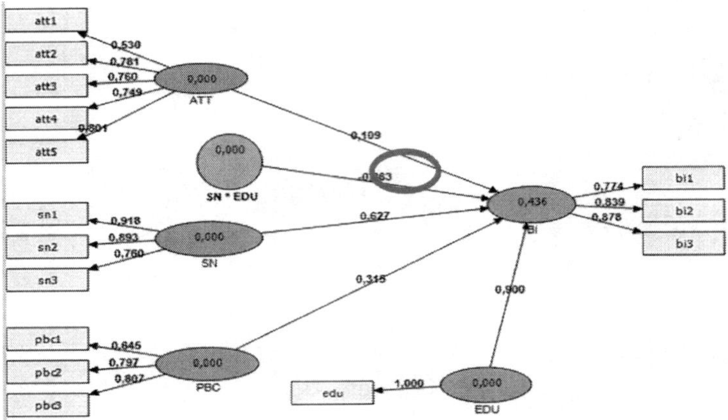

Furthermore, as we can see in Figure 4.10 living in a village has a negative moderating effect (β=-0.871, p<0.05) on the positive influence of Perceived Behavioural Control on Intention to use technology. Direct influences of Attitude, Subjective Norm and Perceived Behavioural Control account for approximately 39.7 percent of the variance in Behavioural Intention (R^2= 0.397).

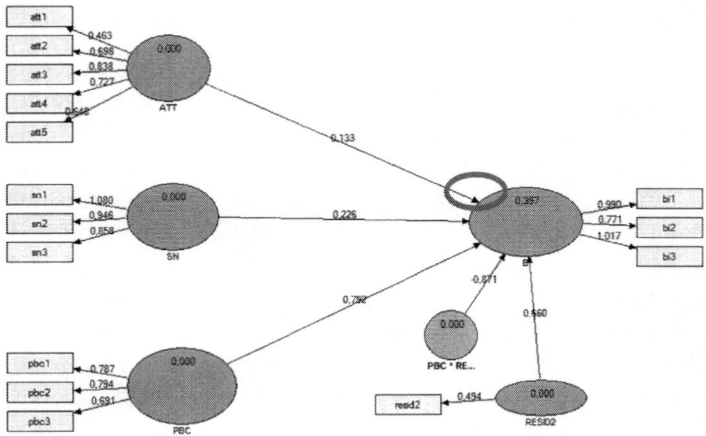

The remaining nineteen non-significant moderating paths are omitted from the results presented in Figure 4.9 and 4.10.

Hence, hypothesis 5 that the moderation of Attitude, Subjective Norm, and Perceived Behavioural Control is expected to be significant with age, with level of education, with residence area, with marital, economical and professional status upon to Intention to use computer technology is partially rejected.

4.3.3 Results of TAM Method

Reliability of questionnaire

Reliability results from testing the measurement model are reported in Table 4.4, where inter-item reliabilities for each multi-item instrument are calculated using Chronbach's alpha. The data indicates that the measures are robust in terms of their internal consistency reliabilities as indexed by their Chronbach's alpha results, based on the average inter-item correlation.

Table 4.4: Reliability of the scale Chronbach's alpha

Variable constructs	Chronbach's alpha
Perceived Ease of Use (PEOU)	0.78
Subjective Norm (SN)	0.83
Perceived Usefulness (PU)	0.87
Computer Self Efficacy (CSE)	0.77
Behavioural intention (BI)	**0.56**

The reliability of the four different measures in the model ranges from 0.77 to 0.87, which exceeds the recommendation of Fornell and Larcker (1981); and the Chronbach's alpha for each measure exceeds 0.70. As recommended, the internal consistency reliabilities are higher than 0.7 except from the behavioural intention. Consequently, these reliability coefficients are considered satisfying. The reliability of the variable BI is considered to be of medium standard; but for research purposes, an internal consistency reliability of 0.56 is acceptable.

Data analysis and results

Table 4.5: Descriptive Statistics

Rodopi-Xanthi sample N=137		
Construct	**Mean**	**Std. Deviation**
Behavioural Intention (BI)	8.57	1.316
Perceived Ease of Use (PEOU)	26.07	4.952
Computer Self Efficacy (CSE)	16.46	3.544
Perceived Usefulness (PU)	77.63	12.193
Subjective Norm (SN)	7.43	2.226

The mean score on the Behavioural Intention scale was high: (mean= 8.57, possible range 5–10) implying that women strongly intended to use computers in the future. Women trainees appraised computers to be moderately easy to use (mean=26.07, possible range 14–35). The checklist assessing magnitude of perceived usefulness indicated that overall women appraised computers to be very useful (mean=77.63; possible range 45–100). The subjects perceived themselves to be highly self efficacious using the computers: (mean=16.46; possible range 4–20), where they revealed a positive view of their cognitive capacities in dealing with computers. They appraised the Subjective Norm to be quite important (mean=7.43; possible range 2–10), indicating a motivation to comply with the expectations of others significant to learn computers.

A Pearson's correlation analysis was computed in order to detect the relationships among the variables and to stress the differences or similarities among the Muslim minority women as shown below (Table 4.6).

Table 4.6: Correlation Matrix of Psychological Variables in Greece

	PEOU	*PU*	*CSE*	*SN*	*BI*
PEOU		0.47**	0.33**	0.30**	0.36**
PU			0.23**	0.41**	0.50**
CSE				0.11	0.33**
SN					0.25**
BI					

Source: Author's Field Survey, 2009 Notes: **p<0.01, *p<0.05

116

Hypothesis 6: *There will be a positive relationship between Perceived Usefulness, Perceived Ease of Use and Behavioural Intention to use computers.*

During the statistical analysis of the data collected, a positive relationship was found between Perceived Ease of Use and a significant positive relationship between Perceived Usefulness to Behavioural Intention (r=0.36 and 0.50 respectively, p<0.01). In other words, when women think of computers as being easy to use and useful they adopt the use of this technology.

Hence, hypothesis 6 that there will be a positive relationship between Perceived Usefulness, Perceived Ease of Use and Behavioural Intention to use computers is accepted.

Hypothesis 7: *There will be a positive relationship between Perceived Ease of Use and Perceived Usefulness to computer use.*

A significant positive relationship between Perceived Ease of Use and Perceived Usefulness (r=0.47, p<0.01) was also examined.

Hence, hypothesis 7 that there will be a positive relationship between Perceived Usefulness, Perceived Ease of Use and use of computer is accepted.

Hypothesis 8: *There will be a positive relationship between Subjective Norm and Behavioural Intention, Perceived Usefulness, Perceived ease of use towards using computers.*

Subjective Norm was found to be significantly associated with Perceived Ease of Use and Perceived Usefulness (r=0.30, r=0.41, p<0.01 respectively). On the other hand Subjective Norm was not highly correlated with Behavioural Intention (r=0.25, p<0.05).

Hence, hypothesis 8 that there will be a positive relationship between Subjective Norm and Behavioural Intention, Perceived Usefulness, Perceived Ease of Use towards using computers is partially accepted.

Hypothesis 9: *There will be a positive relationship between Computer Self-Efficacy and Behavioural Intention, Perceived Ease of Use, Perceived Usefulness, Subjective Norm towards using computers.*

Computer Self-Efficacy was significantly related to a positive Behavioural Intention (r=0.33, p<0.05) and to Perceived Ease of Use (r=0.33, p<0.01). This indicated that the more efficacious the women perceive themselves to be, the stronger their intention is to use computers and think that are easy to use. Computer Self-

Efficacy and Perceived Usefulness were not correlated in a high level (r=0.23, p<0.01).

Hence, hypothesis 9 that there will be a positive relationship between Computer Self-Efficacy and Behavioural Intention, Perceived Ease of Use, Perceived Usefulness, Subjective Norm towards using computers is partially accepted.

Pearson's product-moment correlation coefficients calculated show that most variables are strongly interconnected. Reliability results and correlation results provide a favourable condition to test the Technical Acceptance Model with regression analyses.

Regression analyses -Measurement of ß-coefficients to test TAM

In order to detect the causal linkages between the psychological variables and Behavioural Intention to use computers, a regression analysis was conducted as shown in Table 4.7.

Table 4.7: Regression Analysis

Dependent Variable	R^2	Independent Variable	B	Standard error of b	β	T
Perceived Ease of Use	0.11	Computer Self-Efficacy	0.459	0.114	0.328	
		Constant	18.512	1.912	–	
Perceived Usefulness	0.17	Subjective Norm	2.245	0.430	0.410	
		Constant	60.949	3.335	–	
Perceived Usefulness	0.29	Perceived Ease of Use	0.874	0.196	0.355	
		Computer Self-Efficacy	0.284	0.263	0.083	
		Subjective Norm	1.617	0.414	0.295	
		Constant	38.153	5.670	–	
Behavioural Intention	0.28	Perceived Ease of Use	0.026	0.023	0.10[a]	
		Perceived Usefulness	0.042	0.009	0.39*	
		Computer Self-efficacy	0.075	0.029	0.20*	
		Subjective Norm	0.048	0.048	0.04	
		Constant	3.244	0.713	–	

Notes: **p<0.01; *p<0.05

Perceived Usefulness and Computer Self-Efficacy had a direct effect on Behavioural Intention and emerged significant (β=0.39, and β=0.20 respectively, p<0.05). Perceived Ease of Use and Subjective Norm had no direct effect on Behavioural

Intention (β= 0.10, and β=0.04, respectively). All the variables taken together explained a 28 percent variance in behavioural intention, the indicator of technology acceptance (Figure 4.11).

Significant causal linkages were found for two sets of variables: 1) Computer Self-Efficacy was a significant determinant of Perceived Ease of Use (β =0.33, p<0.05), implying that when a woman sees herself as competent, she views computers easy to handle; 2) Subjective Norm was a significant determinant of Perceived Usefulness (β=0.41, p<0.05), that is, when women feel that important people in their lives expect them to learn computers, they assess the technology in question as useful.

In Table 4.8, the indirect effects of psychological variables to Behavioural Intention are presented and they provide a further insight.

Table 4.8: Direct and Indirect Effects of Psychological Variables on Behavioural Intention

Variable	Direct Effect	Indirect Effect	Total Effect
PEOU	0.10	0.26	0.36
PU	0.39	0.11	0.50
CSE	0.20	0.06	0.26
SN	0.04	0.21	0.25

The overall effect of Perceived Usefulness increased to 0.50, with an indirect effect of 0.11 through all other psychological variables. The overall effect of Perceived Ease of Use had a significant effect too (0.36, p < 0.05) when combined with the indirect effect through Perceived Usefulness (0.26). The overall impact of Computer Self-Efficacy (0.26) and Subjective Norm (0.25) to Behavioural Intention was significant through all other psychological variables.

The mediating effect of beliefs about computers, definitely Perceived Usefulness and Perceived Ease of use, was additionally explored as shown in Table 4.9.

Table 4.9: Results of Sobel z test Assessing Mediation of Perceived Usefulness in Determining Behavioural Intention to Use Computers

| Dependent Variable | Independent Variable | Mediating Variable | Sobel z |
			Females Greece (N=137)
Behavioural Intention to use computers	Subjective Norm	Perceived Usefulness	3.89****
	Perceived Ease of Use	Perceived Usefulness	3.91****
	Computer Self-Efficacy	Perceived Usefulness	2.53[a]

*p<0.005, ****p<0.0001, [a]p<0.0115

As we read in Umrani's (2007) research, according to Baron and Kenny (1986), Sobel z, a statistics to assess mediation effect, is computed to examine whether the other variables are contributing to Behavioural Intention indirectly through the mediation of Perceived Usefulness. This research has clarified that the effect of Subjective Norm (z = 3.89, p<0.05), Perceived Ease of Use (z = 3.91, p<0.0001), Computer Self-Efficacy (z = 2.53, p<0.0001) on Behavioural Intention to use computers is mediated significantly by Perceived Usefulness.

Benefits

The women who participated in the research were asked to list benefits in the order of priority. They reported an average 5.64 of the benefits of the eight they were asked to list, with 69.3 percent reporting five or more benefits and 30.7 percent reporting four or less.

Table 4.10: Frequency and Rank of Categories of Benefits of Computer Use

Category	Frequency	Rank
Seeking information	177	1
Entertainment	157	2
Communication	113	3
Personal/family gain	76	4
Job/career	76	5
Personality	44	6

Category	Frequency	Rank
Convenience	43	7
Social gain	32	8
Information storage	27	9

Seeking information was ranked as the first most important benefit by women as they became aware of the potentials of access to information through computers. Entertainment was cited as their second most preferable choice, and use of computers for communication, and connecting with family and kin the third, which emerges as crucial and will be further presented in the qualitative research.

Figure 4.11: Path Diagram of the Effects of Psychological Predictors on BI

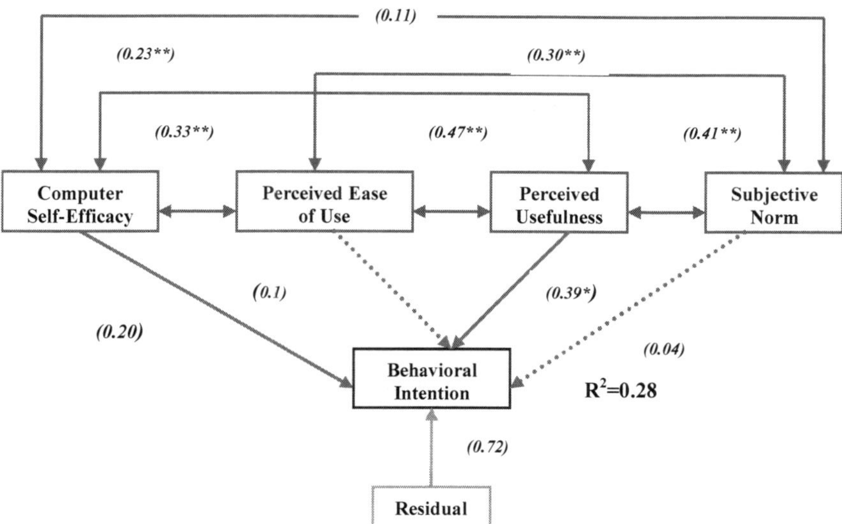

Notes: **p<0.01; *p<0.05 numbers in parenthesis represent correlation coefficients between the variables.

4.4 Qualitative Research

This part of the study is qualitative in nature and focuses on exploring the connection of ICTs to the social empowerment of Muslim minority women in Thrace. Data for this part was collected from 28 individuals, a sub sample drawn from the parent sample of the initial part of the study. The selection of the subjects was based on their availability and relation to ICTs as this was detected from the questionnaires designed for the initial research. Four women from the area of Xanthi and five women of the area of Rodopi did not want their voices to be recorded. A total of 11 hours, 38 minutes and 22 seconds of recorded voices was transcribed into text.

4.4.1 Demographics of Women

Of the 28 women interview participants, fifteen live at the Rodopi administration, thirteen at the Xanthi administration, thirteen in villages and fifteen in towns as illustrated below.

Figure 4.12: Residence area

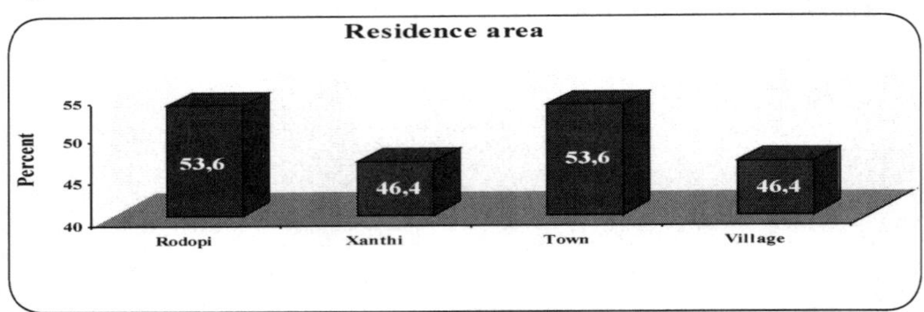

The mean age of the sample was 35; the median of the age range was 31–40 years; 12 were young adults (20–30 years), six were mature adults (31–40 years), eight were middle aged (41–50 years), two were in the older group (51–60 years). As for their marital status, the overwhelming majority was married and had children.

Figure 4.13: Marital Status

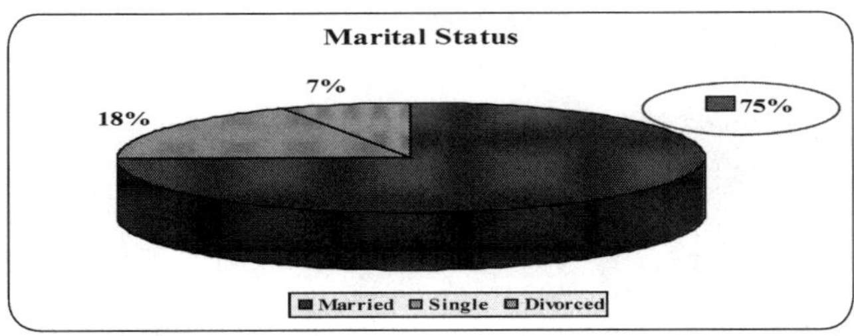

The fact that the highest rate of their parents' education level is that of primary education is worth mentioning as it describes the educational level of the biggest part of minority members all the past years.

122

Figure 4.14: Parents' Education

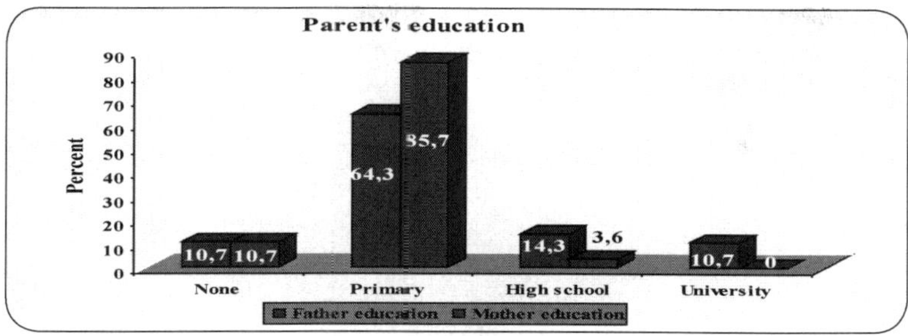

As illustrated in Figure 4.15, an overwhelming majority of the interviewees studied in a minority elementary school and only a small percent studied in a state school.

Figure 4.15: School of Primary Education

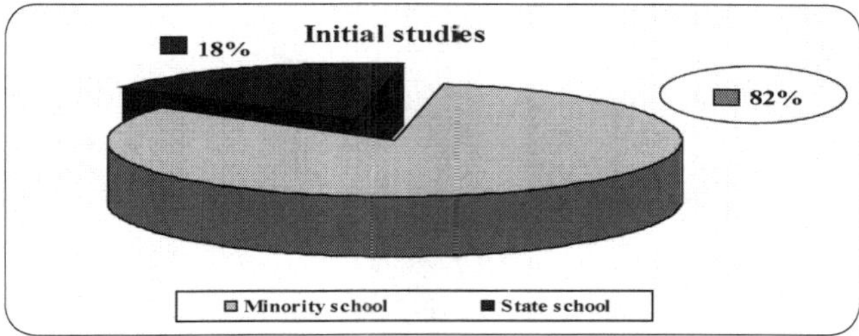

Interviewees were of different educational levels, but one fourth of them was of primary education and the same number of tertiary education. We tried to make our sample consist of different educational levels in order to obtain a pluralism of the views we were about to select.

Figure 4.16: Interviewees' Studies

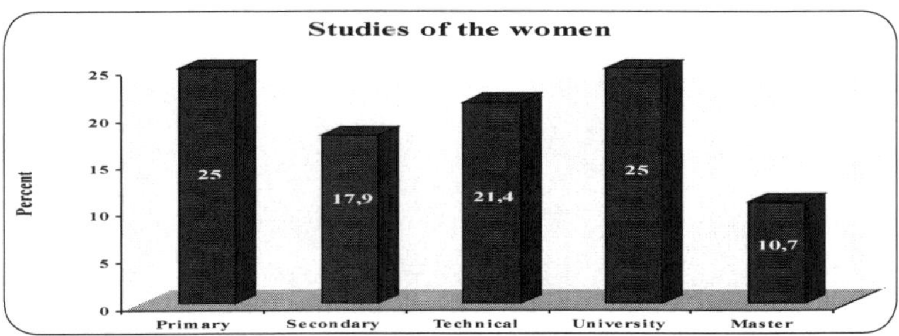

Of the interviewees, 27 speak Turkish (one was of Pomak origin and was raised in the Greek territory but outside Thrace), 26 speak Greek and 15 of them can speak English. Only half of them work. Most of them are of middle income.

Figure 4.17: Economical Status

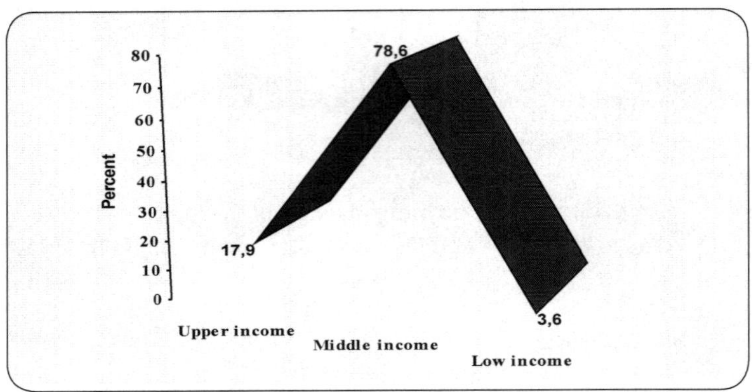

4.4.2 Experiences on ICTs

In Figure 4.1 the findings on the interviewees' experiences on ICTs are presented with bars with dominants those of cell-phone, computer and Internet.

Figure 4.18: Relations to ICTs

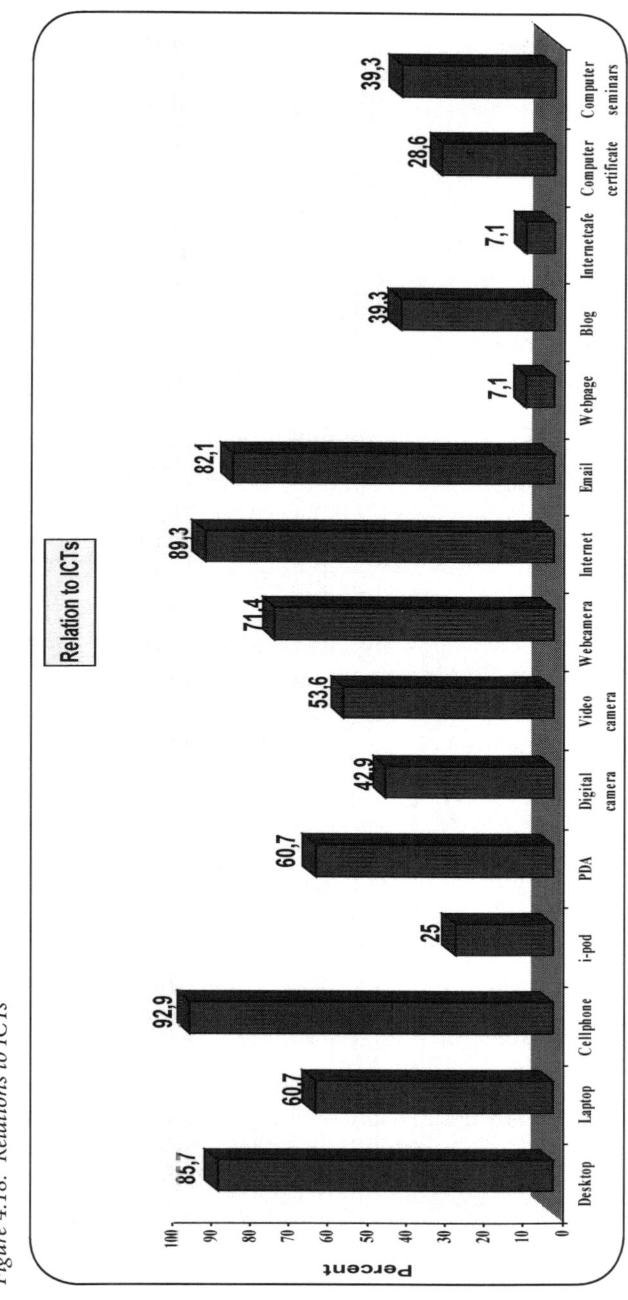

The findings on the interviewees' experiences on ICTs that emerged from this study show that an overwhelming majority of the interviewees own cell phones, desktop computers and laptops, have Internet at home but only 39.3 % of them have Internet at work as only half of the interviewees work. An overwhelming majority own personal digital assistants (address books, blackberries), web-cameras for their chat connections and most of them have email accounts. Many of them have their own face book accounts, which can be connected to the efforts women make to become extrovert. Almost 40 % of the interviewees has participated in seminars on computer use and obtained certificates for their attendance. In Greece, whenever applying for a job, such certificates and skills give bonus to the application. Most of the interviewees 22 (78.6 %) said they used the computer daily. Seventeen of the interviewees (60.7 %) said they usually went online several times a day; and six of the rest eleven interviewees, 3–5 days a week. Of the interviewees, the overwhelming majority of them 25 (89,3 %), use the Internet a lot and 18 (64.3 %) use both the Word and the Messenger a lot, fifteen use the Excel a little to a lot, the majority of the women do not use the Photoshop, the AutoCAD, the Outlook, the FrontPage, the Access, the PowerPoint.

Women interviewees connected the term ICT to computers, mobile phones and web cameras since these are the gadgets they commonly use. In general, their view on ICTs is positive as they have had the above experiences; they have described ICT as something new, something that provides quick communication, something that helps in their learning procedure, something that makes their life easier. This is brought out by Vildan's, Alev's, and Bikek's comments respectively in the order quoted below:

> *"It is something that scares me, but on the other hand it is something necessary."(Vildan)*

> *"It makes my life easier, helps me a lot to make things much easier, provides me with knowledge, and it changes my life."(Alev)*

> *"ICT is something good, a development for the human kind. I used to write with a pen, now I write with a computer."(Bikek)*

4.4.3 Infrastructure

Almost all of the interviewees (96.4 %) say there are cyber cafés in the area they live, and 82.1 % say there are training centres in the area they live in with a proximity to 15–30 minutes of the centre. Majority of them do not visit cyber cafés as these places usually function as cafes or bars in the area of Thrace and mostly in villages. This finding is similar to what Gurumurthy (2005) claims: *"Cyber cafés, for example, often have a predominantly male customer base and tend not to provide a separate space for women and may not be open the times convenient for women who have heavy domestic responsibilities, especially in the dark night."*

Information on computer seminars is usually obtained from the interviewees from KEP (Centres for Citizen's Service). KEP is the most favoured choice of women of all ages with primary, secondary and technical education, and especially of village dwellers. University graduates prefer the Muslim Youth Association and those with a master's degree all the choices: (library, association, adult education centres, newspapers and Internet); except KEP.

Figure 4.19: Areas where Information is received

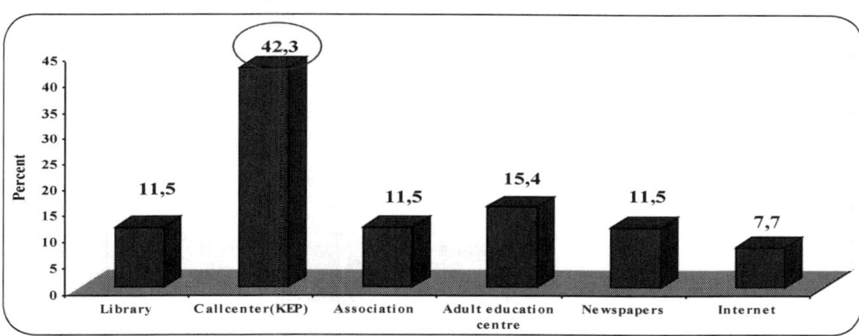

Almost half of the women, especially the older ones who live in villages, learned the use of the computer at home or in their family shops with the contribution of their husbands, siblings, sons or daughters. Young women learned how to use the computer in high schools in Greece or those who studied in Turkey, in universities. Some women attended seminars in private schools (KEK) and others attended seminars on computer use in the private club of the Muslim Youth's Association. In addition to the above, information of the efforts a woman of the minority makes to learn how to use the computer is worth mentioning.

Hatice, a young woman who was brought up in Germany and received only secondary education in a German state school, when describing her efforts, she exhibits all the agony of a young woman who wants to become skilled and to be able to help her children.

> *"I learned computer at home on my own. I attended online lessons on computer use through the Internet. In the afternoons, I attended lessons at the 2nd Chance School and at the technical school following the programs provided for the adult education."*

Twelve of the women showed a preference to state or minority schools as the place where they could attend programs on computer use, with private centres for professional training following their choices. Remarkable is the fact that women from Xanthi also selected the choice "Association", stating by this choice the importance of the minority women's association that functions in the area.

In addition, data of the interviews gave us the information that women who took part in the study from the Province of Xanthi were more informed on the function of private centres for professional training and the EU funded programs they provided. Findings of the study display that women are interested in expanding their knowledge by attending seminars and computer programs or learning the Greek language. Most of them state that the minority women need to achieve a better social position, to change their family status quo, to be able to help their children, and to gain their personal fulfilment, social gain and empowerment.

> *"A woman has to understand that life is not only marriage, a husband, and kids, but she has to be creative in other parts of life". (Sabahat)*

> *"I am learning for my own good and interest and to be able to help my children in the future." (Hatice)*

> *"The "Second Chance" schools help a lot. I believe that after finishing this school you have a chance to continue your studies at the university. Knowledge has nothing to do with age." (Alev)*

Women were aware of the existence of state schools for adult education (the Second Chance School) and pointed out that this kind of school had to be established in every Municipality easily accessible or transportation must be provided for easy access. This finding comes as no surprise because the time saved on travel enables women to balance their educational aspirations with family and household responsibilities.

4.4.4 Multiplier Impact

During the research the interviewees were asked about their family members who were computer literate and the answer that received the highest rate was that of the "husband", followed by the "brother" and then "son", findings being illustrated in Figure 4.20. Although in the quantitative part of this study, the same question had a different order of the answers with some differences, the choices were almost the same as the background of these women is characterized by at least one computer literate family member who contributes to the computer literacy of the others and plays the role model that can be observed or imitated.

Figure 4.20: Interviewees' Relatives who Use Computer

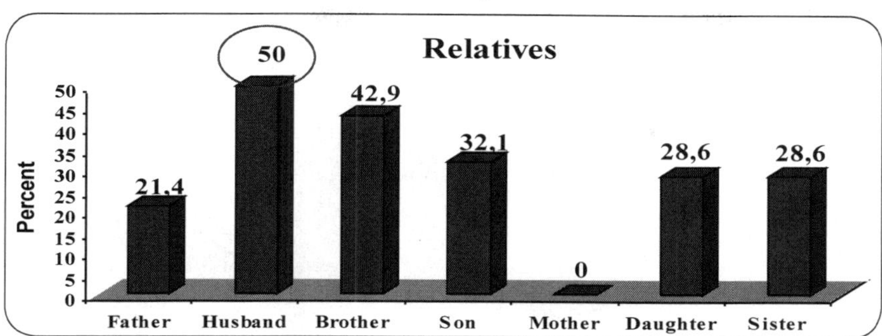

The main factors that influenced them in learning the computer use were their peers, husbands, their children, then their mentors and finally their interests.

The interviewees' acquisition of technical skills results in computer literacy of other family members and consequently computer awareness in the family as the majority of the interviewees (67.9 %) has encouraged members of their family to learn the computer use. They usually teach computer skills and serve as a role model by talking about computers to their female friends and neighbours, their sisters, mothers and daughters, and their unemployed friends. For instance, Aynur, a scarf clad woman, said

> *"I taught the computer use to my mother, to my mother in law, to my friends and especially to my young students as I teach them the Koran via Internet."*

Furthermore, Hatice, a young woman, added another parameter to the dialogue which was expressed several times by different women pointing out in this study,

> *"I persuaded my friends to learn to use the computer to help their children."*

Ayla, a mature woman well informed, working in a government position said,

> *"I have encouraged unemployed friends to attend seminars (OAED and EU projects). They even received a certificate. I told it to 10 people, only 2 attended."*

Deniz, a very active housewife, explained, *"I taught my husband how to use it.*

> *"All the time I keep telling my friends that they should learn how to use it. We went once to attend lessons all together."*

4.4.5 Reasons for Computer Use and the Internet

When women were asked to state reasons they use the computer, according to the multiple answers they were provided with, "Internet" was the one with the highest rate of choice compared with the others. "Communication" was their second choice, followed by "Profession" and "Game/Entertainment" equally as their third choice.

Figure 4.21: Reasons for Computer Use

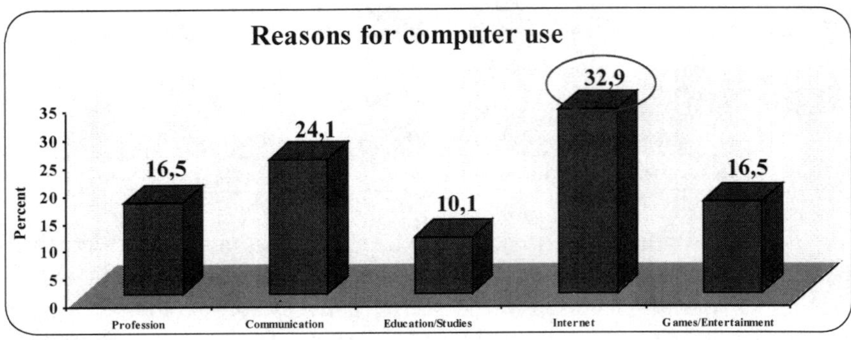

A cross tabulation between the reasons for computer use and the residence area has revealed a significant percentage for "Communication" for ones who live in a town and for "Internet" for those living in both prefectures, and in villages. The choice "Profession" is mostly preferred by those living in Komotini, the Rodopi prefecture and town. "Education/Studies" gained an equal percentage with all possible parameters they are cross tabulated. "Games/Entertainment" is mostly preferred by town dwellers and it is the highest preference among all the others for village dwellers.

Figure 4.22: Reasons for Computer Use and Residence Area

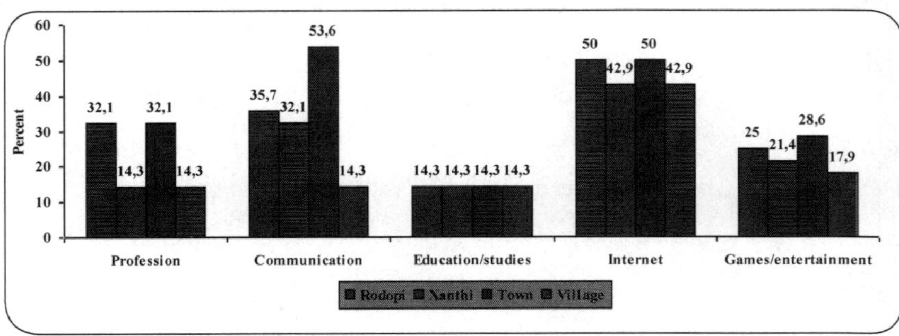

A cross tabulation between the reasons for the computer use and the educational level (primary, secondary, technical, tertiary, master's degree) revealed a significant percentage for Internet, Communication, Profession, Games/Entertainment for the women of tertiary education, and for Internet for those of primary, secondary and technical education. The women who held a master's degree revealed a significant percentage for Education/Studies.

Figure 4.23: Reasons for the Computer Use and Educational Level

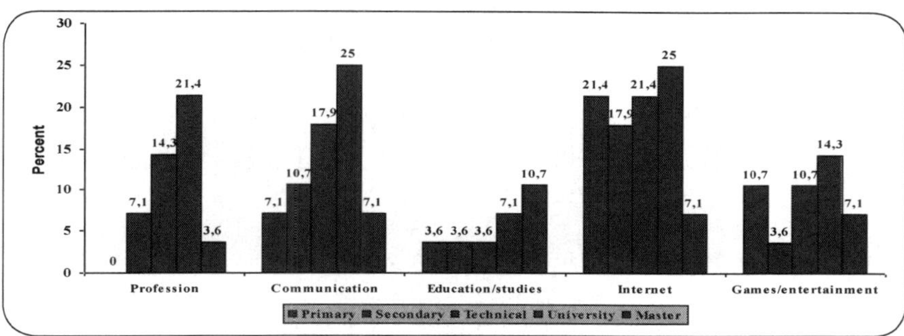

A cross tabulation between the reasons for computer use and the age of the interviewees revealed a significant percentage for Internet and Communication for the ages 18–30. The choice Education/Studies was chosen only by the ages 18–30 and 31–40 whilst profession was chosen even by the ages 41–50. Internet and Communication was the only choice for the ages over 50.

Figure 4.24: Reasons for Computer Use and Age

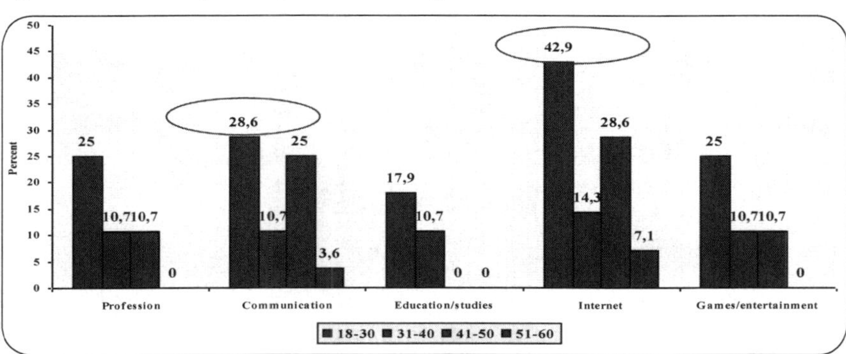

When women were asked to indicate what sort of information they got from the Internet, according to the multiple choice they were provided with, "News" scored the highest percent of choice compared to the others. "Chatting" was their second choice followed by "Work" as their third.

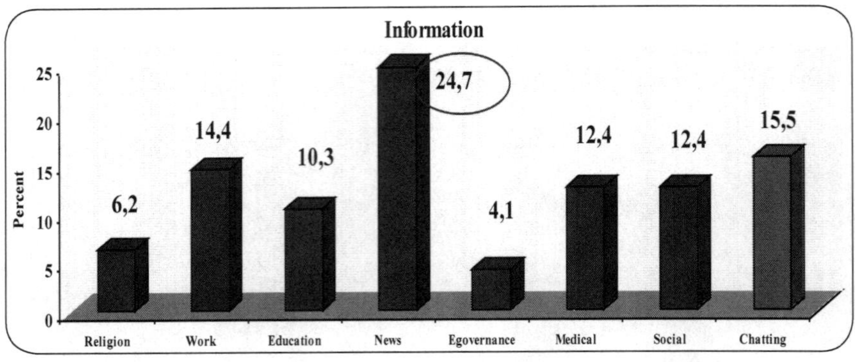

Figure 4.25: Information Received from the Internet

A cross tabulation between the information from the Internet and the residence area revealed a significant percentage for "News" as the mostly preferred with the choice "Work" following. Residents of the Rodopi prefecture and town dwellers chose "News" at 60 %, and "Work" at almost 40 %. Information on medical issues was chosen in a high percentage 36 % by town dwellers, followed by the same category of information on social issues 32 %.

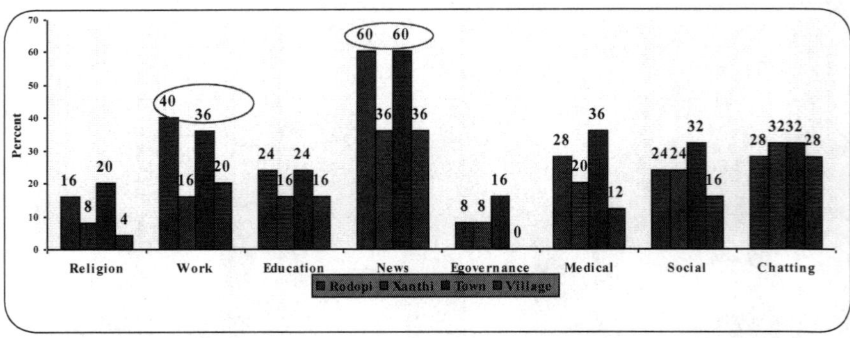

Figure 4.26: Information from the Internet and Residence Area

A cross tabulation between the information from the Internet and the educational level (primary, secondary, technical, tertiary, master's degree) revealed a significant percentage for "News", followed by the choice for "Work" from the ones of tertiary education and technical education. The choice "Chatting" was mostly preferred by the one of primary education. E-governance was only preferred by the ones who received high levels of education.

Figure 4.27: Information from the Internet and Educational Level

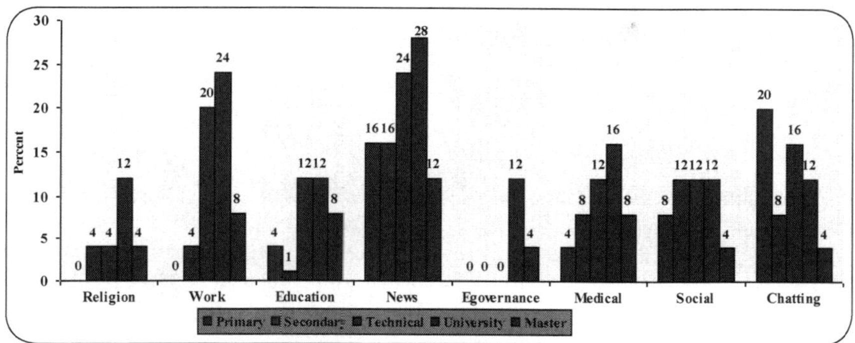

A cross tabulation between the reasons for computer use and the age of interviewees revealed a significant percentage for the choice "News" (40 %) and for the choice "Work" (36 %) from women at the ages of 18–30. As for the ages of 41–50, there was a significant percentage for the choice "News" (32 %). The highest rates for all choices derived from women at the ages of 18–30.

Figure 4.28: Information from the Internet and Age

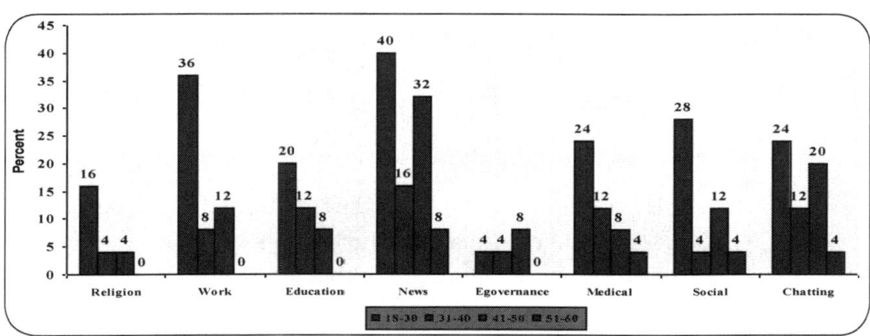

The interviewees explained that they mostly communicated with their friends and relatives abroad via Internet as most minority people have relatives who live in Turkey or in many other European countries.

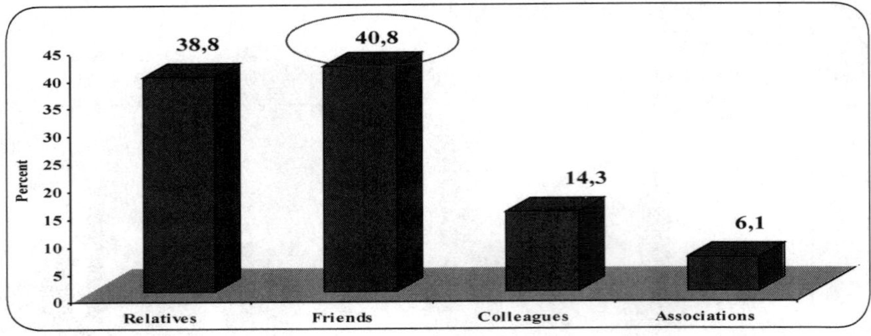

Twenty options, all manageable through the Internet, were quoted to women interviewees. They were asked to rank their ability to use these 20 options. Of the 28 women, 3 did not respond to the question. The numbers in Figure 4.30 represent the percent of the women for each option.

The answers that received the major preference were as follows:

- Get news on line.
- Connect to their friends and Learn new things (at the same level).
- Connect to relatives abroad.
- Look for information about movies, books, etc.
- Look for information about a hobby or interest.
- Browse for fun.
- Look for information about health, medical issues, enjoy hobbies, and download music files.
- Do their job.
- Information for a place to live; share online artwork, photos, etc.

Their choices did not include or were not of high range for the following options: to manage your personal finances, the e-government, to work with others in your community or in groups you belong to and the telemarketing.

134

Figure 4.30: Reasons for Using the Internet

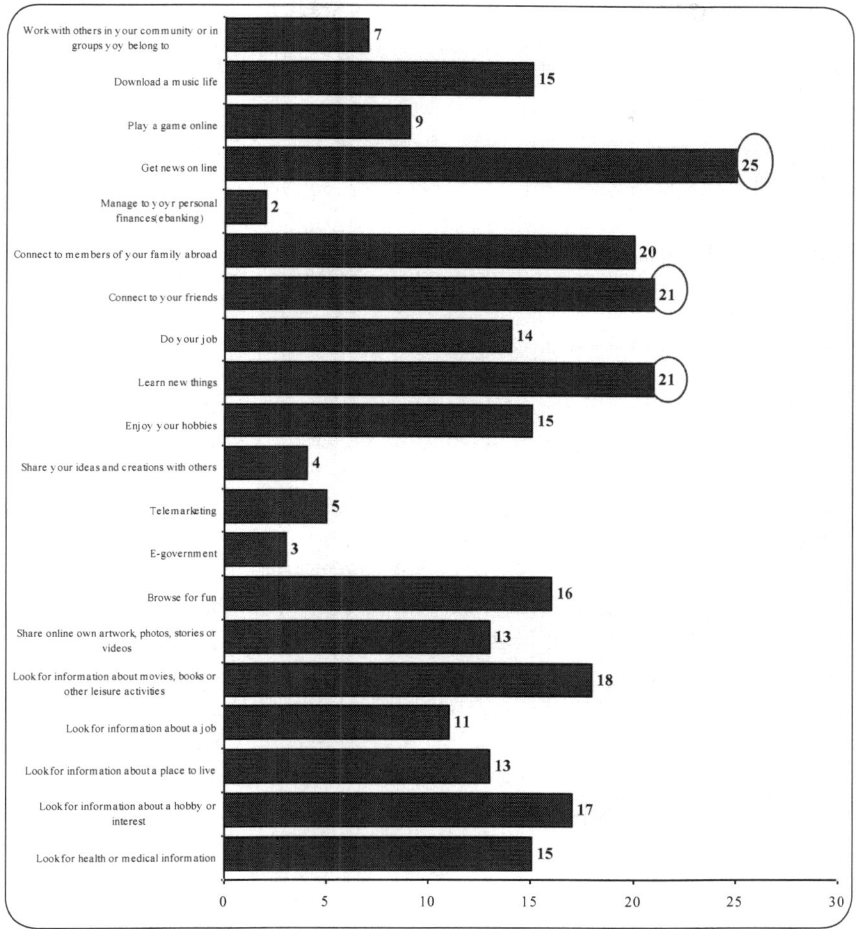

A cross tabulation test between the frequencies of the options and the demographics of the women verified the above range. For the cross-tab analysis, we recoded the degrees "a lot" and "some" together and the degrees "only a little" and "not at al" together.

A cross tabulation between the functioning of the 20 options and the residence area (town-village) of the interviewees revealed that both town and village dwellers chose the option "Get news on line" as their first choice. The village dwellers preferred as their second option "Connect with relatives abroad", this can be explained by the high percents of emigration observed among the members of the minority who live in villages, especially the ones living on the mountain area. Another most preferable option for the village dwellers was to browse for fun or play games. The town dwellers used the Internet more to find information on books, movies, to enjoy their hobbies, and to find a job.

A cross tabulation between the functioning of the 20 options and the age of the interviewees revealed the choices "Get news on line" as their first choice, followed by the choice "Connect with friends" or "Connect with relatives abroad". The younger women showed a preference for looking up information about books, movies, downloading music, browsing for fun, seeking information for a job or working through Internet.

A cross tabulation between the functioning of the 20 options and their studies revealed that those with high levels of education used the Internet for multiple choices, almost all the ones provided by the researcher; and those with primary or secondary education were oriented more to "Get news on line" as their first choice, followed by "Connect with friends" or "Connect with relatives abroad". Those with primary education used the Internet a lot for "Health and medical information" and for "Fun". The option "Information about a job" was mostly preferred by the more educated.

A cross tabulation between the functioning of the 20 options and the profession revealed that those who worked did their job through the computer or the Internet. The languages the interviewees said they used mostly for reading webpages on the Internet was Greek and Turkish in almost the same rate and only one third of them used English. This finding may seem contradictory as the mother tongue of the interviewees is Turkish, but the web-pages they usually search for information about jobs, scholarships and state services are Greek websites.

Figure 4.31: Languages Used for the Internet

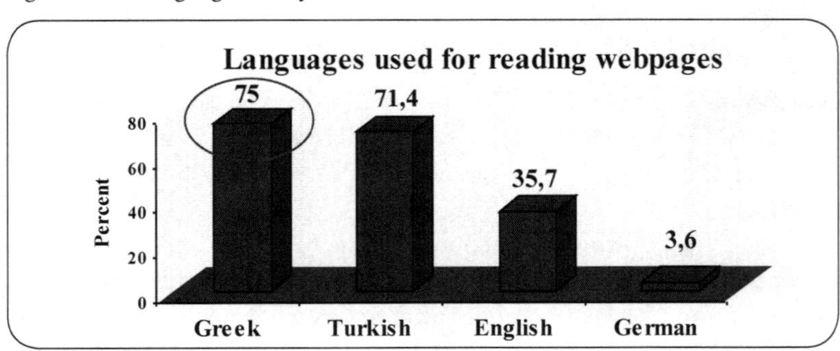

When the interviewees were asked to give information about the websites they commonly use, they provided a variety of websites. They preferred reading Turkish newspapers to receive news from Turkey. They also read the minority Turkish phone daily press which includes many newspapers published everyday in Komotini and Xanthi. They watched Turkish television and all the programmes they missed from Turkish channels. They chatted with friends, relatives, or with the opposite sex. Some of them bought products on line.

There are many sites that deal exclusively with women issues, such as pregnancy, fertility, jobs, home business, home investing, breastfeeding, depression, relationship issues among families, caring for the aged and adjusting to families settled abroad. Women of the Muslim minority in Thrace confront similar problems as many Muslim women do all over the world. As the importance and the safety provided by the networking becomes known, more and more Muslim women are finding the Internet as boon.

One of the interviewees participates in online Turkish communities, exchanging ideas and views about theater plays, directing a play and reciting poems. Some women find food recipes from both Greek and Turkish websites. Most women trying to find a job refer to Greek searching machines or Greek websites of ministries or organizations.

The following Table 4.11 contains the web pages mostly accessed by the women interviewees.

Table 4.11: Websites Commonly Accessed by Women Interviewees

Turkish newspapers	www.gazeteler.com www.milliyet.com.tr www.haberturk.tr www.hurriyet.tr www.hurriyet.tr www.diziizle.tr www.trakyaninsesi.com	www.dergiler.tr www.gundemgazetesi.com www.sabah.tr www.bultengazetesi.com www.rodopruzgari.com
Greek newspapers	www.paratiritis-news.gr www.ethnos.gr	www.xronos.gr www.focus.gr
Searching tools	www.yahoo.com www.facebook.com www.alfavita.gr www.gmail.com www.meteo.gr www.google.gr www.hotmail.com	www.in.gr www.msn.com www.wikipedia.org www.skype.com www.youtube.com www.googleearth.com

Religious papers	www.diyanet.gov.tr	
Information for jobs	www.diorismos.gr www.proslipsi.gr	www.asep.gr www.iky.gr
Cooking Diets Child-nutrition Decoration Theater Entertainment Shopping online Cinema- films Social matters Feminist matters Psychology matters NGO s Payment of bills	www.vefa.gr www.kraloyun.com www.tiyatroonline.com www.antoloji.com www.yemek24.com	www.linewite.com www.ebay.com www.muziklerim.tr www.webshot.com www.dergiler.com http://horoscopes.pathfinder.gr/

4.4.6 Social and Psychological Impact

From the content analysis of the interviews, it was found out that interviewees experienced social and psychological gains from computer education in terms of change in self-perception as they expressed an increased self-confidence and positive self-view and a feeling of knowledgeable and contemporary sense. Computer education had an economic impact as it helped eight of the interviewees to find a job and made them feel assured. It opened up new opportunities to them to use the Internet for job related information. As stated above, the use of the Greek language to read websites is connected to surfing job portals or job circulars sent out on the Internet.

This is brought up by Belgin's comments, a scarf and light long coat clad interviewee who helps her husband in their shop, works at home with three computers while she runs the Photoshop very efficiently.

"Computer education helped me in various sections. First of all, I work at home. I started learning many things from the Internet. I can help my child more. I have self confidence and economical existence. Usually covered women are confronted with prejudice because we are considered to act only as housewives and nothing more. The fact that I am working with the computer and contribute to the family income gives me more confidence. I can buy whatever I want without asking my husband. I just ask him to give me the money."

The majority of the interviewees believe that ICTs can help, to obtain knowledge, to achieve communication, to become more efficient to your work, to gain self confidence, to evaluate your education and studies, and to increase your social

138

participation. Being aware of the potential empowerment through computer education the interviewees quoted some of their motives for attending a computer seminar. These were: knowledge, communication, skills, money, feeling contemporary. Their choices and the order they placed them are an indicator that women have further awareness of the demands of the society they try to plug in.

Zekie, a dweller on the Xanthi mountain, a woman with special characteristics, who is very smart, interested in learning new things to change her life, who integrates technology in her life and does not have a problem to be integrated in the local society she lives in, who wonders whether she can attend the university wearing the scarf, with her own face book account, comments:

> *"I feel much better being computer educated. I learn new things and I can help my child in many things as everything is being done through the computer nowadays."*

Many women reported that computer education helped them to communicate with friends, with their children who study abroad and their relatives. Alev's and Ayla's opinion, almost identical, conclude all the above.

> *"Through the computer I stay in touch with contemporary society, I learn the news, I search for new things, I stay in touch with friends and relatives. This is the easiest way to get information."*

In Chapter 2 it has been presented that Muslim minority women are the basic victims of the distinction between the two worlds they live in. The literal and the symbolic closing of the minority women in the urban areas and their exclusion from the different outside world seems to be the price they pay with their psychological disturbances and their recourses to psycho-medicines in high rates (Tsibiridou, 2005).

In contradiction to this, we submit Didem's comments, the most unexpected of all the interviews we have managed to collect as Didem is a village dweller, almost 50 years old, with only primary education and clothed with a scarf and a black gown:

> *"The computer helps me to communicate with my children and relatives abroad and also fight my loneliness as my husband is out of home the whole day. I feel less lonely in this way. I watch Turkish soap operas and listen to hundreds of the songs I have stored on my computer. I communicate through the Skype with my daughters and grandchildren who all live in Turkey. Before accessing to the Internet, I had to pay 300 euros for telephone calls every two months and my husband was furious. Now I give only 100 euros."*

Elvan, also a village dweller but with a west oriented dress code and very strong personality comments:

Gulden, almost at her 60s, in a humoristic way but expressing her real feelings says:

At this point while describing the social impacts of computer education on Muslim minority, three of the memos kept during the interviews that took place in three villages on the mountains of Xanthi are worth mentioning. The researcher wants to highlight one of the observations she has made during the interviews to give the reader of this thesis the sense of interesting and revealing situations that exist inside the minority. The researcher has observed a different dynamic among women village dwellers on the mountains and this can be captured in the following raw data:

MEMO 1: At the beginning of the interview, when we started our conversation, the women at the Kentavros village, gathered in their sewing club, seemed to be much "closed". They were afraid to speak and seemed to be reluctant about this procedure. In the beginning their only answers were *"I don't know"*. One of them could be described as an aggressive one. After speaking to them in Turkish, explaining that I had traveled all the way up to the mountains to meet them, I asked them to help me, they finally decided to speak. Our conversation continued in Turkish. There was a woman who spoke Greek, but at the end she refused to speak. They did not want to speak about the Pomak language; they said there were no books written in this language, but they admitted that they used this language. They seemed to be seriously interested in the future of their children. They said they wanted to learn the computer use in order to help their children. They were positive to the possibility to participate in computer use seminars. They wanted to protect their children from the Internet. They used a card to get connected to the Internet as there was not an Internet connection in their villages.

MEMO 2: In the village of Oraio the next day, we met Sehrazat, who was a spontaneous and vivid speaker. She could drive a car but she didn't have a driving licence. She had a 4x4 jeep and a motorbike. Her husband helped her a lot for that. Here the husbands encourage their women to do things as their main concern is the family income and the whole family has to contribute to this.

140

housewife only. Now things have changed; things are different from what they used to be in the past. It is not easy for me to pay extra money (150 euros) for her studies, but tomorrow my daughter has to go on has to move forward. Things can't go on the way they used to. At the village of Sminthi, there is a Second Chance School but I can't go there as I don't have time because I work in the tobacco fields. Every Sunday my daughter takes an exam for the ECDL certificate. Now all jobs can be done with the computer. If we had the Internet, we could manage our jobs more easily. We intend to leave the village and go to live at Xanthi just to be next to our daughters. We are planning to set up an association, a women's club, and start an online shop selling our products. We are not informed about programs funded by EU. Our life is very difficult here in the village. Information is not widely provided in the area. When a seminar started we were informed just one day before. But ten women from our village and other women from other villages finally attended it. I hope many seminars will be done. Five women who did not have transportation reacted as a group and they gathered money which was given to one woman to pay the expenses for receiving a driving licence. This woman owned her husband's car, who had immigrated to Holland to work there. In this way, the five of them could be transported to the village where the seminars took place.

MEMO 3: In the village of Miki we met again with young women in their "cutting and sewing clubs" where a woman in charge, their "tailor teacher" was supervising everything that was going around. These "cutting and sewing clubs" function as the vehicle to spread Turkish tradition as the women who act as mentors give instructions how to embroider Turkish traditional products. On the other hand the young women could also speak very well Greek. They were afraid to speak for them selves. They reacted better in groups. They mentioned several times that they are not left to have relations with the boys. Women in the street, wearing traditional clothes, didn't want any pictures to be taken and they got angry about this. They want to be supported in order to apply for the Greek universities. They said that experts on counseling and psychological support should come and visit in order to help them choose departments in the universities or give an orientation in their lives.

Moreover, Tuba at the age 18–30, clothed with the traditional mountain dress, describes a typical young girl's life that lives on the area:

"Things are difficult in the house. My father doesn't work. I want to help. The old ones take care of the babies, cook, stay at home, and cultivate tobacco. My father doesn't let me take a trip to Turkey with the club although we will not pay for it. I want to go to Istanbul, as I see it only on the pictures we have on the walls here in the club, but my father doesn't give his permission for that. They don't let us go alone even to Xanthi. I listen to music that I have stored in my computer and I see the pictures we take with the cell phone. We want to have a wireless Internet connection in the village. We want a club just for women with free Internet. We want to learn how to drive a car. We want to be together with Christian women in the seminars as in this way we could improve our Greek."

Interviewees were asked to quote eight benefits they believed they would result from the use of computer. Their answers gave the impression that they seem to know the empowerment potential of accessing information. Their answers can be categorized in three main patterns. The women interviewees reported personal and family gain, communication and receiving information as the three topmost benefits of using computers, a pattern similar to that found in the quantitative part of the research. The empowering feeling they perceive through computer use can best be described in their words. Pinar stated: *"I learn the news, I feel updated, I communicate with people, I manage and organize my job in a better way, I find answers to almost everything, and help my child for education matters."*

As shown in the case of communication what Bikek and Nur explained respectively is an example:

"Knowledge, communication, information, amusement; Old friends of mine got in contact with me through the face book. I became a member of a theatre group, I found a new world. I can search for historical dates and learn new things, I watch a lot of films on the Internet and it is like having a movie at home. I watch all the Turkish films online on the computer." (Bikek)

"I communicate with friends that I have not seen for a long time. Computer is the medium for widening your mind. I speak through SKYPE with friends and my son can find very easily information." (Nur)

Personal/family gain included benefits that have implications for women themselves as well as their family: *"Job, economical support and independence, helping the child, personal satisfaction that I offer it back to my family."(Sabahat)*

The answers they gave come to support the expectations a woman has for her self through computer education. Their answers are very genuine and characterize the changes that are hatched up in minority's life:

"We need professional training and vocational counseling on female entrepreneurship." (Elvan)

"If a woman knows the Greek language she can work she doesn't depend on her husband. When they cannot speak Greek they are afraid, they ask. They ask their neighbor to pay the electricity bill, the telephone bill. Even at the hospital they cannot reply to the doctor or to the nurses. For this reason they search for doctors from the minority or they go to shops where there are people who speak the Turkish language."(Ceyda)

"Everything they learn can help them. If they learn things in a right way this is good, otherwise I am afraid they should be careful. For example chatting is a little dangerous if their name is discovered. If they look things for their studies and their education this is helpful. I believe that you have to be educated to look for right things."(Bikek)

"The Second Chance Schools help a lot. I believe that someone has to finish the secondary education and enter the university. Knowledge has nothing to do with age. I prefer to continue learn new things." (Alev)

"I believe that things inside minority women's head should change. They will be educated and become more open-minded."(Deniz)

"Family status, a mother can help the children and also her husband. The man goes out and he can see things. Women are closed in the house and through the computer she can learn things. Especially the housewives who have their eyes closed."(Gulden)

Women reply that they learned the computer use mostly for themselves and secondly to be able to help their children and get in contact with them when they are abroad. The following comments highlight these points:

"I have learned the computer use for my own good and interests. Also, just to be able to help my children."(Hatice)

"I learned the computer use for myself. My parents did not want me to study and become educated. This was succeeded after a big fight." (Alev)

I did it for myself in order to feel contemporary. I was embarrassed when I did not know what @ is. If you want to live in reality you must know how to use the computer." (Bikek)

"For myself, to be in touch with my children settled abroad and not feel isolated." (Didem)

Their future plans connected to ICT use include the choice to *"encourage and promote other women of your community"* that was mostly selected, followed by *"apply for documents to civil services"*, *"career decision"* in both administrative areas but the first choice was mostly preferred by town residuals (60 % of the town dwellers) and the second by village dwellers in order to avoid the distance that separated them from the civil services. Also the choice *"offer help and information to your community"* were chosen by women who lived in towns.

4.4.7 Education Impact and Educators

During the interviews, minority women reported that computer education has influenced them to try to receive further education. Majority of the interviewees, 20 (71.%), said that they would definitely continue to do more intensive lessons in order to expand their knowledge on computer use, expressing in this way their ambition to become skilled and competitive.

Interviewees said they would like to learn more things about computer use and almost all of them gave exact and straight answers to this question as if it was thought of their future with computers. More specifically, they expressed the desire to learn more about programs, applications of Microsoft Office (Power-

Point, Excel, Access, Internet), montage of photos and web designing, networking, programming, mining information, information about the hardware of the computer just to be able to repair it. Aynur's comment, illustrating these aspects of educational impact is as follows: *"I want to learn how to prepare websites and web logs and also search for things that concern the minority education."* She is a scarf clad women nearly at her 40s.

Nine women village dwellers and twelve women town dwellers had no preference for the structure of the class in computer seminars. Four women, village dwellers, wanted a single sex training group of women only, eleven wanted a mixed sex students group, and nine wanted a student group composed by women both from the minority and the majority populations.

Women interviewees gave the characterstics of the trainer they would prefer emphasizing knowledge of computers, ability to adjust to the training needs of the trainee, inclination to help the novice ones, patience, ability to communicate and teach in a simple way, and for some of the women the knowledge of the Turkish language.

Zekie stated:

> *"He must be interested in teaching. He must have knowledge and must want to share it. Not like Takis (a computer teacher at the Second Chance School, who does nothing, and he is not interested at all, and he talks all the time on his cell phone."*

Ayla's reply was much more descriptive:

> *"Establishes good communication, adapts to class needs, communicates well, and explains things in a simple way without clinging solely onto books and terminology."*

Sehrazat gave an answer expressing the agony of minority women who could not speak Greek for many reasons as explained in the preceding, and as a consequence of it they have to bend on others:

> *"He/she must speak both languages Turkish and Greek. When you speak Greek is better because you feel freer to "open". For five days during the seminar I spoke Greek and I felt more self confident because you can talk with other people."*

Hilal, a sharp village dweller, gave an answer that was in another spirit as she stated:

> *"I want the educator to be a young one who can speak Turkish in order to understand him in a much easier way."*

4.4.8 Opinions on Key informants

It was interesting to see what women interviewees think about and wait from members of the minority, who have a leader and eminent role inside the life of the minority to act for their social empowerment; the key informants of the research. Bikek said she waits: *"Nothing!!!"* from them, Hilal was more demanding as she stated: *"They should provide help as they ask for our vote"*, Ayla was suspicious and ironic with her comment: *"There is much distance to be covered until we have such aspirations"*, Alev was indifferent to them and as she said she waited nothing: *"Nobody can help you if you don't want to do it on you own"*, and Aynur was the most descriptive by describing her reality with caustic words:

> *"The leaders don't support the empowerment of women. Only the state does things. My husband helped me. Our leaders are only fine words. They don't want people to be educated. They don't benefit if people are educated. When I started my master only my husband helped me. If the education level of the minority changes that would help the children of the minority."*

The majority of the interviewees expressed their opinions about members of their community in administrative positions how they should act for women's social empowerment and emancipation. Sabahat, Vildan and Nur had almost identical thoughts:

> *"They have to know better the conditions under which the women live, to be personally interested in the problems women face, to be interested in our progress, to look in front, to establish associations and clubs in every village.*

Deniz, Aysun, Pinar, Elvan and Ceyda expressed their ideas for computer seminar:

> *"To help for more seminars to be materialized. They should support programs that concern women, for receiving knowledge without having to pay, and inform the community about the programs (a housewife has difficulty in receiving the information). They must help women of the minority to understand that life is not only children, husband and cooking but women can be also creative and meet other aspects of life. But although there are many women who studied they still don't work and live an ordinary domestic life. They believe that the husband must work and they avoid in this way the tiredness of working."*

The answers the interviewees gave when they were asked to quote services their community should provide to help them learn the use of the computer were in the same tone with the previews thoughts: Bikek once again gave critical comments as she believes that: *"They don't have the willing to do something to help the women."*

4.5 Key-Informants' interviews

The total of the 30 key informants included government officials, political activists, NGO representatives, religion leaders, professionals and media personnel. The interviews stated in Chapter III, were tape recorded with the approval of the participants. Then the tapes were transcribed into text and then translated from Greek into English. A total of 17 hours, 6 minutes and 4 seconds of recorded voices were transcribed into text.

4.5.1 Demographics

Key informants included 30 individuals living mainly in the prefectures of Rodopi and in the two towns, Komotini and Xanthi. Ten of them (33.3 %) were women and twenty (66.7 %) were men. More specifically, the group of stake holders consisted of nine mayors, seven presidents of associations, four deputies (ex and formers) in Greek Parliament, four journalists, three muftis, and three vice prefects.

Figure 4.32: Key informants' Social Status

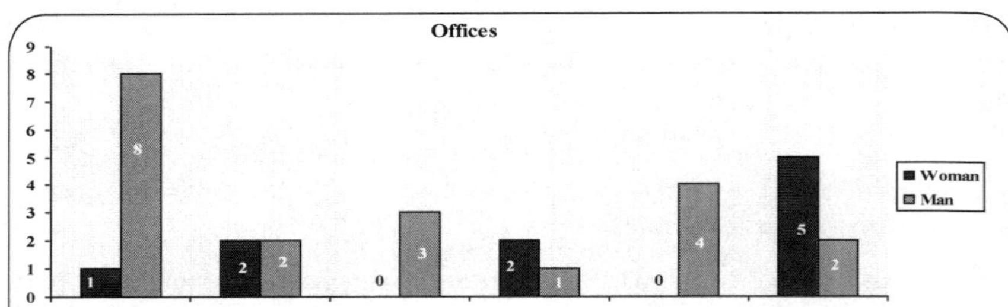

Figure 4.33: Key informants' Residence Area

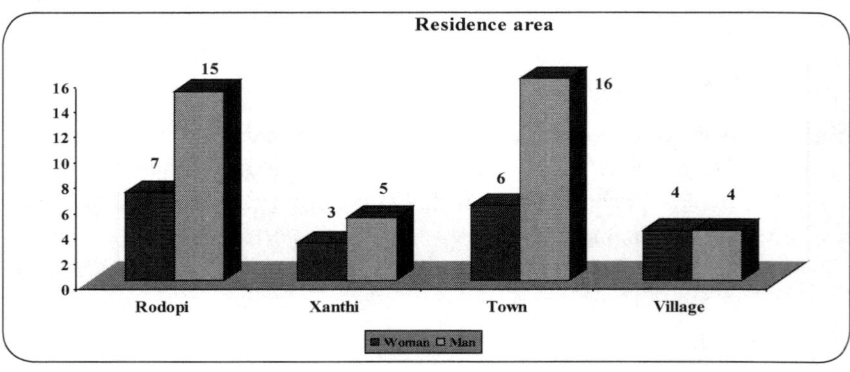

The mean age of the sample is 43; the median of the age is the range of 31–40 years.

Most of the male key informants are at the age of 41–60 and the female key informants at the age of 31–40.

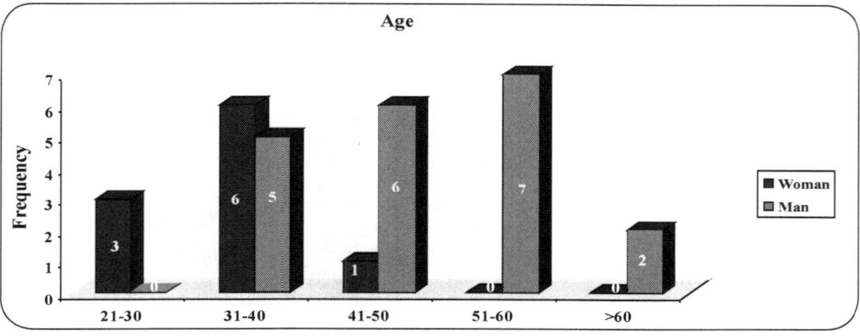

The overwhelming majority of the key informants have received high levels of education. Of the 30 participants, 16.7 % are of a low level of education, 73.3 % have a university degree, and 10 % have master's or PhD's degrees.

Figure 4.35: Key informants' Education Level

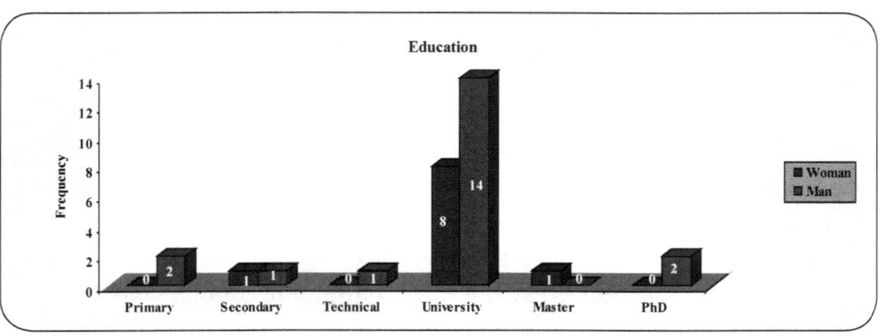

As to their marital status, 93.3 % of them are married. Of the 30 key informants, nine (30 %) speak two languages; seventeen (56.7 %) speak three languages; three (10 %) speak four languages and one (3.3 %) speaks five languages. They all speak Turkish and Greek; additionally, seventeen (56.7 %) speak English; five (16.7 %) speak Arabic; two (6.7 %) French; two (6.7 %) German; one (3.3 %) Pomak.

4.5.2 Relation to ICTs

The analysis of the collected data for this part, revealed that the overwhelming majority of them, 90 %, own computers; 86.7 % have access to Internet; 83.3 % have an email account; on the other hand 70 % of them do not have a computer skill certificate and 63.3 % do not own a website or blog. The following figure presents the above, using frequencies according to the sex of the key informants.

Figure 4.36: Relations to ICTs

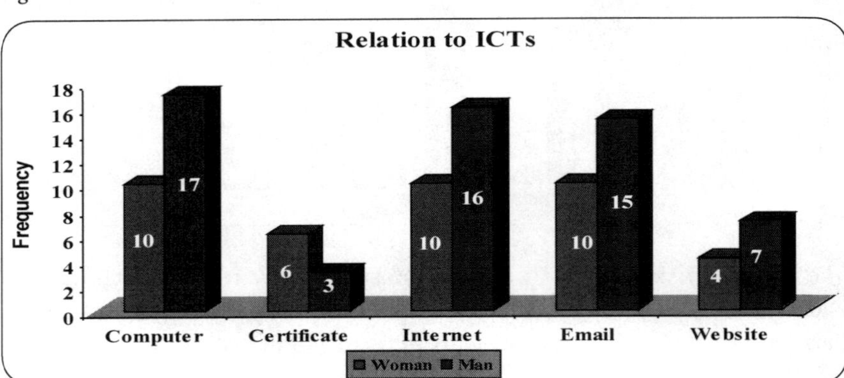

Twenty one (70 %) them said they used their computer daily; four (13.3 %) sometimes during the week; three (10 %); one (3.3 %) 1–2 times a week; one (3.3 %) rarely; Ten (33.3 %) of them used three languages to read the websites on the Internet; twelve (40 %) used two languages; five (16.7 %) used one language and three (10 %) did not use any language at all; twenty four (80 %) of them used Turkish; twenty three(76.7 %) used Greek; eleven (36.7 %) the English; one (3.3 %) French and one (3.3 %) Arabic.

The responses the key informants' gave when they were asked for the reasons they use the computer, were analyzed with a multiple response cross tabs analysis with gender, age, place of living, office. After that we arrived at the following results:

Twenty four (88.9 %) of the key informants who belonged to all age ranges from all the offices we focused on nine (90 %) of the women and fifteen (88.2 %) of the men, from all educational levels used the computer for their work,; 23 (85.2 %) of the key informants, nine (90 %) of the women and fourteen (82.4 %) of the men, more specifically 100 % of the village dwellers, the 100 % of the Xanthi dwellers and 80 % of the Rodopi dwellers from all the offices we chose, from all educational levels used the computer for communication; eleven (40.7 %) of the

148

key informants, six (60 %) of the women and five (29.4 %) of the men, ten (50 %) of the Rodopi dwellers and 1 (14.3 %) of the Xanthi dwellers, nine postgraduates, one with a master's degree and one with a PhD degree used the computer for web-search; three (11.1 %) of them, 10 % of the women key-informants and11.8 % of the men key informants, all Rodopi dwellers, one mayor, one deputy and one association president between 31–50 years old, one of primary education, one postgraduate and one with a master's degree used the computer for games on-line; two (7.4 %) of the key informants, one man and one woman, both Rodopi dwellers at the age of 31–40, one journalist and one deputy, both postgraduates used the computer for tele-work; two (7.4 %) of the key-informants, one (10 %) of the women, one (5.9 %) of the men, both living at the Rodopi prefecture, town dwellers, one deputy and one association president, one postgraduate and one with a master's degree, used it for buying products; two (7.4 %) of them, both women, one at the age of 20–30 and one at the age of 41–50, both presidents of associations, two postgraduates used the computer for e-banking; and only one (3.7 %) woman, living at Rodopi prefecture, president of an association, at the age of 31–40 with a master's degree, used the computer for studies.

Figure 4.37: Reasons for Computer Use and Gender

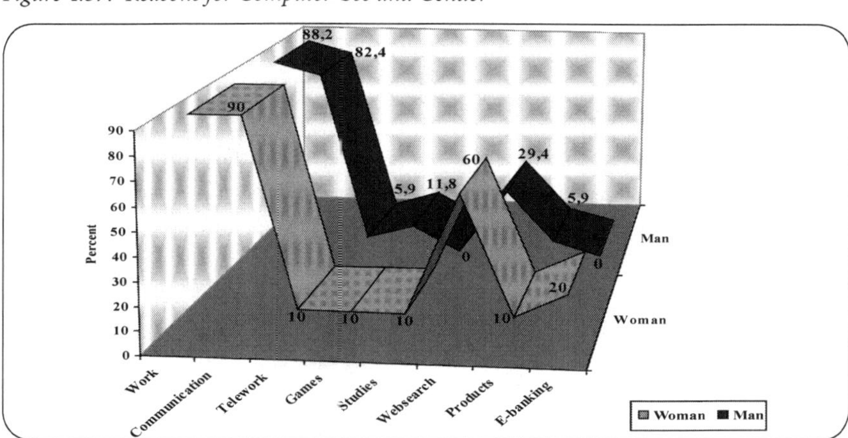

Key informants were asked to classify which of the ICT appliances they used more frequently. They were provided with the following choices: Computer, mobile-phone, TV, CD/DVD player scanner, digital camera, web-camera, MP3, video; they were asked to range them respectively for each choice from not at all, little, enough, much to very much. The most highly ranged in their order of classifica-tion were: Mobile-phone, Computer, TV, CD/DVD player and Fax.

The following table contains web pages mostly the key informants in general use.

Table 4.12: Websites Commonly Accessed by key informants

Turkish newspapers & media	www.gazeteler.com www.haberturk.tr www.hurriyet.tr www.diziizle.tr www.gundemgazetesi.com	www.milliyet.com.tr www.hurriyet.tr
Greek newspapers	www.paratiritis.gr www.avgi.gr	www.naftemporiki.gr www.xronos.gr
Arabic newspapers	www.arab2.com/newspapers.htm	
Searching tools	www.yahoo.com www.alfavita.gr www.kimolia.gr www.meteo.gr www.msn.com www.in.gr	www.facebook.com www.diorismos.gr www.gmail.com www.google.gr www.iky.gr
Greek ministries	www.ypes.gr www.remth.gr www.ypepth.gr	www.minagric.gr www.et.gr
Religious papers	www.diyanet.gov.tr www.acevakfi.tr	www.ilahi.org
Political parties	www.pasok.gr	www.syn.gr
Associations	www.bttadk.gr www.abttf.org www.un.com www.tkdf.org.tr	www.btaytr.com www.httdd.org www.osce.org www.i-gunler.com/Turkey
Job	www.nomologia.com www.agrotipos.gr	www.dsxanthi.gr www.veterinerhekimiz.com
Dictionaries, cooking, NGO, books, articles, theater, cinema films, social matters, feminist matters, commerce, psychology matters		

Key informants are mainly interested in Turkish and Greek local newspapers, job related information via Internet, pages of associations and pages of ministries and political parties.

150

4.5.3 Key Informants' Views on Women relation to ICTs

The answers received in the third part of the interview will be presented in two parts. The first part, Part I, will present data from six close-ended questions with multiple choices answers in a statistically descriptive way. The second part, Part II, consists of data selected from seven open-ended questions. The content of the answers receive was evaluated with the method of capabilities approach.

When the 30 key informants were asked to give their opinions about the skills demanded now days to enter the labour force, they chose firstly computer use, secondly postgraduate studies, and thirdly knowledge of foreign languages. In the following figure, the choices of the key informants are quoted in frequencies.

Figure 4.38: Skills for Labour

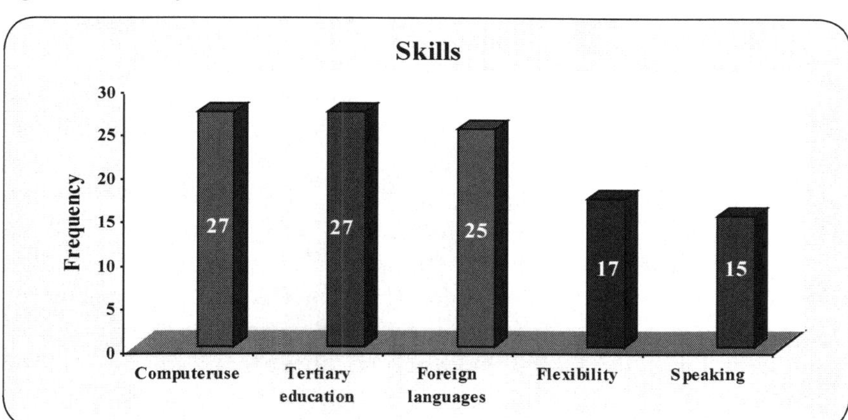

We analyzed the responses the key informants' gave when they were asked about the skills, with a multiple response cross tabs analysis with gender and residence area (village-town) simultaneously. The results of this analysis showed that women key informants living in villages and towns were more positive than men key informants in the perspective of obtaining the above skills for entering the labour market.

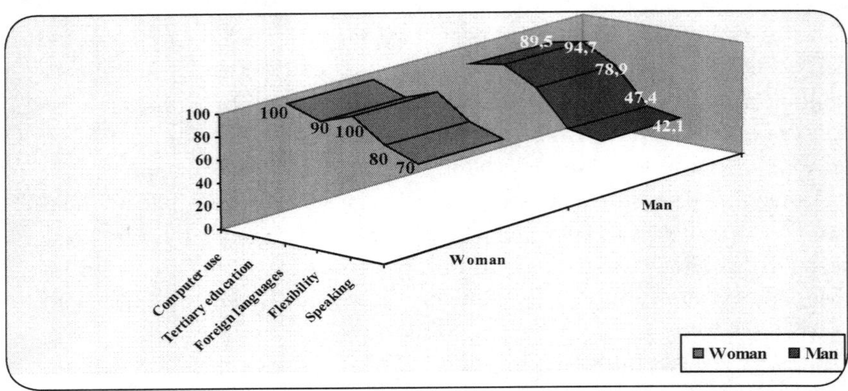

For the seminars on computer use, the key informants are mostly informed about the seminars offered by the state (80 %); Twenty five of them, (92.6 %) receive information from the Internet, eleven (40.7 %) from call centres and only two (7.4 %) from libraries.

The largest part of the key informants, sixteen (55.2 %) of them, town dwellers at the Rodopi administration, mostly men, mainly at the age ranges of 41–50 and over 60, believe that seminars on computer use should be materialized inside State schools; fifteen (51.7 %) of the key informants, the largest part of them, mostly village dwellers at the Xanthi administration, mostly women, especially the ones at the age range of 20–30 and 31–40 years old, express that seminars should be carried out by NGOs. On the other hand, a very small percent four (13.8 %), of them, but with interesting qualitative characteristics, including two women, two men, one village dweller and three town dwellers at the Rodopi administration, non-Arabic speakers (they are taught the Arabic to read the Koran), one with secondary education and three postgraduates, three at the age ranges of 31–40 years old and one at the age range of 51–60 years old, one mayor, one vice prefect, two journalists, but none of the three muftis, agree that seminars should be provided inside the mosques.

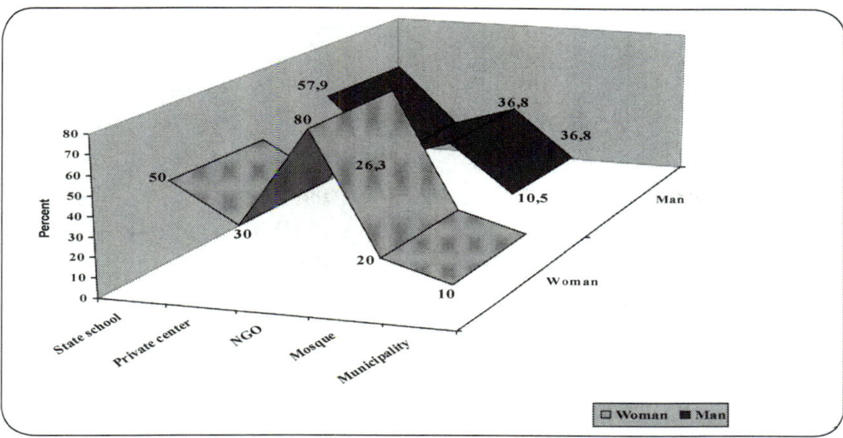

Eighteen (62.1 %) of the key informants, when they were asked how they would contribute to providing information to women, proposed that gathering events would be more suitable, 60 % of the women and 63.2 % of the men key informants, mainly at the age ranges 31–40 and 41–50 years old, postgraduates, especially the mayors and the presidents of associations. Thirteen (44.8 %) of the key informants chose the radio, 60 % of the women, 36.8 % of the men, all town dwellers, mainly at the age range of 31–40 years old, postgraduates, especially the mayors and the presidents of associations.

At this point, we have to make comments on the choice of preaching in mosques as none of the women key informants agreed on that choice, which, on the other hand, gained 21.1 % of the men key informants, choice at the age ranges of 31–40 and 51–60 years old; two mayors, one mufti, one deputy, one of secondary education, two postgraduates, one with a PhD degree.

The third choice was the newspapers, mostly accepted by women, at the age ranges of 31–40 years old, two mayors, four journalists, one vice prefect, eight (31.8 %) of the postgraduates and one (100 %) with technical education.

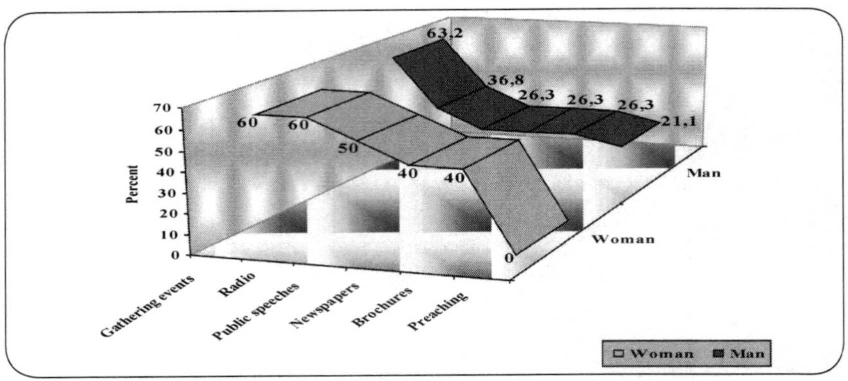

Trying to detect what the key informants think that minority women expect to receive from training programs, the answer mostly appointed was money, twenty two (75.9 %) of the key informants, 70 % of the women and 78.9 % of the men, 87.5 % of the village dwellers and 71.4 % of the town dwellers, all of primary, secondary education, and the largest part of the postgraduates from all offices and 100 % of the journalists.

Their second choice was knowledge appointed from sixteen (55.2 %) of the key informants, preferred mostly by men, in all residence areas, of the age ranges of 41–50 years old, mostly by mayors and vice prefects.

The third mostly preferred choice was communication from ten (34.5 %) of the key informants, by five (50 %) of the women and by five (26.3 %) of the men, mainly by the young ones at the age ranges of 21–30 years old.

The above three choices were selected by key informants from all educational levels. The choice plugging in the local society was selected by nine (31 %) key informants, only by those who were postgraduates and those who had a master's degree, and work by eight (27.6 %) key informants, mostly preferred by those with primary education, and 100 % by those with a master's degree, by more women than men, and mostly by journalists and vice prefects.

Figure 4.42: Reasons for Attending Seminars

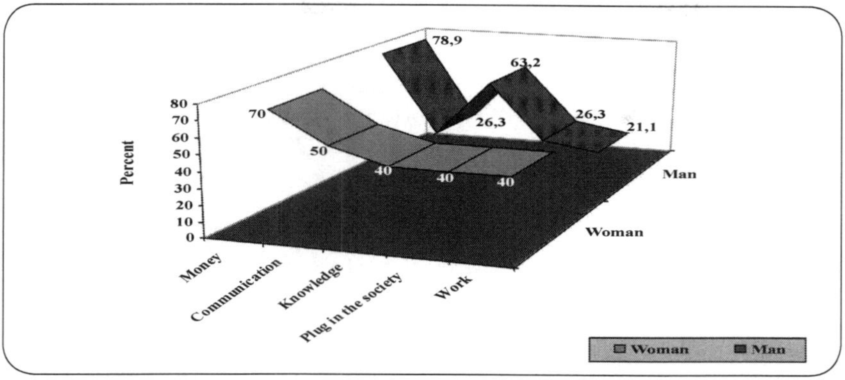

4.5.4 Problems encountered

Capabilities approach was used as the evaluative framework of social policies since it provides the appropriate tool for measuring people's well being. The factors that obstruct opportunities conversion into real capabilities were classified into five different levels which are:

1) knowledge/awareness (knowing the existence of specific opportunities)
2) means (absence of realized capabilities)
3) external factors (conditions that constrain a person's development)
4) aims of action (previous circumstance that make a person reject new choices)
5) education as capability of development.

The five levels which were used as codes for identifying similar concepts contained also several sub-codes for grouping and sub-grouping the information the questions: no18, no19, no20, no21, no27, no28, no29 and no30 of the interview questionnaire provided. Under every sub-code of the 17 chosen the researcher prepared memos which play the role of an internal dialogue going on during the research.

4.5.4.1 Knowledge/Awareness

Gaps in the minority

A major problem stated several times during the research with the women interviewees and with the key informants' themselves is the existence of minority members with a leadership position who try to manipulate the mass of the minority in order to establish their control. Consequently, the information oriented to the minority is usually filtered.

As Naim explains:

"There is a different culture, tradition and values among members of the minority. The culture of the people of the minority of Turkish origin is the ruling one and the other groups of the minority try to be identified with the sovereign group. This group that can be described as the avant garde group consists of educated people, university graduates, working people."

Aslan states the dimension of this problem in a more descriptive way:

"One of the largest problems we have inside the minority is that people who know things, who receive any kind of information do not distribute it to others. There is a minority inside the minority."

Fulya contributes to this by saying:

"Only a part of the minority receive information, i.e. the relatives of mayors, deputies and on the other side the people who are in a desperate need to receive knowledge and money are excluded. We need more and better information. Criteria for choosing women to attend seminars must be legislated."

Koray was astonished to hear from the researcher about minority women heavily using the computer in their everyday life and about village women chatting through Skype.

Ten of the key informants admitted that they did nothing to inform women about the benefits of information society or the seminars offered all the past years and funded by EU. The researcher was astonished to hear Sadik, a mayor deputy, saying:

"I am not doing anything as I don't want to be in the middle of having to choose. Women quarrel about who is going to participate in the seminars in order to earn money."

Gulbahar, from another aspect, gives her own point of view:

"We have to approach women and we need women to do this. We have not done anything. In the future we have to think of it as a project of the minority women's association."

Generally, the largest part of minority women is usually occupied in field work with all the consequences of this limitation. Murat explains the causes of this situation very effectively:

"The position of the woman inside the minority is formed and shaped by the feudal system that still rules the life of the minority. Women are kept in the field work."

Past researches, and we hope this one also, exhibit another point of view for minority women's social status. Changes in the policy towards minority that started in the 1990s had their impact on the status of minority women but the exclusion still exists *as* Naim explains:

> *"The emancipation of the women of the minority has already started. In some groups of the women of the minority, this is very obvious; in others it doesn't exist. There is an internal gap. Some people have come across with new things and these brought a lot of changes to their lives."*

Nilufer believes that:

> *"People of the minority can't understand that women can improve and become better. In my opinion, when there are not any other problems and they suddenly stop children from going to school. If old mentality disappears, and if women get out of their houses, then things will improve."*

On the other hand, the problems of the minority in Thrace are much more complicated as Kadir, a journalist, says:

> *"Women through computer use can achieve to have communication and information. People have to know and understand that the computer is and must be a part of their lives. I don't think that we have yet understood what the information society is. We write in our articles, we publish in our newspapers about problems like education, problems with the mufti, the tobacco. We transfer the problem to the model of minority life. A part of the minority lives in villages where there is no drinkable water, there are no roads. We speak about nursery schools. The Internet and new technologies come after our major problems."*

Lack of information from the state

One of the problems as quoted by the key informants is the lack of information that the state provides about seminars and training programs. Zeki, in a few words, gives the dimension of the problem: *"We face lack of concern by the state."* Aslan, as the president of one of the biggest associations of the minority expresses the problem in the way they face it:

> *"When we learn something, we believe that the members of our association should get the news. We have 850 members, more than 300 being women. Nobody sends us any information about programs or seminars funded by EU."*

Kadir, who expects the state to inform people, says:

> *"People who have been cultivating tobacco for the last 30 years, what can they do now? People of the minority are not informed. Half of the population doesn't understand and doesn't speak the Greek language. Eighty percent of the minority lives in rural areas and women are mostly occupied with the cultivation of the land. The women of the minority don't have the same access to ICTs as the women of the majority do. The children of the minority don't receive a proper education compared to that the Christians receive and they don't have the same access to ICTs."*

4.5.4.2 Means

Lack of education and skills

When the key informants were asked about what they thought the problems the minority women faced were, almost all of them referred to lack of education. Adem, who is a mayor and a very cultivated person, gave in a very fluent way a reply that briefly explains the whole situation:

> *"First of all, women confront the problem of illiteracy, lack of education. Most of them have not finished high school although in Greece in the last 20 years graduating from high school has been compulsory. Women of the minority are excluded from education even today. There was and still exists a high drop-out rate. This is a very important problem for their future. Secondary education is necessary. There shouldn't be even one woman of the minority without having received secondary education. As you can understand these women don't have many chances to find a job. All the above also means lack of knowledge of foreign languages, of computer use. It is not only that they do not have qualifications; it is that they didn't even receive primary compulsory education. I cannot hire women to work in the municipality with no diplomas as the female population in the area is over 60 and the candidates for the jobs are women who have finished only primary school. In the municipality there were 17 positions for jobs and I could not hire anybody as there were not any people qualified to apply for them. This situation describes in general the life women of the minority live in villages. Things in the towns are better for women as there they live under different circumstances."*

Financial problems – Unemployment- Need for money

Another problem minority women face is lack of money and unemployment. Birol explains *"In my opinion, the largest problem among women is unemployment."* Many of the key informants, when they were asked to describe the motives they believed women had for attending the seminars, they replied that women were not really interested in receiving knowledge but only money and subsidies from the seminars. Sadik believed that:

> *"Women are interested in money. They quarrel who is going to attend the seminar if it is funded in order to earn money. They are not interested in programs that are not subsidized. As all people could not attend the programs offered in private centers, I had lost votes because we could not satisfy the demands of every woman. They started screaming at the end "We are left illiterates", but this was not their aim. The aim was the subsidy."*

Lack of money for the women of the minority is a problem, which has other dimensions too. Women's main interest, as it was confessed variously in the women's interviews presented above, is their children. Nowadays the minority demands better education, skills, jobs for their children and the mothers are seriously interested in their children's development. Nilufer quoted her thoughts on this situation:

> "Women wait to receive only money; they are not interested in anything else. 30 % of them would go to Second Chance Schools; but their aim now is to help their children to study. They have a great need for money. They save money; they try to find money in order to afford their children's studies. They send them even to swimming classes in order for their children to be equal with the rest part of the society. They say "What we did not receive, our children must get it." They want to improve their children's lives. They start to help them from the age of 5. My children are 5 years old and I send then for swimming since the age of 3.5 years old. They also attend a ballet class. We want for the next decade now to improve our children's lives."

Other skilled women want to be able to speak the Greek language, and as consequence they are eager to attend seminars of the Greek language.

Emine comments:

> "When the seminars they attend are for learning the Greek language, women don't want to get money because they just want to learn the language."

The main financial problem of the minority is the one which Kadir describes:

> "Let me explain one big problem now the minority faces and will face in the immediate future. People of the minority mainly earn money from tobacco cultivation. During the past years they would earn good money from this product as the cultivation was subsidized. This subsidy is reduced and will expire by 2013. People of the minority have not managed their money in a wise way. They became big consumers of material goods and did not invest the money in their children's education; they did not invest it on the future. They don't take the long view of something. And now they just want money to fulfill their immediate needs. When their families had enough money, they considered all these useless, and no one was interested. Do you understand what the real motive of women to attend seminars is? ...Money."

Lack of infrastructure

The bulk of the minority live in villages, many of which are remote. Consequently, there is lack of infrastructure for Internet connection, for TV and radio channels, other technological infrastructure and transportation. Zafer claims:

> "I receive information from the Internet. Libraries, info-kiosks, information centers don't exist in my village except from Internet cafes at Arianna. Things that are established and exist in the city should also normally exist in the village so that isolation and exclusion can become eliminated. We don't have quick Internet in the area I live. We first have to think of villages that are remote, far from the center; and village dwellers don't have access and lack information. We need better transportation."

Usually seminars are not connected to the labor force of the area where they are materialized or whatever concerns the minority; they do not take into consideration the traditions, the way women function, the lack of facilities the minority experiences. Sadik made some comments which can be helpful for the future policy makers:

> *"The seminars and the EU funded programs must be connected with the area women live in, with the economical level of the participants, with the labor force. For instance, on the mountains we have nut products. Seminars organized in this area must be connected to this product. The state must create infrastructure for Internet, ADSL connections, antennas to watch the Greek channels or the local channels."*

Internal family problems

Women of the minority work in the fields and provide house services, they confront problems with domestic violence and more commonly verbal domestic violence as Fulya comments and they experience high dropout rates from school. On the other hand, their husbands are free due to social reasons to stay out of the house in the evenings and be in circulation. Women feel lonely and neglected and face psychological problems as the relations with parents- in-laws are usually suppressive, i.e. they usually live all together in the same courtyard. This is what Emine states, *"Women have a lot of social pressure from their relatives and familiar environment, especially in villages"*. Timur presented a very characteristic habit that most men of the minority usually have: *"Men neglect their wives and go to the bars with Russian women"*.

Can explains:

> *"Women feel lonely. There is a high percentage of internal family violence problems. But now many women are trying to find a job"* and Sadik concluds, *"Men leave their families in order to find a job. Many young minority men work in shipyards. This job brings a lot of money but also other problems. Women feel neglected."*

Aslan added that:

> *"Women face psychological problems due to social exclusion and lack of information. Men leave them alone in order to find a job and after that the problems start. Minority woman is isolated; she can't even go out for a coffee."*

Gulbahar as a young woman who tries to help women of her community when they face domestic violence knows very well the situation women of the minority experience especially those on the mountains:

> *"Psychological problems. Their husbands immigrate to other countries and they send to their wives, who are left behind alone, a lot of money which the women cannot manage. They live with their parents in law alone. They spend the money without thinking of the*

Ekrem mentions also another problem that the youth of minority faces as young people usually work from their childhood in the family business and contribute to the family income by helping their parents:

> "When I was studying in the medical school, during my summer vacations I was working in the fields; and even nowadays many women who are enrolled in the tertiary education come and help during summer at the tobacco fields. I think that working in the family environment is a disadvantage for our society. Young people don't have the social status they should have and are not considered at the level they should be."

Associations

Women of the minority have their own association as part of the Association of the Scientists of the minority. The researcher interviewed women who were, and some still are, presidents of this association. Gulbahar brought for the need the women of the minority had for information,

> "Women must be better informed. I, as the president of the women's association, have to contribute to this. We have to start; not just wait from the state, the EU and the municipalities. We have to start something and the help will come." Timur adds that "Minority women's associations should be funded to organize new activities."

Kaan believes that educated members of the minority have to provide information to women regarding the use of ICTs. The radio as the most common means of media can help in distributing information as women of the minority listen to the radio a lot.

Ekrem gave an encouraging message by saying

> "Cooperation among policy makers and local institutions is needed. Every region has its own characteristics which are better known by the locals. Many things can be done and I believe they will be done."

4.5.4.3 External Factors

Social pressure

Naim believes that minority women are after the seminars for different reasons, such as

> "The initial motive is to get off the "zone" of the clog, the second is the money and third the settlement in their career. They went to learn new things by getting out of the "ring".

Deniz claims that minority women are in an inferior position compared to that the majority women live. Adem describes clearly the situation many minority women live in:

> "They usually get married; and even if they are not happy in their marriage, they have to stay in it; they cannot have a divorce as they are afraid where they will go after the divorce; they cannot express themselves as they don't have any economic entity; so they stay next to their husband to help them in the fields. These women cannot live their own lives; they live in the shadow of their husbands and just work in the fields. I am speaking about women of the villages, but these descriptions also fit in general most women of the minority."

Esrin adds that *"Minority women do not have self-confidence and they experience conjugal oppression."* Kadir comments about the fact that in Thrace you cannot find a job easily, as mediators are needed in order to succeed in this, especially if you are a woman and a member of the minority.

State

A matter that concerns the minority these days and is discussed seriously is the establishment of bilingual nursery schools in the area of Thrace where both Greek and Turkish languages will be taught. This subject could not be avoided in the conversations we had with the key-informants. Sadik puts this in a perspective view as he combines the demand with the final success of the minority students in the university.

> "Things must change from the nursery school not at the end gaining the quota in order to study in the university. And then, what; when you enter the university you cannot finish it."

Adem explains the reasons why women should receive information through the local channels:

> "Women at the age of 30 or 40 need the Internet; but in my opinion, women should receive messages from the TV. They should receive information on EU funded projects from the local channels. People of the minority should have a motive to watch the Greek television. TV programs should provide information on feminine matters, alternative ways for cultivating the fields and others matters."

Another problem in terms of the key informants' views is that the Greek language is not taught properly in minority schools. Through this problem which deplored many generations of the minority, the mistrust to the Greek state has been augmented. Evren described his thoughts:

> "As minority women have lost their chances, they must have new ones. Teachers were coming to schools with orders not to teach the Greek language. I learned the Greek language when I was thirty years old, when I joined the army. I studied in Turkey because we were en-

tering the Jelal Bayar with a lottery system and we could not succeed in Greek state schools. Now this policy has changed and they can achieve better in Greek state schools. They do this in order to attract the minority children from going to the minority high school."

4.5.4.4 Aims of Action

Feelings of fear

The consequence of the situation as described above is feelings of fear and mistrust minority members have towards the Greek state and its policy. This is brought out by Kaan's comments:

"We, as a minority, we are still afraid. What are we afraid of; what do we believe in as a minority from what we hear? The state wants to do something, according to EU demands, but the state still decides and order. We have fear as a minority. The state believes that they know what is better for us. They do something for the minority and they don't even ask us. After that we cannot believe and trust the Greek state regarding its intention."

Hakan, a man from another generation than that of Kaan, gave another aspect of how things are developing:

"I believe that after 2000 people of the minority want to stay here in Greece and many who left for Turkey want to return to Thrace. When the policy of the Greek government changed, the feelings of the people changed and this makes them want to come back."

Lack of trust

Tuba describes the experiences she had during the elections as she was running as a candidate:

"We have to get over the suspiciousness between the Christians and the Muslims. I had a very hard time during the elections. We have to get over the hate between the two communities. Although many of them say that they have gotten over it but it still exists and it is there waiting. There is a lot of hate between the Muslims and the Christians in Thrace. While I was running my campaign for the elections, I had to face anger and prejudice. Old people of a prefecture where there were no minority dwellers wouldn't even shake my hand."

Evren explained in a pessimistic way that mistrust, lack of knowledge of the Greek language due to the policy of the Greek state all the past years, are the main factors that have influenced his life. Koray believes that even if he has the qualification and the ambition, he will never be able to become the General Secretary of the Prefecture in Thrace because he is not considered to be trust worthy.

Ekrem, trying to overcome softer this situation, gives some hope suggesting:

"An environment of trust between the minority and the state has to be cultivated. Thrace must not be considered as a problematic area. It is for Greece's interest to have an educated and cultivated minority, with men and women not easily manipulated. Educated people

know better what they do. For the women of the minority special programs have to be materialized so that that they become skilled and able to find jobs. They have a tremendous need for a job. Programs offering lessons on the Greek language is a priority. These lessons should be materialized after a communication with the minority, not just for the interests of political parties, but with a target to succeed in something."

This mistrust is kept even when the state or private institutions provide seminars for minority as we can deduce from Zeki's words, a village dweller:

"We are very cautious about the seminars. We talk all the time about the projects, but nothing appears up in the area we live."

or Adem's saying in the same vein:

"Quick steps must be taken. I believe that the state doesn't really intend to help minority people especially those living in villages. I believe that in the next coming years, village dwellers will abandon villages and live in towns. All the issue we discuss is an economic issue."

Although minority women are aware of private or public institutions which provide seminars on computer use and programs for learning Greek, still the key informants insist that these programs will be organized in cooperation with the minority, with the minority women's association and that the teachers will be Turkish speakers. Thus, Emine remarks:

"Women of the minority feel more comfortable coming and asking in our associations i.e. when the seminar will start than going to a private centre or to OAED (Organization of Occupation of Labour Force, If we organize such a program they will not have any language problem."

Kadir speaks about NGOs:

"Seminars can be organized everywhere, but it has to be done with the cooperation of minority NGOs, with the association of minority scientists"

and Kaan adds:

"Our people who know the language and are most trusted must teach the members of the minority."

Mosques

When the key informants were asked whether seminars on computer use would be held in the mosques or in areas around the mosques, mostly all of them were negative to such a proposal explaining that the mosque is just a location for praying.
Tuba and Bairaq said:

"The mosque is a wrong choice. You cannot do seminars at the mosques. People have to believe that seminars are for their own good. Mosques and medreses are areas for only religious matters." Moreover Timur comments: *"Women don't come to the mosque. The only thing you can do in the mosque is pray. I think that the radio can play an important role to provide information to women as minority women listen a lot to the radio."*

4.5.4.5 Education as Capability of Development

Education of children

Key informants favor the fact that minority women want to continue their studies in Second Chance Schools, and many of the mayors especially in villages try to establish Second Chance Schools in their local areas. Adem, a mayor, shows his interest by saying:

> *"I agree with the idea of the Second Chance school because I think that if women are educated, they can then help their children to have a better life. A parent who is educated will go to school to converse with the school teacher about the child in order to help him/her more and will take care of the problems the child faces. I want to say for the Second Chance schools that we have to support the parents to attend lessons in these schools and have the experience of a school, in order to be able to help their children."*

Communication

Key informants believe that ICTs (computer, TV, radio, mobile phone) help women to communicate, to receive information, to work, to become educated, to be better informed in order to protect their children, to communicate with the young, to become skilled, to become able to find a job, to manage their emancipation. These thoughts are supported by what many of the key informants say.

> *"Women come in touch with the information society. They come in touch with each other all over the world. Through ICTs I can get in touch with young people and learn how they think, what their thoughts are about the environment and other major problems. I have good relationships with young people and this is totally different from the relations with the old people." (Ekrem)*

> *'The use of ICTs would help women to their emancipation. As they live in a society where women are more isolated than men are, the use of ICT could help them learn the world outside the "ghetto" they live in. The minority has the characteristics of the ghetto."(Naim)*

> *"Women learn from their children. I have a friend 47 years old and her children study in Turkey. Because of her need to speak with her children she learned how to use the computer and communicate with them online. She writes with one finger and she has finished the 4th degree of primary school."(Tuba)*

> *"ICTs may help women to find a job and thus improve their position in the family and then inside the minority." (Kadir)*

The key informants were also asked to describe what they had done from their position in charge in order to help minority women to improve their access to ICTs. This was actually the most important question that was addressed to them as the aim of involving the key informants in the research was to guarantee their contribution to computer education of minority women. Although ten of them admitted they did nothing to this respect the rest seemed to be interested and willing to help women become computer educated as they could evaluate the contribution of computer literacy in general. Some spoke about lack of infrastructure, absence of Greek channels on TV, lack of ADSL connections, lack of information provided. They had a leading role in organizing seminars on computer use and the Greek language, in establishing Internet cafes and associations or women's clubs, in spreading any information about seminars or the Second Chance School, asking for antennas for TV or influencing women to continue with their studies.

All these are brought by what Adem said:

"As a Mayor, I established an Internet café (received money from EU), and there were many people coming there. Women were quarrelling with boys because they were smoking. After that, we had to make a separate place for boys and another one for girls. Now it is closed because we are trying to find a larger place. People are interested in such places. Women at the age of 30 or 40 need the Internet, but in my opinion, women should get news from the TV. They should receive information on EU funded projects from the local channels. People of the minority should have the motive to watch Greek television"

by Nilufer's remarks:

"I have founded a women's association. Last year I became a mayor's assistant. Now I have time. In this association we gather twice a week. We discuss our problems. We are going to ask for some help from doctors and psychologists to provide information; I have many ideas and I am thinking of new ones. There should be seminars on ICTs provided for women. My colleagues treat me very well. Especially men colleagues treat me equally. The mayor helps women to go on excursions. We plan to go sightseeing the museums."

By Kaan's comments:

"In the mosque, I tell them to learn Greek, Turkish, English and the use of the computer. Our country is Greece; otherwise we will stay farmers and shepherds."

By Aslan's statement:

"As president of the association, I have created a group of 4–5 women members of our association to provide information to people living in remote villages."

and by Fulya's recommendation:

> *"Mothers have to learn the computer use in order to protect their children. I have helped and advised many women to go to the 2nd chance school. Through my job I try to convince minority women to continue with their studies."*

Language matter

Key informants recognize that one of the major problems minority women face is that of lack of knowledge of the Greek language. Hakan described the situation stating:

> *"Most women can't speak Greek. Women don't want to go shopping, they don't want to go a doctor, they are not open minded especially in villages and more in the area of Evros."* Zeki said: *"Women must learn the Greek language very well in order to be able to integrate in this society."*

and Ekrem added by saying:

> *"If minority woman wants to have the position that she deserves, then she must obtain a promising and sufficient education."*

Some of the key informants expressed that the Turkish language should be integrated in the procedure of teaching during the seminars in order to ensure the participation of minority women. Guner, in this vein pointed out:

> *"Women should be informed about the programs; but most of them don't know Greek and for this reason some programs must be bilingual, both in Greek and Turkish or in the mother tongue."*

and Ekrem referred to the information usually offered in the seminars by saying:

> *"We must have a target. Women must learn again how to make bread or to receive new skills? If she obtains the second, she will do also the first. Women of the minority know how to cook, to make sweets. The main problem is how these women will acquire knowledge. For this you must know your mother tongue and also the language of the country you live. In villages where Muslim people live the seminars should be taught in Turkish. Also, in seminars mixed groups of Christians and Muslims should work together so that existing relations among them might improve."*

Scarf issue

During the conversations some of the key informants referred to the issue of the scarf, which lately has been under discussion in Europe. The key informants agreed that the scarf had to be a religious symbol, not a means of policies.

What Ekrem said on this subject is very interesting; it reflects one part of the minority who is in favor of minority women wearing scarves or being covered.

Can and Murat respectively present the other part of the minority who is not in favor of such traditions and believe that by influencing women to wear scarves or cover their bodies and faces and escape from a west-oriented model of life, in this way other means are being served which do not benefit the minority. Can was very critical of the situation is being established in the last years in the area as the number of scarf clad minority was increasing lately:

"Religion and fundamentalism has increased; but here in Thrace we are in a transitional situation. We can see many women wearing colorful scarves, but this is something that has come and will pass. Women here are influenced by the pictures coming from Turkey. They see how the Turkish Prime minister's wife dressed is and they want to resemble her. But even Erdogan's wife (Turkish Prime minister's wife) wears the scarf since this serves some means. And the main mean is the money. They don't really believe in what they are doing."

Murat trying to explain the phenomenon put forth,

"Women try to keep their identity and this drives them to adopt the scarf. But the problem is for them to be in peace in the area they live. Here people of the minority are not so religious. They are more west oriented."

Halil's believes on Islam, are presented in an unprocessed way as it is generally difficult to approach this key informant, give another aspect to what usually considered to be the religion of Islam:

"Islam doesn't discriminate women and men. They can use both the ICTs; they can both be educated and can become doctors. Even flying with an aero plane is permitted. The first woman pilot was a Muslim woman. Additionally they have to help other women as obstetricians, to help other women with medical issues. Women whatever want they can find it on the Internet. He said that they are open in new things and sometimes they can be more progressive than the ones who want to react as progressives. They are open in new ideas in order to help people but their economical situation is their only problem. Things can be done in the mosque as it can function in another way but they don't have money to materialize their ideas. They could even materialize programs and seminars. He is not negative in such a prospective. We want to contribute to strengthening women's rights but we don't have the economical ability. Islam doesn't slander women. I am against the word "prohibition". Islam doesn't prohibit. In Iran, Egypt, Maroco there are even women judges. There are women who are professors in universities. In a society, the right people must be

educated and trained with no discrimination. I believe that women and men are equal. Muslim minority women, contrary to what people believe, have the right of the divorce. When a woman can prove that her husband is an alcoholic or a drug user she automatically can get the divorce. In Islam woman can join the army. This started 1400 years ago. But in the West the gender equality was succeeded 100 years ago. We want to translate the family laws of SARIA in English and in Greek but we don't receive any economical aid for that."

Changes from past-Cultural transformation -Emancipation

The researcher's experience has been her motive to start searching about the minority women and their computer literacy:

"I work at KEKs and it is the first time all these years to see women dressed in black gowns, covered with feretzes to come there or even their husbands to bring them on motorbikes to attend consulting lessons. So I thought these people must be in great trouble in order to abolish their tradition to get over old methods."

During their interviews, the key informants said that the situation for the minority women was changing. Naim described the situation as it was formed today in a very perspicacious way.

"After 1991, the psychological part of the minority changed as the policy of the Greek government towards the minority changed and became more clarified. As a consequence, now minority people want to invest here in Thrace. The new generation watches all these changes and becomes more claiming, dispended from the complexes of the past. I am astonished at the number of women, even the ones who wear a scarf, driving a car, riding a bike, using ICTs. I believe that the question "whether women of the minority have to work" is unnecessary in the research. All my life, I have been fighting for the rights of women to work."

Zeki, a young mayor who was afraid to speak openly said,

"Things are not like as they used to be in the old days. I think that women of the minority need support. We have to sit down all together, mayors, deputies, policy makers to put things in order to provide a substantial help. We have to change our mentality in the way we confront women because during the past years the situation has been ridiculous. I don't want to give any examples."

Nowadays girls who finish primary school continue their studies at the secondary education. Minority women study in the universities and enter the labor force in different fields. Today they go after the chances, but also they have the chances to live better and in equality compared to men. In the past, they did not have the chances and as for this their needs were not so important. Aslan commented:

"Now, how families think about girls is changing. A graduate from the university can manage things in a better way and the changes must be activated quickly."

Family structure has changed. Deniz contributed to the conversation saying,

"Our women also get divorces, and the reason is that a woman who is financially independent cannot tolerate and suffer a husband or a mother in law or relatives of husband as it used to be in the past. I think that they are not so "closed" as they used to be. This situation now has been left behind."

The TV has played an important role in women's emancipation and moreover the ICTs as they function like a window to the outside world giving them the chances to compare things. Murat supported this by saying:

"The TV brought many changes. Old communities were much closed but nowadays technology has brought many changes."

After that they don't want a life similar to their parents'. A key informant mentioned that they live in a transitional period in which women of the minority are expected to be bolder. Defne comments:

"The structure of the family has changed. A woman can work if she has good studies. Nowadays, due to financial problems the number of working women who come from villages increases." Kadir added *"I believe that in the next 10 years, we will not have such problems. The time in the middle of the 90s was a milestone for the history of the minority. The minority obtains a new face in the local society."*

Key informants were positive with regard to minority women's intention to work and contribute to the family income as this was unavoidable due to the economic crisis and due to financial problems the minority family faces. Timur stated,

"Of course, they should help and support the income of the family as their children have more expenses because of their studies."

And Birol coloured the real intentions of the minority as he mentioned that,

"Basically they want to find a job or more specifically to find a job in civil services. Now days they can think even of that. For example we have a mayor assistant who is a woman."

Even those in religious positions were positive as they explained that religion put no obstacles to a woman if she wanted to work as Kaan and Hakan admitted:

"I am positive about this. Women are free to work. Islam doesn't forbid women to work; it sets them free. Mohamed's wife was a merchant. But we, as men, have to feed our wives."

Adem, a mayor in a rural area, gave in his answer the image of the contemporary minority:

"Yes, I agree that finally women have torn apart the curtain. Economic problem is very big and we don't know if they will eventually do this because they want to get information or just money. I believe that the Greek state has to support all the people of the minority who are interested and in this way to give a push to the general situation of the whole minority."

And finally Sadik concluded:

> *"I believe that the revolution in the minority; connected to transformation and integration of the minority in the social context avoiding the old ghettos and margins; will start from the women. It will not start from the young ones despite the fact that the young men of the minority are now educated, they go to Greek universities and they come back and work, nevertheless I believe that only women can change the situation because men have been brought up in a different way."*

Chapter 5: Discussion

5. Introduction

The previous chapter presented the findings of this study by organizing data from various sources into categories to produce a readable narrative.

The study was carried out in three parts by using a combination of quantitative and qualitative methods so as to provide richer information about the problem being addressed:

- The initial part, was was devoted to empirically validate the Technology Acceptance Model (TAM) and the Theory of Planned Behaviour (TPB) and analyze how it varies across computer attitude.
- The second part assessed the benefits of computer education in terms of the nature and extent of empowerment experienced by 28 women of the minority.
- The final part, explored through 30 interviews the thoughts and the attitudes of the key informants about the potential of social participation of minority women through computer education.

Finally, Muslim minority women's perceptions of how the computer education could lead them to pathways for their social participation were explored, and, moreover the contribution of members of their community in administrative positions, to this effort was detected.

The purpose of this chapter is to provide interpretative insights into these findings as it attempts to reconstruct a more holistic understanding. The discussion takes into consideration the literature on empowerment of women through ICTs.

5.1 TAM and TPB Metod

A significant difference in computer ownership was found between dwellers of the prefectures of Rodopi and Xanthi, with a higher percentage for those in Rodopi, and between town and village dwellers, with a higher percentage for those in towns. This may be due to different economic levels of minority people living in te Rodopi prefecture, since the middle class of the minority is mainly gathered in this area, and usually in urban areas whilst minority's status from the point of residence is more rural and mountainous in the prefect of Xanthi.

Trainers, in their role as a measure of institutional support in attending lessons, were not found to hold gender-stereotyped views. Significant difference was not found in the preference of the gender of the trainer connected to the family status of the women or connected to their residence area. *"He/she must be interested in teaching. He must have knowledge and must want to share it. Good communication, adaptability to the class needs, explaining things in a simple way, without clinging solely on books and terminology"* are some of the characteristics women expect a trainer to have. The finding in this research contradicts some experiences of tele-centres around the world that have shown that women are more comfortable with women trainers and, in some cases, able to participate more effectively in women only training environments (Jorge, 2000). Huyer (2006) mentions the critical need for experienced gender experts to work in the field of ICTs with policymaking agencies and at regulatory bodies. Additionally, the need for accurate sex disaggregated data and indicators to understand gendered trends of participation in the information age, must be emphasized (Hafkin, 2006a).

Depending on the place where women of the sample use the computer, it is found out that they mostly have access to a family computer. The background of these women is characterized by at least one computer literate family member who contributes to the computer literacy of the others and plays the role model that can be observed or imitated. In general, a small percent of the women use their computer out of house. The Muslim minority women interviewees, with limited or non-existing presence at cyber cafés say they usually access the computer at their houses, and this is a result of high rate of computer ownership at homes, and due to social restrictions and structure of the minority society. Researches have showed that women usually do not frequent cyber cafés as these places function in such ways that women are not comfortable visiting (Gothoskar, 2000; Gurumurthy, 2004; Melhem et al., 2009). On the other hand, Umrani's (2003) research in India among Muslim minority women describes an opposite behaviour as women there mainly access computers in training centres and cyber cafes due to lack of computer ownership as a consequence of their economical situation.

Seeking information was ranked as the first most important benefit by women who were aware of the potentials of access to information through computers. Entertainment was cited as their second most preferable choice; and the use of computers for communication and connecting with family and kin, the third, which was the most mentioned during the interviews. People have always sought to communicate and to gain information that will sustain their livelihoods, increase their opportunities, and improve the quality of their lives. And ICTs can provide the tools to do this (Nath, 2006; Huyer, 2005, 2006; Hafkin, 2003a, 2006). Their networking is mainly with friends and relatives as women focus on narrow social groups. This is not surprising as it has been observed that social relations of Muslim women center on family and kin. Yet this can be a first step for their potential empowerment through ICT use to participate in social networks and linking up with others to form coalitions to influence decision making mechanisms at all levels of society (Nath, 2006).

5.1.1 TPB Method

The TPB model is used in Greece in several researches to validate the influence of psychological variables as Subjective Norm, and Perceived Behavioural Control to Intention to use technology. There are studies among students or teachers (Koutromanos & Papaioannou, 2008; Koutromanos, 2006; Koutromanos & Kibirige, 2006; Koutromanos, 2009; Koutromanos & Zisimopoulos, 2009), among bank employees investigating the knowledge-sharing behavior (Chatzoglou et al., 2010), among employees in a company investigating the use of e-learning (Tsakiri, 2007), among Greek users of the Internet investigating their attitudes to e-commerce (Kanios, 2009), or students' relation the Internet, the confidentiality of data and their consuming behavior (Ferekidou, 2007).

In this research, among Muslim minority women in Thrace, Attitude toward technology, Subjective Norm, and Perceived Behavioural Control are all found to be significant positive determinants of Intention to use technology with a positive influence on Behavioural Intention. **Perceived Behavioural Control and Subjective Norm** are the two most significant positive determinants of **Intention** to use technology respectively. TPB is validated in this study, explaining approximately 37.5 percent of the variance in Behavioural Intention.

Moderation of Subjective Norm is significant with the level of education upon Behaviour Intention to use computer technology. This finding is harmonious with the findings of older researches in which the same determinants have been validated (Fishbein and Ajzen, 1975; Ajzen, 1991; Taylor and Todd, 1995; Venkatesh and Davis, 2000; Venkatesh et al., 2003; Yu et al., 2005; Baker et al. 2007). As we read in Baker et al. (2007), this finding supports Hartwick and Barki's (1994) assertion that the relative influence of Subjective Norm on Behavioural Intention is significant even when users have only limited direct experience from which to develop attitudes about ICT adoption and usage. Higher levels of education had a negative moderating effect on the positive influence of Subjective Norm on Intention to use technology. This negative moderating effect suggests that with increasing levels of education, the influence of Subjective Norm on Intention to use technology is muted. That means the more educated someone is, the less he is influenced by the perceived social pressure to use or not technology.

Moderation of Perceived Behavioural Control is significant with the level of residence area (village-town) upon Behaviour Intention to use computer technology. Living in a village has a negative moderating effect on the positive influence of Perceived Behavioural Control on Intention to use technology. This negative moderating effect suggests that living in a village mutes the influence of Perceived Behavioural Control on Intention to use technology. Perceived Behavioural Control is defined as the perceived ease or difficulty of performing a behaviour (Eagly and Chaiken, 1993 in Umrani, 2003); that is, of using the technology. That can be explained as someone who lives in a village has not benefited at such a level from using the technologies; that is, they are less adept at using technology.

Non-significance of age, of resid1 (the Rodopi and Xanthi prefects), of marital status, of economical and professional status as moderating variables on Attitude, Subjective Norm, and Perceived Behavioural Control are worth mentioning as they affect Behaviour Intention to use technology. These findings, especially with respect to age, marital and professional status, were not unexpected. To gather the sample of the research, we approached women familiar with computer use, of different ages, (half of them were in the 20–30 age range and the median of the age was the range of 31–40 years), overall of them married, of a mixture of educational levels (from primary education to holding a master's degree); but finally this blend of social characteristics did not act as moderating variable giving the sense of a homogeneous sample.

5.1.2 TAM Method

TAM theorises that an individual's actual technology usage is determined by intention, which, in turn, is determined by perceived usefulness and perceived ease of use. The TAM model has been tested across a wide range of computer settings and has been shown to be a robust predictor of computer use (Taylor & Todd, 1995; Venkatesh & Davis, 2000). Pavlou (2003) investigated consumer's acceptance of electronic commerce using the TAM method. Rigopoulos et al. (2008), evaluated user's attitude towards adoption of decision support systems with the TAM model. Kourakos and Kaouni (2009) examined the technology acceptance of electronically mediated learning by adult learners in KEE (Centres of Adult Education). In Aggelidis and Chatzoglou (2009) study the original TAM has been extended to include some exogenous variables in order to examine HIS acceptance by Greek hospital personnel. The results indicated that Perceived Usefulness, Ease of Use, Social influence, Attitude, Facilitating conditions and Self-Efficacy significantly affect hospital personnel's Behavioural Intention. Koutroumanos (2009), in his research, about the examination and prediction of university students' decisions to acquire access to Broadband Internet for personal and educational purposes, states that TAM was used in very different settings; for example, to test the acceptance of Internet utilisation behaviour (Shih, 2004 in Koutroumanos 2009), online shopping (Vijayasarathy, 2004 in Koutroumanos 2009), online learning (Saade & Bahli, 2004 in Koutroumanos 2009), Internet banking (Lai et al., 2005 in Koutroumanos 2009) and so on.

Umrani (2007) remarks that while the TAM method explains 45 to 71 % variance in Behavioural Intention to use it in the United States and Europe (Davis et. al. 1989; Venkatesh & Morris, 2000; Venkatesh & Davis, 2000), the results are mixed when tested in countries outside the West like China (Mao & Palvia, 2001), Japan (Straub, 1994; Straub et al., 1997), Arab countries like Jordan, Egypt, Saudi Arabia, Lebanon and the Sudan (Rose & Straub, 1998) and Hong Kong (Hu, Chau, Sheng & Tam, 1999).

In our research, all the variables taken together explained a 28 percent variance in Behavioural Intention, the indicator of technology acceptance, which is much lower than the typical about 40 to 60 percent usually found. This difference can be explained by way of the sample characteristics, level of technological advancement, and cultural variations. Earlier studies were conducted on students, professionals, and high-end computer users in the West. The present study was conducted on women computer users of different ages, different reside areas, different educational level, with a family and social background which usually directed minority women to exclusion all the past years.

The findings of this research showed that the mean score on the Behavioural Intention scale was high implying that women strongly intended to use computers in the future. Women trainees appraised computers to be moderately easy to use; overall of them appraised computers to be very useful. They also perceived themselves to be highly self efficacious using computers where they revealed a positive view of their cognitive capacities in dealing with computers. They appraised Subjective Norm to be quite important, indicating a motivation to comply with the expectations of significant others to learn computers as individuals tend to take significant referents' opinions into consideration when assessing usefulness of a technology.

The results of the present study indicated that for the overall sample **Perceived Usefulness** and **Computer Self-Efficacy** were the significant predictors of **Behavioral Intention** to use computers. Perceived Usefulness and Computer Self-Efficacy had a direct effect on Behavioural Intention and emerged significant. In other words, when women think of computers easy to use and useful, they adopt the use of this technology. The more efficacious the women perceive themselves to be, the stronger their intention is to use computers and think that are easy to use. Perceived usefulness in other countries had a primary role in determining intention for computer use. This choice highlights that people are motivated to become computer educated when they connect this new literacy with a practical utility.

Perceived Ease of Use and Subjective Norm had no direct effect on Behavioural Intention as they were not highly correlated to Behavioural Intention.On the other hand, Subjective Norm was found to be significantly associated with Perceived Ease of Use and Perceived Usefulness. In this research, it is observed that the effect of Subjective Norm, Perceived Ease of Use, and Computer Self-Efficacy on Behavioural Intention to use computers is mediated significantly by Perceived Usefulness. This last finding is confirmed by Lin et al. (2003) as their research indicates that subjective norm is an important determinant of technology acceptance, and behavioural intentions and factors, such as perceived usefulness, may mediate the effect of subjective norm on technology acceptance.

Subjective Norm has been of particular interest in Asian and African researches where cultural factors are highlighted to explain its relevance in determining Behavioural Intention to use computers (Umrani, 2007). Zakour (2004) and Straub et al. (2001) state that in societies with feminine culture people usually take in serious consideration the opinion of the others. In such societies the role model often comes from peers-husbands, relatives and neighbours.

Significant causal linkages were found for two sets of variables:

1) Computer Self-Efficacy was a significant determinant of Perceived Ease of Use, implying that when a woman sees herself as competent, she views computers easy to handle.
2) Subjective Norm was a significant determinant of Perceived Usefulness, that is, when women believe that significant others want them to use computers, it not only results in stronger intention to use computers but also influences their beliefs about usefulness of the technology as the effect of subjective norm is also mediated through perceived usefulness

We can conclude the analysis of quantitative findings by saying that in terms of the researches explained above, Muslim minority women in Greece exhibit a more West-oriented Behavioural Intention to use computers; that means they have the intention to use the technology as long as they feel capable of doing it and think it is useful. They take into consideration the opinion of the others, which also influences their beliefs about the usefulness of the technology.

5.2 Women's Interviews

The second part of the study was qualitative in nature as women were interviewed to assess their potential empowerment after receiving computer education and to figure out the ways for their social participation. Women's empowerment is defined as a multi-dimensional process of civil, political, social, economic, and cultural participation and rights. It is conceptualised in terms of the achievement of basic capabilities, of legal rights, and of participation in key social, economic and political domains (Moghadam, 2003). In the following discussion, we shall detect which of the above terms are satisfied through the research we have carried out among Muslim minority women in Thrace.

5.2.1 Experiences on ICTs

Interviewees were of different educational levels, but one fourth of them were of primary education and the same number of tertiary education. We tried our sample to consist of different educational levels in order to obtain a pluralism of the views we were about to select.

The overwhelming majority of the sample belonged to middle income group (14.000–30.000 €). As only half of the interviewees work, this income was defined as family income, not their personal income. Those who are employed earn sufficient money and contribute to the total family income. Some of the women who are not employed in public or private sector contribute to the family income by working in the fields next to their husbands or in family business. The level of economical status declared by the interviewees excuses the high family purchase of computers, laptops, cell phones and Internet connection at home, recorded and succeeded through financial assistance from family or relatives. Women interviewees connect the term ICT to computer and mobile phones and web-cameras as these are the gadgets they commonly use. Traditional technologies continue to be important for large numbers of people around the world, particularly in rural areas. However, new technologies have a vast potential for empowerment (UN, 2005). Interviewees mostly use the Internet, the Word and the Messenger from the applications of Microsoft Office. Majority of them use the computer daily and have an account on Facebook. Their networking is mainly with friends and relatives as many members of the minority are living either in Turkey or immigrated to other countries in Europe. In general, their social relations centre on family and kin; but this can be the beginning and also the fuel for participation in wider groups as was highlighted in Chapter II from examples among Muslim women in different countries. It is likely that for the start, women focus on narrow social groups but gradually widen their horizons to participate in other networks. Just like as one of the interviewees said, she participates in online Turkish communities, exchanging ideas and views about theater plays, directing a play and writing poems.

5.2.2 Reasons for Computer Use and Internet

When the women were asked to mention the reasons they use the computer, according to the multiple answers they were provided to choose from, "Internet" was the one with the highest rate of choice compare with the others. "Communication" was their second choice, followed by "Profession" and "Game/Entertainment" equally as their third choice. When the women were asked to mention what sort of information they got from the Internet, according to the multiple answers they were provided to choose from, "News" was that with the highest percent of choice compared with the others. "Chatting" was their second choice, followed by "Work" as their third. Research has shown that males use the Internet and the World Wide Web primarily to gather information (Gefen & Straub, 1997), while women use them primarily to communicate (Jackson, Ervin, Gardner & Schmitt, 2001). Women are online primarily for email (Jackson, Ervin, Gardner & Schmitt, 2001; Van Slambrouch, 2000; Wilson, 2000). Using technology for communication is a female gendered tendency while using technology to gather information is a male gendered tendency.

Interviewees were asked to rank their ability to function 20 options by using the computer. The answers that received the major preference were get news on line, connect to friends and learn new things (at the same level), connect to relatives abroad, look for information about movies and books, look for information about a hobby or interest, browse for fun, look for information about health, medical issues, hobbies, download music files, do their job, find information for a place to live in, share online artwork, photos, etc. Their choices did not include or were not of high range for the following options: manage your personal finances, e-government, tele-marketing, work with others in your community or in groups you belong to.

Both town and village dwellers chose the option "Get news on line" as their first choice. Town dwellers use the Internet more to find information on books, movies, their hobbies, and to find a job. Those who work do their job through the computer or the Internet. Interviewees with high levels of education use the Internet for multiple choices, almost all choices provided by the researcher, and those with primary or secondary education are oriented more to "Get news on line" as their first choice, followed by "Connect with friends" or "Connect with relatives abroad". The ones with primary education use the Internet a lot for "Health and medical information" and for "Fun". The option "Information about a job" is mostly preferred by the more educated. Younger women showed a preference to look up information about books, movies, to download music, to browse for fun, to seek information for a job or work through the Internet. Whatever has to do with seeking information on the Internet Mitter (2000) is very descriptive by saying:

> *"The transferability of information bodes well for traditionally disadvantaged groups that include women. In most societies, including in poorer ones, the advent of information and communication technologies opens up possibilities of access to a 'global' pool of knowledge so long as potential users have access to adequate infrastructure and possess relevant skills. Information about reproductive health over the Internet can, for example, save or improve lives of many women (and men) facing the hazards of AIDS in Asian and African countries."*

The interviewees, by the time they were asked to give information about the websites they commonly used provided a variety of websites. They say they prefer reading Turkish newspapers to learn news from Turkey. They also read the minority Turkish phone daily press which includes many newspapers published every day in Komotini and Xanthi. They watch Turkish television and all the programmes they miss from the Turkish channels. They chat with friends, relatives, or with the opposite sex. Some of them buy products on line. One of the interviewees participates in online Turkish communities, exchanging ideas and views about the theatrical plays, about how to direct a play and how to write poems. Some women find food recipes from both Greek and Turkish websites. Women who try to find a job search Greek searching machines or Greek websites of ministries or organizations.

5.2.3 Infrastructure

The challenge for minority women, who have been documented in the past years the most educationally and economically disadvantaged, the most socially excluded part of the minority, is to introduce the technology to a large number of women's groups in urban and rural areas.

Some of the interviewees mentioned the lack of infrastructure on Internet connection or broadband Internet connection especially in rural and mountainous regions, the lack of infrastructure that facilitates reliable and affordable connectivity, the lack of telephone facilities, frequent breakdown and poor quality of lines, some times lack of electricity and the need for investments in ICT infrastructure. This lack of infrastructure combined with the jobless state of half of them is a mixture that abolishes their right to get information and can lead them to less opportunities and chances for integration (Ekdahl and Trojer, 2002; Nguessan, 2006; NTIA, 1995; Hafkin 2000; Arun and Arun 2002; Prasar 2003; Gurumurthy 2004; Mitter 2005; Hafkin and Huyer, 2006a).

The interviewees, as they were a sub-sample of the women who filled the questionnaires for the initial quantitative research, confirmed the comments made in in the first part of the research, that the majority of the interviewees did not visit cyber cafés which usually function as cafes or bars in the area of Thrace, and mostly in villages. However, women say they visit cyber cafés when they are in Turkey as there they feel freer to react with no restrictions or interventions from the social environment. This finding is in the same vein with the work of Huyer and Hafkin (2007), which demonstrates that there is no correlation between the saturation of ICTs in a country and women's access to those ICTs. Social and cultural factors limit women's access to shared ICT facilities, such as cybercafés, or telecentres, which often become meeting places for young men, and hence deter women's absorption and adoption of ICTs to access information and knowledge.

The interviewees mostly found information about computer seminars at the KEP (Centres for Citizen's Service). These centres (KEP) were established in Greece in 2004 in order to provide quick and full services with limited bureaucracy to citizens of every municipality. It seems that all these years these centres have played an important role providing information, especially to people living in villages who have less resources to receive information.

Ng and Mitter (2005) and Peizer (2005) describe how myriad government-sponsored agencies and non-governmental organizations (NGOs) in South Asia have initiated a host of ICT-based development projects to demonstrate the potential of ICTs, to provide unprecedented social and economic opportunities for vulnerable groups, such as women and marginalized communities. It seems that these kind of centres or telecentres or cyber kiosks are there to contribute to the inclusion of marginalized communities in the emerging rural network society by improving participation in democratic processes and by providing access to expanding social and economic opportunities (Hafkin, 2002; Hafkin and Taggart, 2001; Sharma, 2003; UN,2005b).

Some of the interviewees, living on mountainous villages, had to face problems of transportation by the time they wanted to participate in seminars. As Panousi (2007), claims bad transportation in minority villages, bad land-planning of the centres for training and adult education, unpropitious weather conditions in winter which influence transportation, attitude of minority parents towards girls' education, lack of teachers specially trained to teach an audience of a multicultural synthesis, all together contribute to minimize the opportunities for minority women to receive further training and education. Some of the interviewees' reaction in order to manage their transportation is considered remarkable. This lack triggered five women to react as a group and pay the expenses of the one of them to get a driving licence. Communalism plays an important role in the inclusion of marginalized communities and has been verified in many countries where many projects were funded and implemented aiming to increase voluntarism, to inform of the use of ICTs, to raise awareness on issues of common concern, such as, sexual and reproductive health and drug abuse, to raise awareness on the importance of women's participation in political life, to motivate for networks with counterparts at every level (Wheeler, 2006b; Sreekumar, 2007; VFA; UN, 2005b).

The researcher from the very beginning was aware of the lack of statistics concerning the Muslim minority population. The National Statistic Service did not provide her with data, not even for the number of the minority populations living in Thrace. According to Dodos (1994) in Asimakopoulou and Lionaraki (2002:231) after the quota of 1951 when populations were recorded according to their religion and to their mother tongue, every data that concerns minority populations in Greece is considered to be not announced. In her research Panousi (2007), faced exactly the same problem that drove her to assume the population of the minority from statistics included in various researches from the past. Thus, the researcher had to collect data, on her own, to detect minority women's participation in education connected to ICTs; presented in Chapter II (Geogiadou, 2008). As Hafkin (2006), comments we know very little about women's situation and ICTs in developing countries. Much like the digital divide, a statistical divide exists where the need is greatest: in developing nations (Huyer et al., 2005). Huyer and Mitter (2003) explain that good figures globally on women's use of the Internet do not exist. Most government statistics agencies do not provide a breakdown by gender; therefore globally comparable and consistent data are not yet available. However, we do know that women's access to and use of ICTs is much lower than men's around the world, while several recent project reviews have indicated that women continue to benefit less than men from the implementation of ICTs (Thioune, 2003; Rathegeber, 2002; and Hafkin and Huyer, 2003).

Interviewees were informed of the existence of state schools for adult education (the Second Chance School) and pointed out that this kind of school had to be established in every municipality and easy access or transportation had to be provided. Almost half of them showed a preference to state or minority schools as the place where they could attend programs on computer use, with private centres for professional training following their choices. Remarkable is the fact that women from Xanthi also selected the choice "Association", stating by this choice the importance of the minority women's Association that functions in the area. They also were informed of and participated in seminars provided in both private Centers for Adult Education (KEK) established in the early 1990s (although their participation in these centers started mainly in the mid of 2000s) and in state Centers for Adult Education (KEE), established in 2006–2007 and supported by the Institute of Life Long Training for Adults and the General Secretariat of Adult Training (Georgiadou, 2008; Navrozidou, 2008; Hatzikosta, 2008).

Continuous education and training enhances the chances for learners to participate in the processes of socio-economic development and upgrade their qualifications for the expansion of their employment opportunities. Long time unemployment, limited education, poverty, lack of social solidarity can under-estimate the social cohesion (UNESCO, 1997). In a society with these demands, socially excluded groups with limited education confront a higher possibility for marginalization. The non formal education system has come up as a very promising alternative to the formal education system in an effort to make edu-cational opportunities available to a larger population and addressing the needs of contemporary times (Thompson, 2001). Even illiterates have benefited from non formal education to obtain skills in order to confront needs of contempo-rary life. Programs of "ICTs for community empowerment through non-formal education" in Thailand, Sri Lanka, in Lao PDR, in Uzbekistan, in Sub-Saharan Africa, in India can be considered as examples in the same vein to support all the information presented above and provide data to rely on for ICT policymakers in Greece (UNESCO, 2005; Pye 2003; Mitra, 2000, 2001, 2003, 2005). The needs for knowledge, change, and social improvement are subjects that Muslim minority women want to be a part of them as a contradiction to their usual behaviours. A new face for the "woman of the Muslim minority in Greek Thrace" comes into sight. The impacts and conflicts this matter erupts, have to be considered. Adult education can become the vehicle to support the redefinition of the role that Muslim minority women were forced to adopt. This role, all the past years, has derived from internal social conflicts the Muslim community went through or external actions.

Interviewees made clear that they could also use conventional ICTs, such as the radio to access information sources. This was also supported by the key-informants' interviews as they commented that they used the radio to provide information to minority women. Melhem et al (2009), by providing examples about the community radio station Radio-Ada in south-eastern Ghana and the radio listening group projects in postwar Siera Leone, explains that the radio is used by women to access information sources and communication processes to achieve their development goals both for the good of their households and communities.

5.2.4 Multiplier Impact

Findings of the study point out that women are interested in expanding their knowledge by attending seminars and computer use programs or learning the Greek language. This intention expresses their objective to integrate in the new Greek reality and impresses deeper transformations in social and cultural level.

Interviewees reported that the main factors that influenced them in learning the computer use were their peers, husbands, their children (sons, daughters, etc), thirdly their mentors and finally their interests. Interviewees said that their husbands encouraged them to do things as their main concern was the family income and the whole family had to contribute to this.

The following comment describes the value that the most participants in this study placed on learning the computer use to be able to help their children: *"I am learning for my own good and interest and to be able to help my children in the future."* The interviewees' acquisition of technical skills resulted in computer literacy of other family members and consequently computer awareness in the family as the majority of the interviewees encouraged significant others, such as members of their family to learn the computer use and acquire technical skills. They usually teach computer skills and serve as a role model by talking about computers to their female friends and neighbours, their sisters, mothers and daughters, and unemployed friends. Some women reported that the ones who received their advices reacted and participated in seminars to become computer literate. This finding comes as a complement to previous researches that argue for the benefits of having a computer literate family member (Hafkin & Taggart, 2001; Hafkin, 2002; Umrani & Ghadially, 2003; Wheeler, 2006b; Umrani, 2007).

Their future plans connected to ICT use include the choice to *"encourage and promote other women of your community"*, that was mostly selected, followed by *"apply for document to civil services"*, *"career decision"* in both administrative areas, but the first choice was mostly preferred by town residuals (60 % of the town dwellers) and the second was mostly preferred by village dwellers in order to avoid the distance that separated them from the civil services. The choice *"offer help and information to your community"* lucked of choice by women who live in towns. This attitude of the interviewees was in line with the program "Netcorp Jordan", which helped build an ICT skilled workforce. This program managed to encourage entrepreneurship, voluntarism and benefit of life skills in order to shape a better future for the participants. Women demonstrated skill especially in training others in ICTs. The Net Corps Jordan program has repeatedly demonstrated that if one person is trained, this one person will educate many (Wheeler, 2006b).

5.2.5 Social and Psychological Impact

ICTs, as past researches have showed, are increasingly promoted as a key solution for comprehensive development, poverty eradication and empowerment of historically disadvantaged groups, such as women and minorities (Hafkin & Huyer 2006; Hafkin & Taggart, 2001; Heeks, 1999, Huyer & Mitter, 2003).

In this research, the interviewees' perception for computer education was very positive as the majority of them believe that ICTs can help to obtain knowledge, to achieve communication, to become more efficient to work, to gain self confidence, to obtain better education and studies, and to increase social participation. A majority of the interviewees said they learned the computer use mainly for themselves, and secondly, to be able to help their children and to get in touch with them when they were abroad. The following comment describes the value that most interviewees in this study placed on learning the computer use:

> *"The computer helps me to communicate with my children and relatives abroad and also fight my loneliness as my husband is out of home the whole day. I feel less lonely in this way. I watch Turkish soap-operas and listen to hundreds of the songs I have stored on my computer. I can Skype with my daughters and grandchildren who all live in Turkey."*

Interviewees, being aware of the potential empowerment through computer education quoted some of their motives for attending a computer seminar. These were: knowledge, communication, skills, money, feeling contemporary. Their choices and the order they placed them in are an indicator that women have further awareness of the demands of the society they try to integrate. It can be stated that psychological benefits for these minority women from computer use include positive self-esteem, awareness and feeling contemporary. These findings are supported by many researches in the past which ended up to relative conclusions. Hafkin (2002) interviewed women enrolled in a Cisco Certified Networking Associate (CCNA) course in networking and found out that computer skills had resulted in increased self-confidence and enhanced self-esteem. Marcelle (2000b), points out that ICTs can have positive effects on women's confidence, self-esteem and status and through its use women get access to information which challenges existing gender inequality. Lee (2004) indicated that one year after the completion of the course women experienced considerable change in behaviour, actions and perspectives because they felt empowered after learning computer use; because it enabled them to use the family computer and participate in family conversation on the technology. Most women reported that they could participate in the lives of their children and spouses, contribute to conversations and experiences centred on the new technology, thus modifying their role in the family.

Interviewees, through their experience of participating in seminars and different projects, of using ICTs and communicating out of the house, tried to improve their living conditions and focused on them; they "broke out of the fold", something that was not a feature of Muslim minority women in the past as their orientation in the society was collectively oriented in their family. Muslim minority society was in the past, and in some cases it still is, what Maneja (2002) described an "escalator hierarchy" where younger women had to obey older women whose only concern was to serve males in their youth, to give birth to preferably to sons, to show obedience to elders, and to be excellent housekeepers. The literal and the symbolic closing of the minority women in the urban areas and their exclusion from the different outside world seems to be the price they pay with their psychological disturbance and their recourse to psycho-medicines in high rates (Tsibiridou, 2005).

During the first part of the research where quantitative data was collected and analyzed, it was counted that seeking information was ranked as the first most important benefit by women as they were aware of the potentials of access to information through computers. Entertainment was cited as their second most preferable choice, and use of computers for communication, and connecting with family and kin, the third, which emerged as crucial. It can be assumed that with both methods, through questionnaires and interviews, the most important impact of computer education is observed in its role as the medium for seeking information, managing communication, and the personal entertainment as the second, which by extension can be considered as factors that lead to Muslim minority women's psychological and social empowerment.

Women interviewees reported personal and family gain, communication and receiving information as the three topmost benefits of using computers, a pattern similar to that found in the quantitative part of the research. It is not surprising that the major benefits of learning computers pertain to themselves and their family as half of the sample consists predominantly of women homemakers. Since women are the ones who keep the internal cohesion of the family and are responsible to maintain family relations, their computer literacy can improve the social function of the family. The empowering feeling they perceive through computer use can best be described in their words. Nancy Hafkin (2002) refers to Amartya Sen argues for the centrality of women in the knowledge society, placing emphasis on the agency and capabilities of women. He sees women's leadership as a crucial element in development and notes that expansion of women's capabilities enhances not only women's own freedom and well being, but also has beneficial effects on society as a whole. Sen (1999), concludes by saying:

> *"knowledge is not only for economic growth, but its foremost use should be to empower and develop all sectors of society to understand and use knowledge to increase quality of people's lives and to promote social development. A socially inclusive knowledge society empowers all members of society to create, receive, share and use information and knowledge for their economic, social, cultural and political development."*

The expectations the interviewees have for the social status of the minority from the participation of the minority women in life long learning programs (computer education, language learning, skills etc.) can be summarized in thee words: job-children-knowledge. The answers they give come to support the expectations a woman has for herself through computer education. Their answers are very genuine and characterize the changes that are hatched up in minority's life:

> *"We can find a job with the computer. What I think for my daughter is that I don't want her just to finish primary school. On the contrary, for God's sake, I would like her to study in order to be able to find a job and live a better life than the one I have, not only to become a house wife. Now things have changed, things are different from what they used to be in the past."*

Computer education had also an economic impact as it helped eight of the interviewees to find a job and made them feel assured. Being computer literate, they used the Internet to find information related to jobs. As stated above, the use of the Greek language for reading websites is connected to surfing job portals or job circulars sent out on the Internet. Financial impact of the use of ICTs for women can be supported by many researches globally. ICTs can provide to women the opportunities for personal business development and growth (Hafkin and Taggart, 2001; Jorge, 2002; Huyer and Sikoska, 2002; Huyer and Mitter, 2003; Arun et al, 2006). An interviewee, a mountainous village dweller, remarked,

> *"We are planning to create an association, a women's club, and start an online shop selling our products".*

Tele-working is another growing employment trend that has opened up new opportunities for women using ICT to enable them to work from their homes as it allows flexibility in timing and location of work and increases opportunities to combine domestic and professional lives (U.N., 2005). Mitter (2000) explains that the growth of the e-economy potentially offers possibilities for business and self-employment even to women who are not privileged and are employed in the informal sector of the economy.

5.2.6 Educational Impact

It is generally accepted that education helps women achieve their empowerment as it increases their capability, it raises their self-confidence, it provides them with knowledge to confront problems and situations that arise in their domestic life and supplies opportunities to contribute and act equally as men do (Moulton, 1997). As education has emerged the most appropriate tool for achieving the goal of women's empowerment, it should be made accessible to women through all means (Adwoa, 2008). Information and communication technologies as educational tool promote women's empowerment and advancement in any society. Education, especially technical education, is instrumental in expanding capacities and improving employment opportunities, resulting not only in economic but also personal and social empowerment, such as enhanced confidence levels and social status (Huyer, 2003). We cannot expect that ICTs offer a panacea for social and economical development or can work as a magic wand to make the discriminations women have faced through centuries eliminate, but we can expect ICTs to prevent further ones.

In this research, the educational impact that influenced more women interviewees was their aspiration to continue their computer education with more advanced computer courses. The majority of the interviewees said that they would definitely continue to do more intensive lessons in order to expand their knowledge on computer use, expressing in this way their ambition to become skilled and competitive.

It appears that as the interviewees realize that they need to acquire advanced skills in order to find a well-paid job in the 21st-century job force, the basic skills program will need to alter to more specialized programs. These findings of the research come to full harmonization with the effects of globalization and the impact of ICT on labor conditions aptly captured by Mary Kalantzis (2000):

"The students and the workers of the future cannot rely on learning the stable technical or professional skills base that was until recently necessary and sufficient for work... The pace of technology and organizational change is such today that technical and professional skills need to be constantly updated. More significantly, perhaps, the borderline of technology and culture is being blurred. So, the future of work will require professionals who are multi-skilled and flexible in their response to change... The new workers will not only change jobs more frequently. They will also change career, perhaps even several times. They will change the sector of work, between private, public and sector; and between salaried and self-employed project worker. This spells the end of the career in its traditional form. Instead, we will see the emergence of portfolio worker, whose strength is not career stability and specific content knowledge but range and versatility."

We did not do a period time research in order to check whether women were enrolled in higher programs of computer education; but the intention women expressed can be described as a good omen for the future of the minority and more specifically for their children's. Our respondents' decision to pursue further studies on computer use could be seen as an attempt to break out of the typical female profile of low social position and to advance educationally. The answers of the women about this subject presented in Chapter IV, were of high demand; it triggers of the reader to think that minority today wants to adjust to a continuous changing environment, wants to handle and use every channel for expression and show off matters of education.

Most women did exhibit any preference for the class structure in computer seminars. Unlike previous research, which recommended women trainers (Narayanan, 2002) to promote computer adoption by women, Umrani's research (2007) comes to support the findings of this research (the same questionnaire was used in both researches) as the gender of the trainer was not found to be important in both studies. This can be explained by varied sample characteristics of the studies. Narayanan's work considered rural and semi-urban economically disadvantaged women and men trainees, whereas the Umrani's study focused on metropolitan, educated women. Nevertheless, in this study we considered a mixture of the above groups of women and the findings were similar to Umrani's, as a consequence of a more West-oriented behavioral intention to use computers, the Muslim minority women was proved to have in the initial quantitative analysis.

More than the gender of the trainer, her/his personal attributes emerged as important with the trainees emphasizing knowledge of computers, ability to adjust to the training needs of the trainee, inclination to help the novice ones, patience, ability to communicate and teach in a simple way, and for some of the women the knowledge of Turkish language. The role of trainers as a dimension of institutional support in novice women's computer adoption is a crucial one. Some of the interviewees put in the conversation the subject of the language since this is a permanent problem, especially for female minority members, in order to be able to integrate in the local society of Thrace. As Youngman and Singh (2005) claim the quality of adult learning programmes is influenced by the availability of competent personnel to develop, organise, promote, teach and evaluate modes of learning of adults. Those who educate adults require a particular range of competencies to be effective. These competencies are based on a defined body of knowledge, skills and values, which include such elements as adult psychology, teaching strategies, programme planning, research methods, social and political analysis, sensitivity, empathy and tolerance all relevant to the local situation and culture.

Only three of the interviewees holding a master's degree from the ages 18–30 and 31–40 said they used the computer for further "Education/Studies" in both prefectures of Rodopi and Xanthi. All over the world, gender disaggregated data on education has shown that, compared to their male counterparts, women have attained low levels of formal education. Several reasons, including their productive and reproductive roles, societal perception, and limited economic resources, domestic responsibilities, lack of mobility and socio-cultural practices, have contributed to this low level of formal education among women, most of which could be addressed by providing alternative modes of delivery. The ICTs contribute for bridging that gap through online distance learning by bringing education to the doorstep of people, especially at the tertiary level (Adwoa, 2008; UN, 2005; Ghadially and Umrani, 2004; Huyer, 2006b). A mountainous village dweller in this research describes how she has become computer literate:

> "I learned computer at home on my own. I attended online lessons on computer use through the Internet. In the afternoons, I attend lessons at the 2nd Chance School and at the technical school following the programs provided for the adult education."

In addition, ICTs, as a tool for effective enhancement of learning, teaching and education management allow us to learn anytime, from knowledge sources anywhere in the world, and gain an overview of our relationships and ourselves in different settings (Giddens, 1990); they have been used for various basic education and skill training activities through both formal and nonformal education, covering the entire spectrum of education. Since education and the workplace have been revolutionized by information technology over the past years, the new "technologically oriented" jobs, created in the private and public sectors (Cooper & Weaver, 2003), necessitate functional literacy, numeracy and computer literacy.

5.2.7 Opinions about Key Informants

In interviewees' answers, the reader can detect a sense of doubt and a kind of rejection for key informants as the answers women gave were from very negative to very demanding. In simple words they put on the table of the conversation the fact of the existence of an internal gap inside the minority, which is one of the factors of exploitation the minority members confront. The most interesting finding of the data was that the interviewees exposed critical thoughts and gave concrete answers for solving their problems as they had the chance to express themselves. Twenty women recommend that the leaders of their community should provide to minority women information for seminars, they should work for well planned and scheduled seminars depending on the needs of the participants, they should establish centres with the help of the state where minority women can have free access to the Internet and wireless Internet connection, they should ensure transportation to women for approaching training centres, and try to set up Second Chance Schools in every municipality so that minority women have the chance to continue their studies.

The majority of the interviewees had an opinion about how members of their community in administrative positions should act for their social empowerment and emancipation. This is the importance of this research as women have found a pondium to express their thoughts and become visible. The most important feeling for the researcher was to see that Muslim minority women expressed critical thoughts and opinions about members of their community. They answered autonomously, acting as units inside a group that usually acts collectively. That means we must overcome stereotypical approaches we usually have as members of the majority for women of the minority and try to invent new policies which will increase their behaviours of self-expression. Most of the answers women interviewees gave triggers off thinking that minority today wants to adjust to a continuously changing environment, wants to handle and use every channel of expression and to demand a better education.

5.3 Key Informants' Interviews

5.3.1 Key-informants' relation to ICTs

In the last years, due to the measures taken by the Greek state for the integration of the minority, new conditions have been established. Changes in the social strata of the minority are observed with an intensive social mobility. An important parameter in progress is the formation of new elite of intellectuals and politicians whose political choices and statements influence, in a high range, the self-definition and the general attitude of the minority towards the Greek state (Troubeta, 2001:246–247).

The group of key informants in this research consists of ten women and twenty men, with a median age of 31–40 years, living mainly at the administration of Rodopi and in the two towns of Komotini and Xanthi, of high levels of education, nine mayors, seven presidents of cultural associations, four deputies (ex and formers) in the Greek Parliament, four journalists, three muftis, and three vice prefects.

The key informants, who were interviewed, due to their administrative positions and their high educational and social levels, also exhibited a high economic standard. This can explain the high rate of possession of ICT gadgets. The analysis of the collected data, concerning the relation of the key informants to ICTs, revealed that the overwhelming majority of them owned computers, had access to

Internet, and had an email account. On the other hand, the majority of them did not have a computer skill certificate and did not own a website or a blog. The key informants, when they were asked to classify which of the ICT appliances they used more frequently, they ranged mobile-phone, computer, TV, CD/DVD player and fax in order of classification.

From what the key informants say it could be deduced that they are familiar with ICTs and appreciate their usage. The majority of them state they use their computer daily, mainly for their work and for communication. Web-search and games online are preferred by key informants of different socio cultural levels. The choices tele-work, buying products online, e-banking, studies were marked by a small number of the key informants, mainly preferred by women of high educational level. It is worth mentioning that key informants who use the computer for e-banking are women. This comes to support what Sadik commented: "*I believe that the revolution in the minority will start from the women.*"

They mostly use the Turkish language to read the websites on the Internet; their second choice is the Greek language and their third choice is the English language but not in such levels of use as the other two. Mainly, key informants are interested in Turkish newspapers, in Greek local newspapers, in minority Turkish-phone newspapers, in job related information via the Internet, in web-pages of their associations and in pages of ministries and political parties in Greece.

By the time the 30 key informants were asked their opinion on skills demanded nowadays to enter the labour force, they pointed out the computer use as their first choice, the postgraduate studies as the second, and the knowledge of foreign languages as the third. Women key informants living in villages and towns seem to be more positive than men key informants in the perspective of obtaining the above skills to enter the labour market as their answers include most of the choices and were almost identical. The Information and Knowledge Society founded on wires, optical fibres, digital devices, computers, satellites and all information communication technologies demands constantly from people to obtain knowledge, to acquire social skills, abilities, to improve critical thought, to obtain computer literacy, learn and communicate in foreign languages, have business acumen, which are strong linchpins for economical development.

Kalantzis and Cope (2004) claim that today the challenge is to create learning environments which engage the sensibilities of learners who are increasingly immersed in digital and global lifestyles – from the entertainment sources they choose to the way they work and learn. The wealth of nations is no longer equated on the scale of the quantity of the inherent natural resources but on the quality and strength of the knowledge-based workforce (Akinsola et al, 2005). Continuous education and training enhance the chances for learners to participate in the processes of socio-economic development and upgrade their qualifications for the expansion of their employment opportunities. Consequently, it is the labour market that determines educational politics and choices (Vergidis and Prokou, 2005). In a society with these demands, the socially excluded groups with limited education confront a higher possibility of marginalization.

As for the seminars or lessons on computer use, the key informants are mostly informed about the programs offered by the state. The overwhelming majority receive information from the Internet, half of them from KEP and only two from libraries.

Half of the key-informants, mainly the older men, believe that seminars on computer use should be materialized inside State schools. This choice is excused as for people in of older ages school is the place where knowledge is usually provided. Half of the key informants, younger women, declare that seminars should be carried out by NGOs, which usually play a rigorous role in such matters besides funding from private sectors. Volunteers inside NGOs can provide seminars and lectures about various topics including personnel and employee rights, nutrition, medicine, psychological problems, reproductive health, digital connections, literacy, etc. On the other hand, a very small percent of the key informants, two women and two men, dwellers at Rodopi administration, none of the three muftis, agree that seminars should be provided inside the mosques. The choice of mosque was put among the answers provided to key informants when they were asked to indicate where they would like the seminars on computer use to be materialized as the researcher through bibliography found out that mosques are commonly used as ICTs centres in several countries by Muslims.

We further quote some examples: Putting ICTs in the Hands of the Poor runner-up project was developed inside the Babul-Uloom-Madrasa, an Orthodox Muslim religious school, with the help of a prominent "Ulema" for the women of the Muslim minority of Seelampur who live in extreme poverty, rarely venture out of their homes, and wear the burqa. It was designed to encourage livelihood skills among women through vocational CDs, providing computer skills training, and developing linkages for marketing women's traditional arts and crafts products. In the same vein was the project "Internet Reaches Iranian Village", where the first computer in this new computer centre was purchased with money raised by villagers; a government grant paid for a second and several more came as courtesy of a charity formed by Iranians in London. Villagers who knew about computers volunteered as teachers in the centre, set up in a local mosque where computer skills were taught free to anyone and everyone who was interested. Furthermore, in Malaysia the project "The Masjid as a Neighborhood Centre" aimed to enable a mosque to become the hub of the networked communities around it, working closely with community leaders to provide the 200 neighborhood communities they served with training in various ICT applications. A community website and a Management Information System were designed – the online MIS enabled more efficient mosque administration. Members of the community were also able to visit the website created to access the community database and an online mini resource library.

Most of the key informants indicated that gathering events would be the more suitable means for providing information to women. These events usually take place in the area of the Youth's Association as religious feasts, or gathering events. The radio was the second choice, indicated by half of the key informants, for providing information and mostly preferred as mentioned above by the women key informants. This choice comes to complement the fact that interviewee women have made clear that they also use conventional ICTs, such as the radio, to access information sources. The third choice was newspapers, chosen mostly by women. As we read in Asimakopoulou and Lionaraki (2002:253), the Muslim minority press consists of a variety of newspapers, magazines, radio stations broadcasting in Turkish, and nowadays, electronic press and websites. All the above media include a great variety of publications with political/propaganda, educational, athletic, and professional content.

Trying to detect what the key informants think minority women will receive from training programs, the answer mostly pointed out was money, their second choice was knowledge and the third mostly preferred choice was communication. The above three choices were selected by key informants from all educational levels focusing on "money" and not on "knowledge", showing that material is higher in preference than spirit for minority women. Maybe this is the truth, but the order of the choices, the connection of women firstly with material and secondly with spirit, in a way puts limits to the pursuits of minority women. The key informants seem to know the problems minority women have; but in a way they underestimate these problems projecting on more vital problems minority faces and need prompt solutions. As one of the key informants, a village dweller, said:

"They must learn to use the computer and the Internet but at a level we don't loose them."

5.3.2 Key Informants' Views

Previously stated, in Chapter IV, presenting data from the interviews of 30 key informants would be challenging. The data the key informants provided was very rich and thick of ideas, beliefs and findings. The quality of ideas and the richness of information varied between informants and was related largely to their background. When presenting the data, Bryman's (2004:533) suggestion of not including all the results but only those findings that relate to the research questions of the study so that the thread of the argument is not lost was followed although it was found to be a rather painful process. For coding the data, the open coding technique and the axial coding technique to relate concepts/categories to each other was used. The factors that obstructed opportunities conversion into real capabilities were classified into five different levels which are knowledge/awareness, means, external factors, aims of action, education as capability of development.

During the analysis, interpretation and synthesis of the findings, it was decided not to keep this serial presentation according to the concepts/categories that were presented; but instead to frame the key informants' comments according to the general problems that minority face and usually are focused. Out of this frame, the researcher will exhibit the key informants' reaction to minority women's connection to ICTs. From the following analysis, it will become obvious that the main concern of the key informants is to contribute to improve living conditions and to solve problems of the minority which they exhibited during the interviews despite the questions the researcher asked them but these were oriented in a different direction.

In the past, members of the minority were regarded, through their language and religion, with the hostile identified foreign "other" and consequently could not be accepted as equal. They were given the characteristics of a "second category" citizen and were excluded from participating in the social vested rights (Zabeta, 2003:155–156). Consequently, minority woman were double and triple excluded because of her minority status, because of her gender, because of minority family structure, because of her mainly grass root living conditions. Generally, the largest part of minority women is usually occupied in field work as according to one of the key informants said: *"The feudal system still rules the life of the minority"*, with all the consequences of this limitation.

Relations with majority

Changes in the policy towards minority, which started in the 1990s (Aarbakke, 2000: 548), had their impact on the status of minority and as well on minority women; but the exclusion is still alive under new circumstances. Some of the key informants expressed a feeling of cautious optimism that things were improving and people of the minority *"who left for Turkey want to return to Thrace. When the policy of the Greek government changed, the feelings of people changed, and this makes them to want to come back"*. For others, however the fear still exists:

196

"We as a minority are still afraid." This statement is also supported by Askouni (2002: 317), who claims that this long standing violation of basic human rights for the minority and its marginalization, shelters minority's mistrust to every change, to every new situation even if this change takes place for minority's benefit. A key informant described the situation even more dramatically: *"We have to get over the suspiciousness among Christians and Muslims. I had a very difficult time during the elections. We have to get over the hate between the two communities. Although many of them say that they got over it, but it still exists and it is there waiting."* The consequence of the situation as described above is the feelings of fear and mistrust minority members have towards the Greek state and its policy.

Scarf issue

During the conversation, a subject that lately is being discussed in Europe, the issue of scarf, was reported. It is confirmed from data collected that the scarf has to be a religious symbol, not a means for policies, and this outfit must not be adopted out of pure mimicry. *"Women try to keep their identity, that they are Muslim members of the minority, and this drives them to adopt the scarf. But the problem is for them to be in peace in the area they live. Here people of the minority are not so religious. They are more west oriented"*.

Imam and Tsakiridi (2004:49) claim that the part of the minority who is of Turkish origin are not so religionist; but on the other hand, this part holds the reins of religious, economical, cultural and political area inside the minority. Many of the key informants state that part of the minority who is not in favor of such religious traditions and they believe that by influencing women to wear scarves or cover their body and faces and escape from a west-oriented model of life, as the number of scarf clad minority women is increasing lately in Thrace, other means are being served which do not benefit the minority. *"Religion and fundamentalism has increased in Turkey. But here in Thrace we are in a transitional situation"*, explains one of the key informants.

Zaimakis and Kaparani (2005) confirm that the intention of release from dedication to traditional codes of dressing is in conflict with traditional perceptions, which continues to be in force in the local society. After analyzing the data and by approaching women of different social, economical, educational levels with a scarf or not for the needs of this research, it can put forth that no difference or exclusion or fault was detected for women to use the computer or become digital literate whether wearing a scarf or not. Instead, the scarf clad women were the ones who created the great surprises during the research with their confessions. Margot

Badran, a Senior Fellow at the Prince Alwaleed Bin Talal Center for Muslim-Christian Understanding, Georgetown University explains:

> *"Islamic feminism is spreading infinitely faster and globally via the Internet and the Satellite. It has a vibrant presence in cyberspace reverberating in what Fatima Mernissi colorfully calls the 'digital Islamic galaxy.'"*

Lack of knowledge of Greek language

Minority considers education as the only problem, and priority shows that there are many things that have to be done (Demesticha, 2004:180). A big issue all the past years was that the Greek language was not properly taught in minority schools as Greek teachers worked in these schools like missionaries, with instructions not to teach Greek in an efficient way. *"Half of the minority population doesn't understand and doesn't speak Greek."* Through this problem which deplored many generations of the minority, the mistrust to the Greek state has been augmented.

According to the linguist Sella-Mazi (1999), the basic reasons for the insufficient knowledge of Greek is the weaknesses of the bilingual educational system (despite the changes that have occurred) and the refusal of Turkish-speaking populations to learn Greek with the fear of assimilation. Demesticha (2004:180) comments that concerning the language of the minorities all the Turkish-speakers of Thrace know much less Greek (despite the fact that this is not anymore the case among the youth who graduate from Greek high schools and universities as changes in education observed after 1991 have contributed to helping the adjustment to Greek reality by teaching better Greek) although a large part of the Turkish youth attended high schools and universities in Turkey in the past. The discussion takes into consideration that these days women want to be able to speak the Greek language, and as consequence they are eager to attend seminars on the Greek language. *"If the woman of the minority wants to have the position that she believes she deserves, she must obtain a promising and sufficient education."* There was a suggestion for the Turkish language to be integrated in the procedure of teaching during the seminars in order to ensure the participation of minority women.

A matter that concerns the minority nowadays could not be avoided in the dialogue that was developed during the research. One of the minority's demands from the Greek state is the establishment of bilingual nursery schools in the area of Thrace where both Greek and Turkish languages will be taught: *"… You must know your mother tongue and also the language of the country you live in."*

The mistrust to Greek state, the lack of knowledge of the Greek language due to the policy of the Greek state, the lack of secondary or tertiary level of education, the high drop out rates in secondary education, the lack of transportation to schools, the improper school infrastructure during the past years are some of the main factors that influenced the lives of minority people, the majority of whom still cannot obtain administrative positions in the public sector or as one of them have mentioned the highest levels of administration are prohibited. They can reach only the level of vice positions although there are mayors elected in areas where the minority population is superior. As one of them, explained:

> *"It is for Greece's interest to have a minority educated and cultivated, with men and women not easily manipulated. Educated people know better what they do. For the women of the minority special programs have to be materialized so that these women become skilled and able to find jobs. They have a tremendous need for a job."*

Policy

Women of the minority these days are aware of private or public institutions that provide seminars on computer use and programs for learning the Greek language. It is suggested that these programs should be materialized in cooperation with the minority, with the minority women's association and the teachers should be able to speak the Turkish language.

> *"In villages where Muslim people live, seminars should be taught in Turkish. Also, in seminars mixed groups of Christians and Muslims should work together, so that existing relations among them might improve. Programs offering lessons to learn the Greek language is a priority. These lessons should be materialized after discussions with the minority, not just to serve the political interests of the parties, but with a target to succeed in something."*

Scaling up socially excluded ICT related projects for poverty reduction depends on the project providing useful services that are driven by the real needs of the local community for an adequate training and development of the local people, but it also depends on achieving this with effective local skilled staff that can maintain high levels of community acceptance, within centres that are financially sound.

Mentors from the minority community should be trained to teach in non formal educational programs in order to succeed more efficient tuition, as they will be probably more aware of the level of the students, otherwise, the mission of these programs to innovate and transform will be unfulfilled. The development and improvement of qualification, motivation and performance of teachers to teach socially excluded groups is a challenge. Improving the performance of teachers, therefore, will be an exercise in improving the utilization of scarce resources. As for this, the creation of ICT research centres and training institutions in Greek Thrace should be a priority to provide qualifications to teachers who teach people from socially excluded groups.

Lack of money

Another problem minority women face is lack of money and unemployment. Money and subsidies is considered to be the motive of minority women for attending the funded seminars and not really the knowledge they provide. *"Women are interested in money. They quarrel who is going to attend the seminar if it is funded in order to earn money. They are not interested in programs that are not subsidized."* Demesticha (2004:183) claims that the contribution of the European Union, which funded special projects managed by the Ministry of Labor targeting the Muslims and Christians of the region, are very important. Independent bodies financed and managed other projects concerned with minority women, aiming at improving their fluency in Greek and their professional skills. Especially in the last years small funds aiming at women's economic participation in the society (through OAED) gave the opportunity to many minority women to make their own little business.

Lack of money for minority women is a problem, which has other dimensions too. Women's main interest, as it was confessed variously in the interviews of women presented above, is their children. Nowadays Muslim minority's demands are better education, skills and jobs. *"All the problems, we discuss have economic dimensions."* Minority lives in a transitional period in which minority women are expected to be bolder. In general, minority women show a positive attitude to work and contribute to family income as this is unavoidable due to the economic crisis and the financial problems the minority family faces. Women's main concern and interest is their children's living conditions. They dream and try to provide a better future for their children. Asimakopoulou (2002:334) described how different factors in the past, referring to minority parents' inability to support their children in their studies as the overwhelming majority of them were illiterate, the negative attitude and prejudice on behalf of the Christian majority and the way minority schools in the area functioned, influenced minority's life.

Internal family problems

Women of the minority work in the fields and provide house services, they confront problems with domestic violence and more commonly verbal domestic violence; they experienced and still experience high drop out rates from school. On the other hand, their husbands are free due to social customs to stay out of the house in the evenings and be in circulation. Women feel lonely and neglected, as it is common for Muslim minority men to emigrate in order to find a job in big cities of Greece or other European countries. As a consequence of this, minority women face psychological problems as the relations with parents in law, living all together in the same courtyard, are usually suppressive. The absence of social structures for places where abused women can find shelter is total in the area. Data that came from women key informants revealed situations of domestic violence minority women experienced, especially those living in villages on the mountains.

Social pressure

The unemployment in the region continues to be one of the highest in Greece and it is one of the biggest problems not only for the minority but also for the whole population of Thrace. In Thrace you cannot easily find a job especially if you are a woman and a member of the minority. *"Minority women do not have self-confidence and they experience conjugal oppression."*

Minority women are in an inferior situation compared to that of majority women as described by a key informant: *"Eighty percent of the minority lives in rural areas and women are mostly occupied with the cultivation of land. The women of the minority don't have the same access to ICTs as the women of the majority do. Minority children don't receive a proper education compared to that Christian pupils receive, and they don't have the same access to ICTs."*

Lack of infrastructure

A large part of the minority lives in many remote villages. Consequently there is lack of infrastructure for the Internet connection, for TV and radio channels, for other technological infrastructure and transportation. *"Libraries, info-kiosks, information centers don't exist in my village except from Internet cafes. Things that are established and exist in the city should also normally exist in the village so that isolation and exclusion could become eliminated"*. Usually seminars that took place in the past were not connected to the labor force of the area or the traditional restrictions of the minority were not taken in consideration, or the way women function, or the lack of facilities minority experiences.

A major problem that was mentioned several times during the research by the women interviewees and by the key informants themselves is the existence of members of the minority in a leadership position who try to manipulate the mass of the minority in order to establish their control. Consequently, the information that is oriented to the minority is usually filtered. *"Only a part of the minority receives information, i.e. the relatives of mayors, deputies, and on the other hand people who are in a desperate need to receive knowledge and money are excluded. We need more and better information. Criteria for choosing women to attend seminars must be legislated."*

Ten of the key informants admitted that they did nothing to inform women about the benefits of information society or the seminars that were offered all the past years and were funded by EU. *"I am not doing anything as I don't want to be in the middle of having to choose. Women quarrel about who is going to participate in the seminars in order to earn money"*. On the other hand, minority problems in Thrace are much more complicated as was mentioned:

> *"I don't think that we have yet understood what the information society is. We write in our articles, we publish in our newspapers about other problems like education, problem with the mufti, the tobacco. We transfer the problem to the model of minority life. A part of the minority lives in villages where there is not drinkable water, there are not roads. We speak about nursery schools. The Internet and new technologies come after our main problems."*

Other than internal obstacles to receive information there are also external problems that derive from the state, which does not provide enough information about seminars and training programs. Key informants expressed feelings of abandonment by the side of the state as the state shows lack of concern for the minority.

> *"We have 850 members and more than 300 women scientists in our association. Nobody sends us any information about programs or seminars funded by EU; they do something for the minority and they never ask us. After that, we cannot believe and trust the Greek state for its intention."*

Turning the tide

Globalization with the mechanics of interconnection created by new technologies that combine national economies, easier mobility of goods, capital, services and human resources has influenced the life of Muslim minority after 1990. The concept of multiculturalism is another aspect of globalization. The new media (the Internet, the satellite television, etc.) have permitted the spread of forms of global culture and have facilitated communication to different parts of earth (Demesticha, 2004:12). *"Yes, I agree that finally women tore apart the curtain. I believe that the Greek state has to support all the people of the minority who are interested and in this way to give a push to the general situation of the whole minority."* Development, trust, respect, equality before the law, equality of rights, affirmative action can be the solution to the minority problem in Greece (Demesticha, 2004:227).

From the interviews it became clear that the situation for minority women is changing. *"Even the structure of the family has changed."* Today women of the minority go after the chances but also they have the chances to live better and in equality compared to men. In the past, they did not have the chances and as for this their needs were not so important. Nowadays girls who finish primary school continue their studies at the secondary education. Women of the minority study in the universities and enter the labor force in different activities. According to Imam and Tsakiridi (2004:144–145), tradition is still being kept inside the family of the minority, but old values are changing with the intension of being replaced with new ones. Zaimakis and Kaprani (2005) explain that the status of the woman inside minority is combined with the social development of the minority, with the removal of all discriminations on the shoulders of minority caused from the Greek state all the past years, with the support of intercultural communication.

Minority women want to continue their studies in Second Chance Schools, and many of the mayors especially in villages try to establish Second Chance Schools in their local area as the demand is increasing. *"They want to learn new things by getting out of the "ring".* According to Parr (2000), as we read in Vryonides et al (2008), it has been well documented that women's decisions to return to education have to do with practical and personal reasons but primarily with issues of identity and taking control over some aspects of their lives.

> *"Things are not like they used to be in the old days. I think that women of the minority need support. We have to sit down all together, mayors, deputies, policy makers, to put things in order to provide a substantial help. We have to change our mentality in the way we confront women because during the past the situation has been ridiculous".*

During the interviews, it was supported that educated members of the minority had to provide information to women for the use of ICTs. Educational opportunities (mostly in Greek but also in good Turkish universities) resulted in a more active presence of women (Demesticha, 2004:226). The radio is the media which can help in the distribution of information as women of the minority listen to the radio a lot. Women of the minority have their own association as a part of the Association of the Scientists of the minority which can play an important role in the distribution of information.

> *"Women of the minority feel more comfortable to come and ask in our associations when the seminar will start from going to a private centre or to OAED (Organization of Occupation of Labour Force). If we organized such a program, they would not have the language problem."*

Channels that interact with their way of living must be the informants for their benefits of the information society and of providing them with ICT infrastructure. Also voluntarism for teachers, trainers and mentors who want to offer their knowledge and experiences on ICT use and literacy to members of socially excluded groups could be encouraged by a reduce of their taxes or other subsidies. Learning methods for seminars to illiterate people must be improved and specialized, and knowledge processing strategies must be more diversified. Seminars must be materialized according to age, education level, and even gender of the participants by instructors prepared to teach people of special cultural groups and educationally disadvantaged. Reducing the digital inequality must be an on-going process of education and support with a concrete target.

Finally, as a conclusion of this analysis it can be said that key informants' believe that ICTs (computer, TV, radio, mobile phone) can help women to communicate, to receive information, to work, to become educated, to be better informed in order to protect their children, to communicate with the young ones, to become skilled, to become able to find a job, to manage their emancipation. They believe that TV has played an important role in women's emancipation and moreover, the ICTs as they function like a window to the outside world giving them chances to compare things. Although ten of them admitted they did nothing to this effect, the rest seemed to be willing and interested in helping women to become computer educated. Some spoke about lack of infrastructure, absence of Greek channels on TV, lack of ADSL connections, lack of information to be provided. They played a leading role in organizing seminars on computer use and the Greek language, in establishing Internet cafes and associations or women's clubs, in spreading any information about seminars or Second Chance school, influencing women to continue their studies or asking for TV-antennas to be placed in remote areas.

"Women at the age of 30 or 40 need the Internet, but in my opinion women should receive messages from the TV. They should receive information on EU funded projects from the local channels. People of the minority should have the motive to watch Greek television. TV programs should provide information on feminine matters, alternative ways of cultivating the fields."

Chapter 6: Conclusions and Recommendations

6. Introduction

The purpose of the research was two folds:

- Empirically validate the Technology Acceptance Model (TAM) and the Theory of Planned Behaviour (TPB) and analyze how it varies across behavioural intention to use the computer.
- Explore contribution of computer education to social empowerment of Muslim minority women and detect thoughts and aspects of key informants about the potential of social participation of minority women through computer education.

The conclusions from this study follow the research questions and the findings, and therefore address

1) psychological factors that influenced the Behavioural Intention of women of the sample to use the computer
2) experiences on ICTs that women interviewees had, aspects on infrastructure, multiplier impact, reasons for computer use and use of the Internet, social and psychological impact by the computer use, education impact and educators, women's opinions on key informants action for their computer literacy
3) key informants' relation to ICTs and key informants' views on minority women and ICT and their action on that issue.

Following is a discussion of the major findings and conclusions drawn from this research. This discussion is followed by the researcher's recommendations for further research and finally by the contribution of the research.

6.1 Conclusions

6.1.1 Psychological Factors Influenced Behavioural Intention to Computer Use

This chapter portrayed the psychological factors that influenced the Behavioural Intention of a sample of 137 Muslim minority women to use the computer. The analysis of quantitative findings showed that Muslim minority women in Greece exhibit a more West-oriented Behavioural Intention to use computers; that means they have the intention to use the technology as long as they feel capable of doing it and think it is useful. They also take into consideration the opinion of the others, which also influences their beliefs about usefulness of the technology.

6.1.2 Social Empowerment of Minority Women through Computer Education

The first major finding was that a great part of the interviewees owned computers, laptops, cell phones and Internet connection at home, something that was accomplished through financial assistance from family or relatives.

The second major finding was that the interviewees used the computer and mostly the Internet for communication mainly with friends and relatives who live either in Turkey or have immigrated to other countries in Europe. Through the Internet they keep their connection to Turkey at a high level. Their orientation to Greek web-sites concerns the sites that contain information about jobs. Another reason they use the Internet is for professional reasons and for entertainment.

The third finding was their criticism of the lack of infrastructure on Internet connection or broadband Internet connection especially in rural and mountainous regions and the problems of transportation they usually face as this acted as the main obstacle to their way to seminars or educational centres. Cyber cafés are not of high preference as they usually function as cafes or bars or for game playing in the area of Thrace, and mostly in villages. The lack of statistics concerning the Muslim minority population is a major problem that a researcher confronts.

A fourth very important finding of the study points out that women are interested in expanding their knowledge by attending seminars and computer use programs or learning the Greek language. This intention expresses their objective to integrate in the new Greek reality and impresses deeper transformations at social and cultural level. The educational impact that influenced more women interviewees was their aspiration to continue their computer education with more advanced computer courses. It appears that as the interviewees realize that they need to acquire advanced skills in order to find a well-paid job in the 21st-century job force, the basic skills program will need to alter to more specialized programs. The interviewees mostly found information about computer seminars at the KEP (Centres for Citizen's Service). They were informed on the existence of state schools for adult education (the Second Chance School) and pointed out that this kind of school has to be established in every municipality in order to be easily accessible or transportation must be provided for easy access. They also were informed and participated in seminars provided in both private Centres for Adult Education (KEK) established in the early 1990s (although their participation in these centres started mainly in the mid of 2000s) and in state Centres for Adult Education (KEE).

As the fifth finding, we present the most valuable findings which answer the initial question of the research. Interviewees reported that the main factors that influenced them in learning the computer use were their peers husbands, their children (sons, daughters etc); then their mentors and finally their interests. The interviewees' acquisition of technical skills resulted in computer literacy of other family members, and, consequently, computer awareness in the family as the majority of the interviewees encouraged significant others, such as members of their family to learn the computer use and acquire technical skills. It can be claimed that psychological benefits for these minority women from computer use include positive self-esteem, awareness and feeling contemporary.

Interviewees, being aware of the potential empowerment through computer education, quoted some of their motives for attending a computer seminar. These were knowledge, communication, skills, money, and feeling modern. A majority of the interviewees said they learned the computer use mainly for themselves and secondly to be able to help their children and get in contact with them when they were abroad. This is very interesting as women acted as units and not collectively, targeting their personal elevation. The computer education had also an economic impact as it helped a part of the interviewees to find a job and made them feel assured.

Another last finding of high importance was that most of the interviewees were censorious with members of the minority in administrative positions and with a "leading role" in their community. They do not believe that there is a real concern for women's social empowerment by people of the minority who are in administration or implement policies. They suggested that these members of their community should be interested in providing information to minority women for seminars, should work for well planned and scheduled seminars based on the needs of the participants, they should establish centres with the help of the state where minority women can have free access to the Internet and wireless Internet connection; they should ensure transportation to women for approaching training centres, and try to set up Second Chance Schools in every municipality so that minority women have the chance to continue with their studies.

6.1.3 Key Informants' Contribution to Women's Empowerment through ICTs

Changes in the policy towards minority, which started in the 1990s, had their impact on the status of minority and as well on minority women exclusion is still alive under the new circumstances. Some of the key informants expressed a feeling of cautious optimism that things were improving; but feelings of fear and mistrust of minority members towards the Greek state and its policy still exist.

Overwhelming majority of the key informants own computers, have access to the Internet. Majority of them use their computer daily, mainly for work and for communication. They use mostly the Turkish language to read the websites on the Internet; their second choice is the Greek language and their third choice is the English language. Mainly, key informants are interested in Turkish newspapers, in Greek local newspapers, in minority local Turkish-phone newspapers, in job related information via the Internet, in web-pages of their associations and in pages of ministries and political parties in Greece. Overwhelming majority receive information on seminars or lessons on computer use from the Internet, half of them from KEP.

They believe that ICTs (computer, TV, radio, mobile phone) can help women to communicate, to receive information, to work, to become educated, to be better informed in order to protect their children, to communicate with the young ones, to become skilled, to become able to find a job, to manage their emancipation. They believe that TV has played an important role in women's emancipation and moreover ICTs as they function like a window to the outside world has given them the chances to compare things. Trying to detect what the key informants thought the minority women would gain from training programs, the answer mostly pointed out was money; their second choice was knowledge and the third mostly preferred choice was communication.

Half of the key informants, mainly the older men, believe that seminars on computer use should be held inside state schools, and the other half of the key informants, mainly younger women, reply that the seminars should be carried out by non governmental organizations (NGOs), which usually play a rigorous role in such matter besides receiving from private sectors. On the other hand, a very small percent, none of the three muftis, agree that seminars should be provided in the area of the mosques.

Most of the key informants indicated that gathering events, radio as the second choice and newspapers as the third choice, would be a more suitable means to provide information to women. Money and subsidies is considered to be minority women's motive for attending the funded seminars, not really the knowledge they provide. They believe that computer use, postgraduate studies, and knowledge of foreign languages are qualifications demanded nowadays to enter the labour force.

Many of the key informants represent the part of the minority who believes that the scarf has to be a religious symbol, who is not in favor of religious traditions and who believes that by influencing women to wear scarves and escape from a west-oriented model of life other means are being served which do not benefit the minority. In this research, the scarf clad women were the ones who exhibited great surprises with their interviews.

In general, there is a positive attitude, something out of the question in the past, in the intention of minority women to work and contribute to the family income since this is unavoidable due to the economic crisis and due to the financial problems the minority family faces.

Key informants mentioned the lack of infrastructure for Internet connection, for TV and radio channels, other technological infrastructure and transportation, absence of Greek channels on TV in remote areas, lack of ADSL connections, lack of information especially in villages and mountainous areas where a big part of the minority resides. Usually the seminars that took place in the past were not connected to the labor force of the area or the traditional restrictions of the minority were not taken into consideration, nor the way women function, nor the lack of facilities minority experiences.

The state does not provide minority with enough information about seminars and training programs and members of the minority in a leadership position control the information provided as they try to manipulate the mass of the minority in order to establish their control. Minority women have their own association as a part of the Association of the Scientists of the minority, which could play an important role in the distribution of information. It was proposed that educated members of the minority should provide voluntary information to women for the use of ICTs.

Ten of the key informants admitted that they did nothing to encourage women about the benefits of information society or to circulate information about the seminars that were offered all the past years and were funded by EU. Others explained that they played a leading role in organizing seminars on computer use and the Greek language, in establishing Internet cafes and associations or women's clubs, in spreading any information about seminars or Second Chance School; they influenced women to continue with their studies they asked for antennas for the Greek channels to be placed in remote areas.

6.2 Recommendations

During the last years, dominated by technology advancement, it has become obvious that ICTs affect social and economic structures and expand choices. We cannot expect ICTs to work as a magic wand to vanish discriminations women have suffered through centuries, but we can expect ICTs to prevent further ones. Access to ICT can enable women to gain a stronger voice in their communities, their government and at the global level. ICT also offers women flexibility in time and space and can be of particular value to women who face social isolation, including many women in developing countries.

From the research it became obvious that Muslim minority women, contrary to their past behaviours, are further interested in obtaining knowledge and in managing their social improvement. A new face for the "woman of the Muslim minority in Greek Thrace" comes into sight. This way of living is a combination of influences from internal social conflicts that the Muslim community went through during the past years and external social factors.

Adult education can become the vehicle to support the redefinition of the new standards of living for Muslim minority women. Furthermore, targeting computer education in order to optimize the advantages of computer learning, there is a need to educate women in the potential and versatility of this technology beyond a family agenda. Among others, this may include e-commerce, information technology enabled services, and tele working, which open avenues for economic empowerment of women.

Due to the fact that a part of the women of this community faces various problems, mainly caused by the social status of their community, a web-site can be set up offering advice on domestic violence, diagnosis of psychological depression and therapies, family life, hygiene, citizenship, civic consciousness. Greece is the only country in EU where the Islamic Sharia law[5] is practiced by the Muslim minority in a quite legal way based on law 1920/1991. Consequently, a site that provides information on law issues and posts background articles analyzing women's inheritance, marriage, divorce, citizenship and political rights can be helpful for the women of the Muslim minority in Greek Thrace. The content of the site should speak to women's concerns and reflect knowledge for their daily lives, business enterprises, and family responsibilities (including information on health, agriculture/small-scale production, natural resources management).

Websites should be designed in order to promote and advertise agricultural local products as cherries and tobacco cultivated mainly by minority women, traditional costumes woven by them, local traditional food they cook, tradition and customs they have. Web sites can provide information about the business to potential clients, as well as sell products and services. ICT can reduce administrative costs, speed up business transactions and link local businesses with supply

---

5   The code of law derived from the Koran and from the teachings and example of Mohammed, which deals with many aspects of day-to-day life, including politics, economics, banking, business, contracts, family, sexuality, hygiene, and social issues.

chains. A site with information and links of programs on empowerment of women through ICTs in the Muslim world can provide the opportunity for knowledge to be implemented and transformed to the local society. When some of the proposals quoted are materialized in Greek Thrace, this may improve minority women's lives and consequently the status of the whole Muslim minority residing in the area.

Online training programme for advanced using of the computer, for learning the Greek language should be provided. Virtual classrooms, cutting across geographical space and time especially for the ones on the remote mountainous villages, should function. Infrastructure for ADSL connection should be of high priority. In this way they minority people could overcome the obstacles they have to watch Greek TV channels, especially on the mountains. An information dissemination campaign that includes a wide range of media such as radio and print, on ICT as a tool for the empowerment of women, should be implemented. In order to speed up the adoption process, workshops can be conducted in residential areas and places frequented by women such as schools, health centres, markets, etc., to demystify the technology and inform women of its usefulness to them and their families. Such awareness programs must be fine tuned to the needs of various groups of women as differentiated by class, age, occupational status, and geographic location. With respect to this effort, local scientists and politicians, and people who are planning the development of the area, who are aware of the situations women of the minority live in, can also contribute. Strategies for collaboration on subjects concerning education, empowerment, ICT use among the two communities, the Christian and the Muslims should be supported.

In order to widen access points and encourage technology use amongst those at the edge of the information society, community access points based on the tele centre model should be set up in urban locales. Tele centres provide the infrastructure for people to access computers, Internet, and other digital technologies that enable them to gather information, create, learn, and communicate with others. These services are offered either free of cost or at subsidized rates, thus, resulting in community development. But these tele centres could function also as new "e-cutting and sewing clubs". Women of the minority could bring embroidery designs and patterns to the centre and then computerise those using scanners and digital cameras or design tailoring, embroidery, paintings and other traditional craft and designs using Paint Brush, Adobe Illustrator, Photoshop and Corel.

Researches that concern minority and more especially minority women's social, economical, psychological, political empowerment should be subsidized in order to enable researchers to search during a large period of time and in more detailed way.

6.3 Contribution of the Study

In the beginning of this study it was described the gap in the Greek literature on Muslim minority women and their connection to ICTs. The rationale of the study aims to contribute to fulfil this gap, extending the research to the Muslim minority women living in Thrace. This study contributes to the growth of empirical research in both TPB and TAM methods to detect the psychological factors that contribute to behaviour intention of using the computer. Besides, it is the first time that these two methods are used in a sample in Greece with the qualitative characteristics of Muslim minority women in a West oriented area. This study provides data on the Muslim minority sample in Thrace, thus laying a ground for cross-cultural comparison. The present study uses a combination of quantitative and qualitative methods so as to provide richer information about the problem being addressed.

The basic function of the research, which is the pursuit and the publication of valid data, obtains a political dimension which controls the evident truth and the interests that preserve a cloudy image for the minority. Perhaps the political dimension created the gap of data and the absence of valid information concerning statistics of minority population, of education of minority's children, of information about women, of different kinds of indexes that describe minority's everyday life. This bibliographical destitution and stagnation of social research seems to raise both practical and theoretical difficulties. It seems that the practice of securing problems caused of the existence of a minority by its nature self-restricted in a putative homogeneous country is the reason for transforming a social problem to a political. Thus, the procedure of approaching the dimensions of these problems becomes difficult.

It is the time for the two communities (the Christian majority and the Muslim minority coexisting in Thrace) to face each other in the light of the existing reality and not to keep the constructed ones as a result of propaganda. It is the time or probably the time was left over to create the possibilities for effective dialogue between the minority and the majority communities. Thus, researchers from both sides had to go after finding the truth of each community, trying to overcome the prejudices which are main structural elements of the way they think about each other. The researcher felt like functioning as a channel used to transfer data from one society to another. And this channel had to function with no bias and prejudice. Consequently, initially she had to overcome her own ways of thinking and expressing her thoughts about Muslim minority people, further to identify the inter-bias that exist in the Muslim society, and finally to forward the findings in a negotiable way to members of the majority population.

By giving the women the podium, to speak out and define new conditions that could make the changes that take place more familiar to them or just to speak out for the problems they face, this could act as a motive for improving the way they function. During the interviews there were women who gave bold answers, who got over the collective way they usually act by speaking the truth and by describing people of the minority in administrative positions who act with no real interest to the problems that concern the women of the minority. This reaction figured a new identity for the women of the minority; this of a quiet critical power who doubts, who rejects, who acts on her own and for her own good and tries to succeed a better life.

6.4 Limitations of the Study and Suggestions for Further Research

The findings and conclusions of the study can not be said to be representative for all the women of the minority. We tried to select data from women who have different demographic characteristics and women who live in different parts of Thrace just to manage obtaining pluralistic and more valid data. The generalizability of the findings of this study is limited to the women of the minority whom their family belongs to the middle-income group as the women interviewees were of different educational levels.

An overriding concern is that of researcher bias, framing assumptions, ideas, and perceptions regarding the researcher's origin as a member of the majority in the area of Thrace which in spite of efforts to improve the living conditions of the members of the minority is an example of co-existence of multi-cultural populations under social polarization.

Both models, the TPB and the TAM models, were tested only once to minority women. A periodical test of the models every year for three years could ascertain whether the determinants of behavioural intention to use computers vary with time as social and economic factors in Greece are changing rapidly, especially the last year. Also periodical interviews with the same sample of women for three years could detect the influence of computer education to their vocational rehabilitation and social empowerment and to ascertain how these skills are applied by the women to improve their lives and lives of their families. Other categories like gender could be taken so as to study technology acceptance, empowerment, access and impact among people of different sexes.

List of references

Aarbakke, V. (2000). *The Muslim minority in Greek Thrace. PhD dissertation.* The University of Bergen, Norway.

Adwoa Tiwaah Frimpong Kwapong, O. (2008). *Education at doorsteps of women: Open and distance learning for empowerment of women.* BookSurge Publising, pp. 79.

Agbonlahor, O. R. (2008). Gender, Age and use of Information Technology in Nigerian Universities: A Theory of Planned Behavior Perspective in Revitalization of African Higher Education *Edited by J. B. Babalola et al. ISBN: 978-978-49117-1-9, Herpnet 2008, Published by Higher Education Research and Policy Network and The Postgraduate School,* University of Ibadan, Ibadan, pp. 286–304. Available on: http://www.herpnet.org/revitalization_of_african_higher_education/Chapter%2023.pdf (Accessed 12 January 2010).

Aggelidis, V. and Chatzoglcu, P. (2009). Using a modified technology acceptance model in hospitals. *International Journal of Medical Informatics,* 78(2), pp. 115–126.

Ajzen, I. (1985). From intentions to actions: A theory of planned behaviour. In J. Kuhi & J. Beckmann (Eds.). *Action-control: From cognition to behaviour* Heidelberg: Springer, pp. 11–39.

Ajzen, I. (1991). The theory of Planned Behaviour. *Organizational Behavior and Human Decision Process,* 50 (2), pp. 179–211.

Ajzen, I. and Fishbein, M. (1980). *Understanding Attitudes and Predicting Social Behavior.* Prentice-Hall, Englewood Cliffs, NJ.

Ajzen, I., & Fishbein, M. (1975). Attitudinal and normative variables as predictors of specific behavior. *Journal of Personality and Social Psychology,* 27(1), pp. 41–57.

Ajzen, I. (2006). *Constructing a TpB Questionnaire: Conceptual and Methodological Considerations,* Available on: http://www-unix.oit.umass.edu

Akritidou, D. (2002). Η θέση της γυναίκας στην κοινωνική σύνθεση της μουσουλμανικής μειονότητας της Δ. Θράκης. *PhD dissertation.* Panteion University, Athens.

Ahmed, A., Islam. D., Hasan, A.R., Rahman, N.J. (2006). Measuring the impact of ICTs on women in Bangladesh. In: Hamid R. Arabnia (ed.) on E-Learning, E-Business, Enterprise Information Systems, E-Government, & Outsourcing (Las Vegas, Nevada, USA, CSREA Press), pp. 180–185. Available on: http://74.125.155.132/scholar?q=cache:0NldoIje0R4J:scholar.google.com/+2

2Measuring+The+Impact+Of+ICT+On+Women+In+Bangladesh.%22&hl=el&as_sdt=2000, (Accessed 20 April 2010).

Akinsola, O., Herselman, M., and Jacobs, S. (2005). ICT provision to disadvantaged urban communities: A study in South Africa and Nigeria. *International Journal of Education and Development using ICT, (IJEDICT)*,1(3), pp. 19–41, Available on: http://ijedict.dec.uwi.edu/viewarticle.php?id=57, (Accessed 11 August 2010).

Alam, M.J.B., Hoque, M.M. and Islam, A. (2000). *Impact of Asian Highway on Bangladesh*, Proceedings of the 10th REAAA Conference, Road Engineering Association of Asia and Australia, Tokyo, Japan, September, 2000.

Allaudin, A. Durdana, I. Ahmed Ryadh, Hasan. Nayel, J.Rahman. (2006). Measuring the impact of ICTs on women in Bangladesh. *Proceedings of The 2006 World Congress in Computer Science Computer Engineering, and Applied Computing, Las Vegas, USA 26–29/6/2006 Available on:* http://iec.cugb.edu.cn/WorldComp2006/EEE4168.pdf. (Accessed 12 March 2009).

Alexopoulos, N., Fasoulis, K. And Koutroumanos, G. (2008). Η διερεύνηση της σχέσης ανάμεσα στις συμπεριφορικές πεποιθήσεις και τις προθέσεις των εκπαιδευτικών για την εξέλιξή τους στη διοικητική ιεραρχία της εκπαίδευσης. Ekpaideytiko Vima, V(9),May 2008.

Al-Gahtani, S. (2006). *Information technology adoption, the roadmap to sustainable development: examining three models*, paper presented in the 18th National Computer Conference 2006 held by the Saudi Computer Society.

APC News-a http://www.ehomemakers.net/en/index.php, (Accessed 23 August 2008).

APC News-b http://www.genderawards.net/the_awards/press/index.htm, (Accessed 23 August 2008).

Arend, M. (2002). *Socio-economic analysis and macro-modelling of adapting to Information Technology in Europe,* Work package No. 3 "Social Impacts of ICT" – First Interim Report, Project co-ordinator: Cambridge Econometrics.

Arun, S. and Arun, T. (2002). ICTs, Gender and Development: Women in Software Production in Kerala. *Journal of International Development*, 14(1), pp. 39–50.

Arun, S., Heeks, R., and Morgan, Sh. (2006),. Improved Livelihoods and Empowerment for Poor Women through IT-Sector Invention. Article in Hafkin, N. and Huyer, S. (2006). *Cinderella or Cyberella? Empowering women in the Knowledge Society.* Kumarian Press, Inc. USA, pp. 141–164.

Asimakopoulou, F. and Lionaraki, S. (2002). *Η μουσουλμανική μειονότητα στη Θράκη και οι Ελληνο-Τουρκικές σχέσεις.* Eds: Livanis, pp. 231.

Askouni, N. (2002). Η μειονοτική εκπαίδευση στη Θράκη σαν πεδίο έρευνας: Οι πολιτικές διαστάσεις της έρευνας, Edition by Educational symposium: *Minorities in Greece* (7–9/11/2002), pp. 313.

Askouni, N. (2006). *Η εκπαίδευση της μειονότητας στη Θράκη:Από το περιθώριο στην προοπτική της κοινωνικής ένταξης.* Athens: Alexandria.

Baker, W. E., Al-Gahtani, S.S., & Hubona, S.G. (2007).The effects of gender and age on new technology implementation in a developing country. Testing the theory of planned behaviour (TPB). *Information Technology & People,* 20(4), pp. 352–375.

Bandura A. (1982). Self-efficacy mechanism in human agency. *American Psychologist,* 37(2), pp. 122–147.

Baron, R.M., and Kenny, D. A. (1986). The moderator-mediator variable distinction in social psychological research: Conceptual, strategic, and statistical considerations. *Journal of Personality and Social Psychology,* 51(6), pp. 1173–1182.

Baros, W. and Manafi, G. (2009). Approaching migrant youth marginalization through the capabilities approach: Methodological approaches. *Social and Work Society,* 7(1), pp. 113–121.

Bhatnagar, S. (2006). ICTs to build a vibrant knowledge society. *Information for Development (i4d),* March, pp. 29–30.

Bloomberg, D. L. and Volpe, M. (2008). Completing your Qualitative Dissertation: A road map from beginning to end. *USA: Sage.*

Brislin, R. (1986). The wording and translation of research instruments, in Lonner, W. and Berry, J. (Eds), *Field Methods in Cross-Cultural Research,* Sage Publications, Beverly Hills, CA, pp. 137–164.

Bryman, A. (2004). *Social research methods.* Oxford: Oxford University Press.

Chaffe, E.E. (1985). Three Models of Strategy. *Academy of Management Review,* 10, pp. 89–98.

Chatzoglou, P., Vraimaki, E., Diamantidis, A., and Sarigiannidis, L. (2010). Computer acceptance in Greek SMEs. *Journal of Small Business and Enterprise Development,* 17(1), pp. 78–101.

Chau, Y.K.P. (1996). An empirical assessment of a modified technology acceptance Model. *Journal of Management Information Systems,* 13(2), pp. 185–204.

Cohen, J., West, S.G., Cohen, P., and Aiken, L. (2003). *Applied Multiple Regression /Correlation Analysis for the Behavioural Sciences,* 3rd ed., Lawrence Erlbaum, Hillsdale, NJ.

Cooper, J., and Weaver, K.D. (2003). *Gender and Computer: Understanding the digital divide,* Mahwah, NJ: Lawrence Erlbaum Associates, Inc, pp. 3,4,5.

Corsun, D. L., and Enz, C.A. (1999). Predicting psychological empowerment among service workers: the effect of support-based relationships. *Human relations*, 52(2), pp. 205–224.

Creswell, W. J. (2009). *Research Design: Qualitative, Quantitative and Mixed Methods Approaches*. Sage.

Davis, F.D. (1989). Perceived usefulness, perceived ease of use, and user acceptance of information technology. *MIS Quarterly*, 13(3), pp. 319–339.

Davis, F.D., Bagozzi, R.P., Warshaw, P.R. (1989). User acceptance of computer technology: A comparison of two theoretical models. *Management Science*, 35(8), pp. 982–1003.

Davis, F. D. (1986). *A Technology Acceptance Model for Empirically Testing New End-User Information Systems: Theory and Results*, in MIT Sloan School of Management. Cambridge, MA: MIT Sloan School of Management.

Demesticha, M. (2004). *Minorities in the Balkans in the era of globalization: The case of the Turks in Western Thrace*. Master Thesis, Bogazici University.

Demetriou, O.M. (2002). *Divisive visions: A study of minority identities among Turkish-speakers in Komotini, Northern Greece*, PhD Degree in Social Anthropology, London School of Economics and Political Science, University of London.

Dragonas, T. and Frangoudaki, A. (2006). Educating the Muslim minority in Greek Thrace. *Islam and Christian–Muslim Relations*, 17(1), pp. 21–41.

Eagly, A. H. and Chaiken, S. (1993). The psychology of attitudes. Fort Worth: Harcourt Brace Jovanovich College Publishers.

Eurostat. (2008). Internet access and use in the EU27 in Households and by individuals, Available on: http://epp.eurostat.ec.europa.eu/cache/ITY_PUBLIC/4-02122008-BP/EN/4-02122008-BP-EN.PDF, (Accessed 1 August 2009).

EUMC reports on Muslims in Europe Available on http://eumc.europa.eu/eumc/material/pub//muslim/Manifestations_EN.pdf (Accessed 10 November 2008).

Everitt, B.S. and Dunn, G. (1991), Applied Multivariate Data Analysis, Edward Arnold, London.

Esposito, J. and Haddad, Y. (1998). *Islam, Gender and Social Change*, Oxford: Oxford University Press, pp. xvi.

Ess, Ch. (2001). *Culture, Technology, communication: Towards an Intercultural Global Village*. State University of New York Press, pp. 9.

Ekdahl, P. and Trojer, L. (2002). Digital Divide: Catch up for What?. *Gender Technology and Development*, 6(1), pp. 1–21.

Ferekidou, E. (2007). *To Ιντερνετ, βάση δεδομένων, και η καταναλωτική συμπεριφορά*. Master Thesis, Aristotel University ,Thessaloniki

Fereshteh, N.-S. (2005). Wings of Freedom: Iranian women, Identity, and Cyberspace. In Nouraie-Simone F. (Eds), *On Shifting Ground Muslim Women in the Global Era*, The Feminist Press at the City University of New York, pp. 61–79.

Fishbein, M., and Ajzen, I. (1975). *Belief, Attitude, Intention, and Behavior: An Introduction to Theory and Research*. Massachusetts: Addison-Wesley.

Foddy, W. (1993). *Constructing questions for interviews and questionnaires*. Cambridge University Press, pp. 185.

Fornell, C.R. and Larcker, D.F. (1981). Structural equation models with unobservable variables and measurement error, *Journal of Marketing Research*, 18, pp. 39–50.

Fowler, J.D., and Mangione T. W. (1990). *Standardized Survey Interviewing: Minimizing Interviewer-Related Error*, Newbury Park Cal.: Sage Applied social Research Methods Series 18. pp. 93.

Gefen, D., & Straub, D. W. (1997). Gender differences in the perception and use of e-mail: An extension to the technology acceptance model. *MIS Quarterly*, 21(4), pp. 389–400.

Gem project: Available on http://www.apcwomen.org/gemkit/en/practitioners/reports.htm (Accessed 23 June 2008)

Georgiadou, K., Kalantzis, M., and Kekkeris, G. (2007). Gender and ICTs: The case of Muslim women in Greek Thrace. *International Journal of Interdisciplinary Social Sciences*, 1(4), pp. 182–188.

Georgiadou, K., Kekkeris G. and Kalantzis, M. (2007). Roma women in Greek Thrace: Becoming computer literate. *International Journal of Interdisciplinary Social Sciences*, 2(4), pp. 543–550.

Georgiadou, K., Kekkeris, G., and Kalantzis, M. (2007), Immigrant Women from Former Soviet Republics in Greek Thrace: Becoming computer literate. *International Journal on Technology, Knowledge, Society*, 3(4), pp. 28–36.

Georgiadou, K., Kekkeris, G., and Kalantzis, M. (2007). Gender and ICT: The case of Roma women in Greek Thrace. *International Journal of Interdisciplinary Social Sciences*, 2(4), pp. 543–550.

Georgiadou, K., and Kekkeris, G. (2007). The ICTs implication on the construction of immigrants' identity: The case of women from former Soviet Union in Greek Thrace. *Journal of Identity and Migration Studies*, 1(1), pp. 52–63.

Georgiadou, K., and Kekkeris, G. (2007). Cultural Identity and ICT: Immigrant Women from Former Soviet Republics in Greek Thrace. *Proceedings of the International Conference of MTC 2007 "Management of Technological changes"*, Alexandroupolis, Greece, 25–26/8/2007, pp. 369–374.

Georgiadou, K., Kekkeris, G., and Kalantzis, M., (2008). Inclusion in the Information Society for the "Excluded" Women in Greek Thrace, Lecture Notes in Computer Science, Vol. 5280/2008, Emerging Technologies and Information Systems for the knowledge Society, p. 460–468, ISBN 978-3-540-87780-6, © Springer Berlin Heidelberg 2008.

Georgiadou, K. Kekkeris, G. and Taratori, E. (2008). "Koran" or "Qiran.com"? Impacts of ICTs on the Empowerment of Muslim Women, *Kinitro*, (9), pp. 7–15.

Georgiadou, K., (2008). *Statistics concerning the ICT connection of the Muslim women at Rodopi prefecture*, Paper presented at the "Management of the cultural diversity in education" Conference with International participation, Alexandroupolis 3/12/2008, DUTH.

Georgiadou, K. Kekkeris, G. (2008). *ICTs in non formal education: Computer training programs for Roma women in Greek Thrace and experiences from other countries*, paper presented 4º National Conference of HSSS "Systems for management of information and innovation", Ioannina, 29–31/5/2008.

Georgiadou, K., Kekkeris, G., and Kalantzis, M. (2008). A Discussion of Non Formal Education Training Programs for Roma Women in Greek Thrace: Proposals for a Better Planning", *The International Journal of the Humanities*, 6(9), pp. 79–85.

Georgiadou, K. (2008). Empowerment of Women through ICTs in the Muslim World, *Proceedings from the 6th Pan-Hellenic Conference with International participation "Information and Communication Technologies in Education"* Department of Education, University of Cyprus, Limassol, Cyprus, September 25–28, 2, pp. 15–18.

Georgiadou, K., Umrani, F., and Kekkeris, G. (2009). Muslim minority women in India and Greece: Comparing psychological factors that affect their computer use", *International Journal of Interdisciplinary Social Sciences*, 4(5), pp. 303–318.

Georgiadou, K. Baros, V. and Kekkeris, G. (2009). Motivating Roma women through computer education in Thrace, *Pedagogy*, 3, pp. 87–93.

Georgiadou, K. Dimasi, M. and Kekkeris, G. (2009). Muslim minority women's views on computer educators: Preliminary results of a survey in Greek Thrace. *Proceedings of the ESREA, Conference Inaugural meeting, University of Macedonia, Thessaloniki, Greece*, 6–8/11/2009, pp. 700–706.

Georgiadou, K. and Kekkeris, G. (2010). The role of computer education in the empowerment of Muslim women in Greek Thrace: Ethical considerations and limitations of the research, *proceeding of the Multicultural Education: Migration-management of conflicts-pedagogy of Democracy conference* Alexandroupoli, 7–9 May 2010, pp. 234–241.

Ghadially, R. and Umran, F. (2004) Initiatives among Mumbai Muslims. *I4d-Information for Development.* II (2), pp. 8–13.

Giannakouli, M. (2005). Η μουσουλμανική μειονότητητα τηε Δ. Θράκης και η άποψη από τη μεριά του Ελληνικού τύπου για τις Ελληνο-Τουρκικές σχέσεις κατά την διάρκεια του σεισμού του του 1999 στην Τουρκία, graduate project, TEI , Kastoria.

Giddens, A. (1990). *The Consequences of Modernity.* Stanford: Stanford University Press.

Goldstein, K. S. (1964). *A guide for fieldworkers in folklore.* Hatboro, PA: Folklore Associates Inc., pp. 133–138.

Gothoskar, S. (2000). Teleworking and Gender. *Economic and Political Weekly,* 35(26), pp. 2293–2298. (Jun. 24–30, 2000). Available on: http://www.jstor.org/pss/4409449 (Accessed 5 June 2010).

Gurumurthy, A. (2005). Empowering women promoting skill transfer through ICTs. *Information for development* (i4d), March, pp. 11–12.

Gurumurthy, A. (2004). Gender and ICTs: An overview Report. Available on: www.bridge.ids.ac.uk/reports/CEP-ICTs-OR.pdf, (Accessed 8 August 2010).

Hafkin, N. (2000). Convergence of Concepts: Gender and ICTs in Africa, in Rathgeber, E. and Adera, E.O. (eds), *Gender and the Information Revolution in Africa,* International Development Research Center, Ottawa, pp. 1–15.

Hafkin N. and Taggart N. (2001). *Gender, Information Technology, and Developing Countries: An Analytic Study.* Academy for Educational Development, for the Office of Women in Development, Bureau for Global programs, Field Support and Research, US Agency for International Development, Available on: http://ict.aed.org/_nfocenter/gender.htm or http://www.aed.org/learnlink/Publications/Gender_Book/Home.htm (Accessed 13 August 2010).

Hafkin, N. (2002). Are ICTs gender neutral; A gender analysis of six case studies of multi-donor ICTS projects. *Background paper for United Nations International Research and Training Institute for the Advancement of Women (IN STRAW) "Virtual Seminar Series" on gender and ICTSs.* Available on: http://www.un-instraw.org/en/docs/gender_and_ICTs/Hafkin.pdf, (Accessed 23 June 2010).

Hafkin, N. (2003). *Some thoughts on gender and telecommunications/ICTS statistics and indicators.* Paper presented to the 3rd World Telecommunication/ICTS Indicators Meeting, Geneva, 15–17 January 2003, Available on: http://www.itu.int/ITU/ICTs/wICTs02/doc/pdf/Doc46_Erev1.pdf (Accessed 25 June 2010).

Hafkin, N. (2003) *Gender issues in ICT statistics and indicators, with particular emphasis on developing countries.* Paper presented to the World Summit on the Information Society, *Geneva, 8–9 December 2003,* Available on: http://itidjournal.org/itid/article/viewFile/254/124, (Accessed 18 May 2009)

Hafkin, N. and Huyer, S. (2003). Lessons on Gender in ICT Applications: Case Studies of *info*Dev Projects. Washington, D.C.: *info*Dev. www.infodev.org.

Hafkin, N. and Huyer, S. (2006). *Cinderella or Cyberella? Empowering women in the Knowledge Society.* Bloomfield, CT: Kumarian Press, Inc. USA.

Hafkin, N. (2006). Women, Gender, and ICT Statistics and Indicators. Article in Hafkin, N. and Huyer, S. (2006). *Cinderella or Cyberella? Empowering women in the Knowledge Society.* Kumarian Press, Inc. USA, pp. 49–69.

Hafkin N.J. (2006). *Why the world isn't flat enough: Bringing more women contributors and beneficiaries into information technology.* EMC Women's Leadership Forum, Pleasanton CA.

Harrison, D., Mykytyn, P., and Riemenschneider, C. (1997). Executive Decisions About Adoption of Information Technology in Small Business: Theory and Empirical Tests. *Information System Research,* 8(2), p. 171–195. Available on: http://isr.journal.informs.org/cgi/content/abstract/8/2/171 (Accessed 13 June 2010).

Hartwick, J. and Barki, H.(1994). User participation, conflict, and conflict resolution: The mediation roles of influence. *Information Systems Research,* 5(4), pp. 422–438.

Hatzikosta, M. (2008). Καταγραφή της χρήσης εκπαιδευτικών τεχνικών και στάσεων έναντι αυτών από εκπαιδευόμενες μουσουλμάνες γυναίκες τμημάτων εκμάθησης Ελληνικής γλώσσας του ΚΕΕ Ν. Ροδόπης, Graduate project, Open University, Patra.

Heeks, R. (1999). *Information and communication technologies, poverty and development.* Development Informatics Working Paper Series, No.5/1999. Manchester: Institute for Development Policy and Management, Available on: http://www.sed.manchester.ac.uk/idpm/publications/wp/di/di_wp05.htm (Accessed 24 May 2009).

Hellenic Observatory for the Information Society. (2008). *The identity of Internet users in Greece.* Available on: http://www.observe.gr/files/meletes/InternetUsers2007FINAL.pdf (Accessed 27 July 2009)

Hendelman-Baavur, L. (2007). Promises and perils of Weblogistan: Online personal journals and the Islamic Republic of Iran. *Middle East Review of International Affairs,* 11(2), pp. 77–93.

Hollway, W. and Jefferson, T. (2005). *Doing qualitative research differently.* Sage Publications, pp. 90.

Hu, P.J., Chau, P.Y.K., Sheng, O.R.L., & Tam, K.Y. (1999). Examining the technology acceptance model using physician acceptance of telemedicine technology. *Journal of Management Information Systems*, 16(2), pp. 91–112.

Huyer S. (2003). Gender, ICT and Education. Available on: http://archive.wigsat. org/engenderedICT.pdf (Accessed 12 August 2010).

Huyer, S. (2005). *Women, ICT and the Information Society: Global Perspectives and Initiatives,* paper presented at the conference "Women and ICT", Baltimore, MD, June 12–14.

Huyer, S. (2006). Understanding gender equality and women's empowerment in the Knowledge Society. article in Hafkin, N. and Huyer, S. (2006). *Cinderella or Cyberella? Empowering Women in the Knowledge Society*. Kumarian Press, Inc. USA, pp. 15–47.

Huyer, S. (2006b). Cyberella in the Classroom?. article in Hafkin, N. and Huyer, S. (2006). *Cinderella or Cyberella? Empowering Women in the Knowledge Society*. Kumarian Press, Inc. USA, pp. 95–115.

Huyer, S., Hafkin, N., Ertl, H. and Dryburgh H. (2005). Women in the Information Society. In *From the digital divide to digital opportunities: Measuring infostates for development,* (eds) George Sciadas. Orbicom/ITU: Ottawa. http:// www.orbicom.uqam.ca/index_en.html, (Accessed 5 July 2010).

Huyer, S. and Mitter, S. (2003). ICTs, Globalisation and Poverty Reduction: Gender Dimensions of the Knowledge Society Part I. Poverty Reduction, Gender Equality and the Knowledge Society: Digital Exclusion or Digital Opportunity? Available on: http://unpan1.un.org/intradoc/groups/public/documents/ unpan/unpan037351.pdf, (Accessed 30 April 2009).

Huyer, S. and Hafkin, N. (2007). *Engendering the Knowledge Society: Measuring Women's Participation*. Montreal: Orbicom, WIGSAT, NCR Press, International Development Research Center.

Huyer, S. and Sikoska, T. (2002). *Overcoming the gender digital divide: Understanding ICTs and their potential for the empowerment of women,* INSTRAW virtual seminar series on gender and information and communication technologies. Presented at the UN Division for the Advancement of Women Expert Group, Meeting on ICTs and their Impact on and Use as an Instrument for the Advancement and Empowerment of Women. Seoul, Korea, 11–14 November. Available on: http//www.un-instraw.org/en/docs/gender_and_ict/Synthesis_paper.pdf, or http://www.un-instraw.org/en/research/gender_and_ict/virtual_seminars.html (Accessed 19 August 2009).

Imam, M. and Tsakiridi, O. (2004). *Μουσουλμάνοι και κοινωνικός αποκλεισμός*. Athens: Livanis.

Iosifidis, Th. (2003). *Ανάλυση Ποιοτικών Δεδομένων στις Κοινωνικές Επιστήμες*. Athens: Kritiki.

Jackson, C.M., Chow, S., & Leitch, R.A. (1997). Toward an understanding of the Behavioural Intention to use an information system. *Decision Sciences*, 28 (2), pp. 357–389.

Jackson, L. A., Ervin, K. S., Gardner, P. D., and Schmitt, N. (2001). Gender and the Internet: Women Communicating and Men Searching. *Sex Roles*, 44(5), pp. 363–379.

Jorge, S. N. (2000). Gender perspectives on telecenters. Paper presented to the ITU and Telecom Americas 2000 Telecom Development Symposium on Communications: Universal Access and Community Telecenters, Rio de Janeiro, Brazil, 11 April 2000. Available on: http://www.siyanda.org/docs/jorge_telecenters.pdf (Accessed 12 June 2009).

Jorge, S. N. (2002). The economics of ICT: Challenges and practical strategies of ICt use for women's economic empowerment. Presented at the UN Division for the Advancement of Women Expert Group Meeting on ICTs and Their Impact on and Use as Instrument for the Advancement and Empowerment of Women, Seoul Korea, 11–14 November, Available on: http://www.un.org/womenwatch/daw/egm/ict2002/reports/Paper%20by%20Sonia%20Jorge.pdf, (Accessed 19 August 2010).

Kalantzis, M. (2000). *Designing Futures: Challenges for leaders in Education*. Victorian Association of State secondary principals. Annual leadership conference, Geeolong, 16–18/8/2000.

Kalantzis, M. and Cope, B. (2004). "Designs for learning", *E–Learning*, Vol. 1(1).

Kanakidou, E. (1996). *Η προσωπικότητα της Μουσουλμάνας γυναίκας και η συμβολή της στις παραδοσιακές δομές της Αγωγής και Εκπαίδευσης των Μουσουλμάνων στη Θράκη*. Democritus University of Thrace, Alexandroupolis, Available on: http://alex.eled.duth/eled/phd/kanakidou, (Accessed 22 June 2009).

Kanakidou, E. (1994). *Η εκπαίδευση της μειονότητας στη Δ. Θράκη*. Athens: Ellinika Grammata.

Kanios, Ch. (2009). *Investigating attitudes and perspectives among Greek users of the Internet to e-commerce*. MA Thesis, Xarokopio University, Athens.

Kasotaki, S., and Rousos, P. (2006). The Greek scale of self efficiancy in computer usage. in Psillos, D. and Dadilelis, B. (Eds), *Proceedings of the 5th National Conference* "ICT in Education", Thessaloniki 5–8/10/2006, pp. 726–733.

Katsikas, Ch. (1997). *The illiterates of Thrace*. Available on: http://alex.eled.duth.gr/kroupis/31.html (Accessed 15 July 2009).

Kárpáti, A. (2004), Travellers in Cyberspace: ICT in Hungarian Romani (Gypsy) Schools. *Promoting Equity Through ICT in Education.* ed. A. Kárpáti, Paris: OECD, pp. 141–156.

Keil, M. (1991), Managing MIS Implementation: Identifying and Removing Barriers to Use, Harvard University.

Kennedy, T. Wellman, B. and Klement, K. (2003). Gendering the digital divide. *IT and Society,* 1(5), pp. 72–96.

Khan, F. and Ghadially, R. (2010). Empowerment through ICT education, access and use: a gender analysis of Muslim youth in India. *Journal of International Development,* 22, pp. 659–673.

King, N. (1990*). Innovation at Work: The Research Literature, Innovation and Creativity at Work.* M.A. West and J.L. Farr, Chichester: Wiley, pp. 5–80.

Kourakos, N. Kaouni, P. (2009). Acceptance Factors for Web based learning under the sustainability issues. *Proceedings of the 5th International Conference in Open & Distance Learning -November 2009, Athens, Greece,* pp. 170–178.

Koutromanos, G. (2006). Head teachers' intention and behaviour to support the uptake of ICT in their schools: an application of the Theory of Reasoned Action and the Theory of Planned Behaviour. *Journal of Science Education,* 7(2), pp. 26–28.

Koutromanos, G. and Papaioannou, G. (2008). The Use of ICT in the Teaching of Greek Language: Prospective Teachers' Intention, Attitude, Subjective Norm and Perceived Behavioural Control. *Proceedings of ED-MEDIA World Conference on Educational Multimedia, Hypermedia and Telecommunications 2008,* pp. 1671–1679, Vienna, Austria: AACE.

Koutromanos, G. and Kibirige, I. (2006). *Factors predicting teachers' intentions to use the educational software of road safety education "The Chariot of the Sun".* Paper presented to international conference of the Education Association of South Africa (EASA) and Kenton Education Association, at the Wilderness, Southern Cape, South Africa, 28 Nov – 1 Dec 2006.

Koutroumanos, G. (2009). The examination and prediction of university students' decisions to acquire access to Broadband Internet for personal and educational purposes. *Proceedings of the 5th International Conference in Open & Distance Learning -November 2009, Athens, Greece,* pp. 84–96.

Koutromanos, G. and Zisimopoulos, D. (2009). Digital games-based learning material for mild intellectualdisability students: Factors influencing teachers to use it in their teaching', in L. Gomez Chova, D. Marti Belenguer, and I. Candel Terres (Eds.), *Proceedings of International, Education and Development Conference,* 9–11 March 2009, Valencia, Spain, pp. 3476–3483.

Kramarae, C. and Taylor, J. (1993). Women and men on electronic networks: a conversation or a monologue. In *Women, Information Technology and Scholarship*, edited by H.J. Taylor, Kramarae, C and Ebben, M. Urbana: Center for Advanced Study.

Krishnan, U. and Puvaneswary, S. (2005). E-Homemakers network teleworking moms unite! *Information for Development (i4d)*, March, pp. 14–16.

Kvale, S. (1996). Interviews: *An introduction to qualitative research interviewing*. London: Sage.

Kvale, S. (2007). *Doing Interviews*. Sage Publications.

Latimer, C. (2001). *The digital divide: Understanding and addressing the challenge*. New York, NY: New York State Forum for Information Resource Management.

Lee, J.C. (2004). Access, self image and empowerment. Computer training for women entrepreneurs in Costa Rica. *Gender, Technology and Development*, 8(2), pp. 209–229.

Leggon, Ch. (2006). Gender, race/ethnicity, and the digital divide. in eds. Fox, M., Johnson, D. and Rosser, S. (2006). *Women, Gender and Technology*. University of Illinois Press, Urbana and Chicago, pp. 98–109.

Lepper, M. R. (1985). Microcomputers in Education: Motivational and social issues. American Psychologist, 40, pp. 1–18.

Lin, C., Hu, PJ-H., and Chen, H. (2003). Technology implementation management in law enforcement: COPLINK system usability and user acceptance evaluations. Available on: http://www.diggov.org/dgrc/dgo2003/cdrom/PAPERS/hci_usability/lin_coplink.pdf (Accessed 11 February 2006).

Lister, R. (1997). *Citizenship: feminist perspectives*. London: Macmillan

Loehlin, J. (1991), Latent Variable Models: An Introduction to Factor, Path and Structural Analysis, Lawrence Erlbaum, Hillsdale, NJ.

Loh-Ludher. L.L. (2007). Home workers online: Utilization of ICTSs for home-based work in Malaysia. *EJISDC*, 32(5), pp. 1–14.

Longwez, S. (1999). Women's Empowerment (Framework), in *A guide to gender-Analysis*, OXFAM.

Lopez-Claros, A. and Zahidi, S. (2005). Women's Empowerment: Measuring the global gender gap. Geneva: World Economic Forum, Available on: http://www.weforum.org/pdf/Global_Competitiveness_Reports/Reports/gender_gap.pdf, (Accessed 5 June 2010).

Makrakis, B. (2000). *Τα πολυμέσα στην Εκπαίδευση*. Athens: Metaihmio, pp. 18.

Malhotra. Y., and Galletta, D. (1999). Extending the Technology Acceptance Model to Account for Social Influence: Theoretical Bases and Empirical Validation. *HICSS*.

Malhotra, A., Schuler, S., and Boender. C. (2002). Measuring Women's Empowerment as a Variable in International Development. *International Center for Research on Women and the Gender and Development Group of the World Bank.*

Malkidis, Th. (2005). Η οικογένεια και η γυναίκα στην κοινωνία των μουσουλμανικών μειονότήτων της Ελληνικής Θράκης. Επιθεώρηση κοινωνικών ερευνών (*Review of Social Researches*), *116 A΄*, pp. 51–78.

Maneja, C. A. (2002). *Women, weaving and the web: An analysis of rural Indian women's agency in attaining economic empowerment.* M.A. Thesis, Communication, Culture and Technology Program. Georgetown University, Washington, DC.

Mao, E., & Palvia, P. (2001). *The effect of culture on information technology acceptance.* Proceedings of the 32nd Annual Meeting of Decision Sciences Institute, pp. 672–674,. San Francisco, CA.

Marcelle, G. M. (2000a). *Transforming ICTs for Gender Equality. Gender in Development.* Monograph Series 9. New York: UNDP.

Marcelle, G. (2000b). Getting Gender into African ICT Policy: A Strategic Vie, in eds Rathgeber, E. M. and Adera, E. O. *Gender and the Information Revolution in Africa*, Ottawa: IDRC.

Margolis, J. and Fisher, A. (2003). *Unlocking the Clubhouse: Women in computing.* MIT Press, pp. 22 and pp. 80.

Markauskaite, L. (2006). *Exploring differences in trainee teachers. ICT literacy: Does gender matter?* Paper presented in the Ascilite 2006 – the annual conference of the Australasian Society for Computers in Learning in Tertiary Education, Who's Learning? Whose Technology? Available on: http://www.ascilite. org.au/conferences/brisbane05/blogs/proceedings/51Markauskaite.pdf. (Accessed 13 January 2010).

Marshall, M.N. (1996). The key informant technique. *Family Practice,* 13(1), pp. 92–97.

Mathieson, K. (1991). Predicting user intentions: Comparing the Technology Acceptance Model with the Theory of Planned Behavior, *Information Systems Research* 2(3), pp. 173–191.

Mayoux, L. Empowerment. Available on: http://www.lindaswebs.org.uk/Page1_ Development/Empowerment/Empowerment.htm (Accessed 18 July 2010).

Mavrommatis, G. (2005). *Τα παιδιά της Καλκάντζας.* Athens: Metaixmio.

Melhem, S. and Vivek, Ch. (2006). *Promoting Innovation and Entrepreneurship in the Middle East and North Africa*: Summary of Outcomes and findings from our MNA regional Workshop, Casablanca.

Melhem, S. Morrell, C. and Tandom, N. (2009). *ICTs for Women's Socioeconomic Empowerment*. World Bank Working paper no. 176.

Minges, M. (2003). *Gender and ICT statistics*. Presentation at 3rd World Tele-communications/ICT Indicators Meeting, Geneva. Available on: http://www.itu.int/ITU-D/ict/WICT02/doc/pdf/Doc07_E.pdf. (Accessed 8 July 2010).

Mitra, S. (2000). Minimally invasive education for mass computer literacy, presented at CRIDALA 2000 Conference, Hong Kong, pp. 21–25.

Mitra, S. & Rana, V. (2001). Children and the Internet: Experiments with minimally invasive education in India. *The British Journal of Educational Technology*, 32 (2),pp. 221–232.

Mitra, S. (2003). Minimally Invasive Education: A progress report on the "Hole-in-the-wall" experiments, *The British Journal of Educational Technology*, 34(3), pp. 367–371.

Mitra, S. (2005). Self organising systems for mass computer literacy: Findings from the "Hole in the wall" experiments. *International Journal of Development Issues* 4(1), pp. 71–81.

Mitter, S. (2000). *Women in Knowledge Societies*. WomenAction 2000. Available on: http://www.womenaction.org/gkii/swasti.html, (Accessed 19 August 2010).

Mitter, S. (2003). *ICTs and employment and livelihood opportunities of women in South and Southeast Asia*, Available on: http://www.isst-india.org/SessionIII/Swasti.pdf, (Accessed 4 March 2007).

Mitter, S. (2004). Globalization, ICTs and economic empowerment: A feminist critique. *Gender Technology and Development*, 8 (1), pp. 5–29.

Mitter, S. (2005). Globalization, ICTs, and Economic Empowerment. A Feminist Critique, in Ng, C. and Mitter, S. (eds), *Gender and the Digital Economy: Perspectives from the Developing World*, Sage, London.

Mitter, S., and Sen, A. (2000). Can Calcutta Become Another Bangalore?. *Economic and Political Weekly* 35(26): pp. 2263–2268.

Morris, M.W., Leung, K., Ames, D. and Lickel, B. (1999). Views from inside and outside: integrating emic and etic insights about culture and justice judgment. *Academy of Management Review*, 24(4), pp. 781–796.

Moulton J. (1997). Formal and Non-formal Education and Empowered behaviour: a review of the research literature. Prepared for the support for analysis and research in Africa (Sara) project, (http://sara.aed.org/sara_pubs_list_sara_4.htm).

Moghadam, V.M., and Senftova, L. (2005). Measuring Women's Empowerment: Participation and Rights in Civil, Political, Social, Economic, and Cultural Domains. *International Social Science Journal*, 57(2), pp. 389–412.

Moghadam, V. M. (2003). Engendering citizenship, Feminizing civil society: the case of the Middle East and North Africa. *Women & Politics*, 25(1–2), pp. 63–88.

Moore, G. C., and Benbasat, I. (1991). Development of an Instrument to Measure the Perceptions of Adopting an Information Technology Innovation. *Information Systems Research*, 2(3), pp. 192–222.

Nath, V. (2001). *Empowerment and Governance through ICT: Women's Perspective. The International Information & Library Review*, 33(4), pp. 317–339, Paper presented at the International Conference on Women in the New ICT Era: Challenges and Opportunities, Kuala Lumpur, Malaysia. Available on: http://www.cddc.vt.edu/knownet/articles/WomenandICT.htm, (Accessed 11 April 2009).

Nath, V. (2006). Empowerment of Women's through ICT- enabled networks. Article in Hafkin, N. and Huyer, S. (2006). *Cinderella or Cyberella? Empowering women in the Knowledge Society*. Kumarian Press, Inc. USA, pp. 191–206.

Narayanan, K. N. (2002). Socio-Economic Impact of Subsidized Computer Education. Submitted to Sterlite Foundation. India.

Navrozidou, D. (2008). *Η δια βίου εκπαίδευση και η συμβολή της στην προσέγγιση της μουσουλμάνας γυναίκας του Ν. Ροδόπης*. Master thesis, Department of Primary Education, Duth, Alexandroupolis.

Ng, C. and S. Mitter (eds). (2005). *Gender and the Digital Economy: Perspectives from the Developing World*. New Delhi: Sage.

Niknejad, K. (2005). For young Iranians on the prowl, the Internet is the ultimate veil. Available on: http://jscms.jrn.columbia.edu/cns/2005-05-03/.

Notaras, Y. (1995). *The non-homogeneousness of the population. The development of Thrace, Provocations and perspectives*. K. Zolotas, A. Angelopulos and I. Pesmazoglu (eds.). Athens, Academy of Athens: Publications of the Centre of research of the Greek society, pp. 46.

NTIA (National Telecommunications and Information Administration). (1995). Falling through the Net: A Survey of the 'have nots' in rural and urban America. Washington, DC: U.S. Department of Commerce.

OECD. (2009). *Equally Prepared for Life? How 15 Year Old Boys and Girls Perform in School, Programme for International Student Assessment*. Paris: OECD Publishing.

Pfeffer, J. (1982). *Organizations and Organization Theory*, Boston: Pitman.

Panousi, Th. (2007). *Τα εμπόδια που αντιμετωπίζουν οι γυναίκες της μουσουλμανικής μειονότητατς της Δ. Θράκης κατά την διάρκεια της συμμετοχής τους σε ιδωτικό κέντρο εκπαίδευσης στην Κομοτηνή*. Master thesis, Open University, Patra.

Paraskevopoulos, J. (1993). *Μεθοδολογία Επιστημονικής Έρευνας*. Athens, V(1).

Patton, M. Q. (1987). *How to Use Qualitative Methods in Evaluation*. California: Sage Publications, Inc.

Pavlou, P.A. (2003). Consumer acceptance of electronic commerce: integrating trust and risk with the technology acceptance model. *International Journal of Electronic Commerce*, 7(3), pp. 101–134.

Peizer, J. (2005). *The Dynamics of Technology for Social Change*. Lincoln, NE: iUniverse.

Plexousaki, E. (2003). Κραυγές και ψίθυροι Συγκρούσεις και ταυτότητες στον λόγο μειονοτικών γυναικών στη Θράκη: In (Eds.) Vlaxoutsikou, C. and Kain-Hart, L. *Όταν γυναίκες έχουν διαφορές*, Medousa, Greece.

Poole, E. (2001). Interpreting Islam: British Muslims and the British Press. In: Ross, K. & Playdon, P. (Eds), *Black Marks: Minority Ethnic audiences and media*. Aldershot: Ashgate, pp. 67–86.

Prasar, V. (2003). *Information and Communication Technology for Women's Empowerment in India* Paper presented at the "Women in IT-'WIT 2003", International Conference on Women in the Digital Era: Opportunities and Challenges, 10–12 December 2003 Annamalai University, Chidambaram, India.

Pye, D. (2003). Using ICT to increase the effectiveness of community-based, non-formal education for rural people in Sub-Saharan Africa. The CERP project –final report. Available on : http://www2.dfid.gov.uk/pubs/file/usingictedpaper50.pdf, (Accessed 12 July 2009).

Ramilo, C., Hafkin, N., and Jorge, S. (2005). *Women 2000 and beyond*. Division for the advancement of women, Department of economic and social reforms of the United Nations Secretariat. Available on: http://www.un.org/womenwatch/daw/public/w2000-09.05-ict-e.pdf, (Accessed 2 June 2010).

Rathgeber, E. (2002). Gender and Telecentres: What Have We Learned? Presentation at the Gender and the Digital Divide Seminar, World Bank. Washington, D.C.

Ribas Mateos, N. (2000). Old communities, excluded women and change in Western Thrace (Thracian Greece, the Provinces of Xanthi, Rhodopi and Evros), Universitat Autònoma de Barcelona. Departament de Sociologia Barcelona Spain, mazo@arquired.es., *Paper 60* , pp. 119–150 Available on: http://ddd.uab.cat/pub/papers/02102862n60p119.pdf, (Accessed 14 April 2007).

Rigopoulos, G., Psarras, J. and Askounis, D. Th. (2008). A TAM model to evaluate user's attitude towards adoption of decision support systems. *Journal Applied Sciences*, 8, pp. 899–9C2.

Rose, G., and Straub, D. (1998). Predicting general IT use: Applying TAM to the Arabic world. *Journal of Global Information Management*, 6(3), pp. 39–46.

Rubin, J. H and Rubin, S. I. (2005). *Qualitative interviewing: The art of hearing data.* London: Sage, pp. 95.

Said, E. (1997). *Covering Islam.* London: Vintage, pp. 4.

Saga, V. L. and Zmud, R.W. (1994), "The Nature and Determinants of IT Acceptance, Routinization and Infusion", *IFIP Transaction: Computer Science and Technology*, 45, pp. 67–86.

Schaefer, D. S. (2004). Women weavers on line: Rural Moroccan Women on the Internet. *Gender, Technology and Development*, 8(1), pp. 53.

Schuler, S. R., Hashemi M. S., and Riley P.A. (1997). The influence of women's changing roles and status in Bangladesh's fertility transition: Evidence from a study of credit programs and contraceptive use. World Development, 25(4), pp. 563–575.

Seidman, I. (1987). *Interviewing as qualitative research.* Teachers College Press, Columbia University, New York.

Sella-Mazi, H. (1999). *La minorite musulmane turcophone de Grece; Approche sociolinguistique d' une communaute bilingue.* Athens: Troxalia.

Sen, A. (1999). *Development as Freedom.* New York: Anchor Books.

Sen, A. (2000). Social Exclusion: concept, application and scrutiny. *Social Development Papers* No. 1. Office of Environment and Social Development. Manila: Asian Development Bank. Available on: http://citeseerx.ist.psu.edu/viewdoc/download?doi=10.1.1.100.1010&rep=rep1&type=pdf, (Accessed 18 August 2010).

Sengupta, A., Long, G. E., Singhal, A., and Shefner-Rogers, K. C. (2007). The Sada says "We women have our rights": A gender analysis of an ICTS initiative in Afghanistan. *International Communication Gazette.* Available on: http://gaz.sagepub.com/cgi/content/abstract/69/4/335 (Accessed 3 April 2010).

Sharma, U. (2003). *Women's Empowerment through Information Technology*, Author's Press, New Delhi.

Silvera, S. (2000). New Organizational models. Competencies in a feminine key. CINTERFOR/ILO.

Slappendel, C. (1996). Perspectives on Innovation in Organizations. *Organization Studies*, 17(1), pp. 107–129.

Spender, D. (1997). The position of women in information technology-or who got there first and with what consequences. *Current Sociology*, 45(2), pp. 135–147.

Sreekumar, T.T. (2007). Cyber kiosks and dilemmas of social inclusion in rural India. *Media, Culture and Society*, 29(6), pp. 869–889.

Stewart L. A., C. Avila, G. (2004). *Cultural Dimensions of the Digital Divide: ICT and Brockton's Cape Verdeans.* International Association for Media and Communication Research and Conference Porto Alegre Brazil July 24–30, 2004, Available on: http://www.media.uio.no/prosjekter/ctp/papers/IAMCR-CTP04_S2-2_Lizie.pdf (Accessed 19 December 2008).

Straub, D.W. (1989). Validating instruments in MIS research, *MIS Quarterly*, 13(2), pp. 147–69.

Straub, D. (1994). The effect of culture on IT diffusion: E-mail & fax in Japan and the U.S. *Information Systems Research,* 5(1), pp. 23–47.

Straub, D., Keil, M., & Brenner, W. (1997). Testing the Technology Acceptance Model across cultures: A three country study. *Information Management*, 33(1), pp. 1–11.

Straub, D.W., Loch, K.D. and Hill, C.E. (2001), Transfer of information technology to the Arab world: a test of cultural influence modelling. *Journal of Global Information Management*, 9(4), pp. 6–28.

Tadros, M. (2005*). Arab women, the Internet, and the Public sphere.* Paper prepared for the Mediterranean Social and Political Research Meeting, Florence, Italy, March 2005.

Tandon, N. (2008). Information and Communication Technologies. Thematic Note 4, and Community E-centers in Malaysia, Activity Profile 3, Module 9, *Gender and Agricultural Livelihoods Sourcebook*, World Bank and FAO.

Tannen, D. (1994). Gender gap in cyberspace. *Newsweek May 16*, pp. 40–41.

Taylor, S. and Todd, P. A. (1995). Understanding Information Technology usage: A test of competing models. *Information Systems Research*, 6(4), pp. 144–176.

Thompson E. (2001). Successful Experiences in Non-Formal Education and Alternative Approaches to Basic Education in Africa, paper presented at 2001 Biennial Conference of ADEA.

Thioune, Ramata Molo, ed. (2003). *Opportunities and Challenges for Community Development.* Vol. I, Information and Communication Technologies for Development in Africa. Ottawa: International Development Research Centre and Council for Development of Social Science Research in Africa (CODESRIA).

Tressou, E. (1997). Ειδικές ομάδες αποτυγχάνοντας στην εκπαίδευση. Paper presented in the conference "Human dignity and social exclusion-Educational policy in E.U." Athens, 2–4/10/1997, (Ed.): Ellinika grammata.

Triantafillidou, A. (2007). *Regions, minorities and European policies: A state of the art report on the Turkish Muslims of Western Thrace (Greece).* Project report (D1 and D2) prepared for the EUROREG project funded by the European Commission Research DG, Key Action Improving the Socio-Economic Knowledge Base (contract no. CIT2-CT-2003–506019). Available on: http://www.eliamep.gr/old-site/eliame-old/eliamep/www.eliamep.gr/eliamep/files/State%20of%20art%20Greece%20 FINAL.pdf , (Accessed 23 February 2010).

Troubeta, S. (2001). *Κατασκευάζοντας ταυτότητες για τους μουσουλμάνους της Δ. Θράκης,*. Athens: KEMO and Kritiki.

Tsakiri, K. (2007). *E-learning και οι εταιρείες: η περίπτωση της Pricewaterhousecoopers*. Master Thesis. University of Macedonia, Greece, Available on: http://dspace.lib.uom.gr/bitstream/2159/3734/1/TsakiriMsc2007.pdf, (Accessed 30 April 2009).

Tsibiridou, F. (1997). Woman´s Alterity in Cultural Constructions of Identities: A case study from Greek Thrace. *Mediterranean Journal of Human Rights*, 1(2), pp. 217–237.

Tsibiridou, F. (2005). *Middle Eastern Womanhood: Subaltern subjects or postmodern "oriental" citizen*. International conference on "The Arab World and Islam Identities and Intercultural Interaction", University of Sofia, 2005, Bulgaria.

Turkle, S. (1995). *Life on the Screen: Identity in the Age of the Internet*. New York: Simon & Schuster, pp. 17.

Umrani, F. (2007). *Computer adoption among Mumbai Muslim Youth: Empowerment and impact assessment* , PhD Thesis, Department of Humanities and Social Sciences, Indian Institute of Technology, Bombay.

Umrani, F. and Ghadially, R. (2003). Empowering women through ICT education: Facilitating computer adoption. *Gender, Technology and Development*, 7(3), pp. 359–377.

UNESCO. (1997). 5th International Conference on Adult Education. CONFINTEA, Politics and Policies. The politics and policies of the education of adults in a globally transforming society, Hamburg 1997.

UNESCO. (2005). ICTs for community empowerment through non-formal education, APPEAL.

UNESCO. (2009). Statistics Slow Progress Towards Universal Literacy, and More Literate Women than Ever Before. Available on: http://portal.unesco.org/en/ev.php-URL_ID=5637&URL_DO=DO_TOPIC&URL_SECTION=201.html (Accessed 17 July 2010).

UN. (2005a). Division for the Advancement of Women Department of Economic and Social Affairs. Gender equality and empowerment of women through ICTS. Prepared by Ramilo Ch., Hafkin N. and Jorge S. *Women 2000 and beyond*. Available on: http://www.un.org/womenwatch/daw/public/w2000-09.05-ICTs-e.pdf (Accessed 12 May 2010).

UN. (2005b). *Gender Equality and Empowerment through ICT*. United Nations Division for the Advancement of Women Department of Economic and Social Affairs. Available on: http://www.un.org/womenwatch/daw/public/ w2000-09.05-ict-e.pdf (Accessed 15 April 2009).

UN. (2007). Economic and Social Commission for Asia and the Pacific: Gender Assessment of Selected E-business and Strategies in Asia: The case studies of Malaysia, the Philippines, the Republic of Korea and Thailand. Available on: http://www.un.org/womenwatch/daw/public/w2000-09.05-ICTs-e.pdf (Accessed 14 May 2010).

UNDP. (1995). in http://www.undp.org/energy/publications/1995/1995a.htm.

Uzoka. F., Shemi, A., and Seleka, G. (2007). Behavioural influence on E-commerce adoption in a developing country context. *EJISDC*, 31(4), pp. 1–15.

Van Slambrouck, P. (2000). Web acquires more women's touches. *Christian Science Monitor*, 92(184), pp. 1.

Venkatesh, V., and Davis, F. D. (2000). A theoretical extension of the technology acceptance model: Four longitudinal field studies. *Management Science*, 45(2), pp. 186–204.

Venkatesh, V., and Morris, M. G. (2000). Why don't men ever stop to ask for directions? Gender, social influence and their role in technology acceptance and usage behavior. *MIS Quarterly*, 24(1), pp. 115–139.

Venkatesh, V. (2000). Determinants of Perceived Ease of Use: Integrating Control, Intrinsic Motivation, and Emotion into the Technology Acceptance Model *Information Systems Research*, 11(4), pp. 342–365.

Venkatesh, V., Morris, M. G., Davis, G. B., and Davis, F. D. (2003). User Acceptance of Information Technology: Toward a Unified View. *MIS Quarterly*, 27(3), pp. 425–478.

Verbick, T. (2002). Women, technology, and gender bias. *Journal of Computing Sciences in Colleges*, 17, pp. 240–250.

Vergidis, D. and Prokou, E., (2005). *Designing, Management and Evaluation of Adult Training Programs*. Vol. A, Patra, Greek Open University.

VFA: Volunteers for Africa ICT Programme-East and Central Africa, Available on http://vfa.8m.net/photo.html. (Accessed 13 August 2010).

Vitsilakis, C. (2004). New Forms of Work Organization and Gender. In Nova-Kaltsouni, C., and Kassotakis, M., *Promoting New Forms of Organization and Other Cooperative Arrangements for Competitiveness and Employability*, Athens: National and Kapodistrian University of Athens, pp. 202–216.

Vitsilakis, C. and Eythymiou, H. (2007). *Νέες Τεχνολογίες στην Εποχή της Παγκοσμιοποίησης: Μια Έμφυλη Προσέγγιση*. Scientific Publication on Gender Studies, Publication's director: Vitsilakis, C. Athens: Atrapos.

Vryonides, M. Vitsilakis, Ch. (2008). Widening participation in postgraduate studies in Greece: mature working women attending an e-learning programme. *Journal of Education Policy*, 23(3), pp. 199–208.

Vygotsky, L. (1987). *Thought and language*. (A. Kozulin, Ed.). Cambridge, MA: MIT Press.

Wajcman, J. (1991). *Feminism Confronts Technology*. London: Polity Press., pp. 20.

Wheeler, D. (2001). The Internet and Public culture in Kuwait. *Gazette* Sage publications, London, Thousand Oaks & New Delhi, 63(2–3), pp. 187–201.

Wheeler, D. (2006a). Empowering publics: Information Technology and democratization in the Arab World—Lessons from Internet cafés and beyond. *Oxford Internet Institute, Research Report* No. 11.

Wheeler, D. (2006b). Gender sensitivity and the drive for IT: Lessons from the NetCorps Jordan Project. *Ethics and Information Technology*, 8, pp. 131–142.

Wilson, S. (2000). The anthropology of online communities. *Annual Review of Anthropology*, 31, pp. 449–467.

World Bank. (2000). Engendering development: enhancing development through attention to gender. http://www.worldbank.org/gender/prr/index.htm.

World Bank. (2001). Engendering development through gender equality in rights, resources, and voice, Available on: http://www.wds.worldbank.org/external/default/main?pagePK=64193027&piPK=64187937&theSitePK=523679&menuPK=64187510&searchMenuPK=64187283&siteName=WDS&entityID=000094946_01020805393496, (Accessed 4 May 2010).

Yamane, T. (1973). *Statistics: An Introductory Analysis*. 3rd ed. New York: Harper and Row.

Yoo, Y. and Alavi, M. (2001). Media and group cohesion: Relative influences on social presence, task participation, and group consensus, *MIS Quarterly*, 25, pp. 371–390.

Youngman, F. and Singh, M. (2005). *Introduction in the Strengthening the Training of Adult Educators: Learning from an Inter-regional Exchange of Experience*. Report on the Workshop Held at the CONFINTEA Mid-term Review Conference, Bangkok, Thailand, September 2003, pp. 1-10.

Yu, J., Ha, I., Choi, M. and Rho, J. (2005). Extending the TAM for a t-commerce. *Information & Management*, 42(7), pp. 965–976.

Zabeta, E. (2003). *Σχολείο και Θρησκεία*. Athens, Themelio.

Zaimakis, G., and Kaprani, K. (2005). Μουσουλμάνες γυναίκες και πολιτισμική αλλαγή: Διαφορετικότητα, φύλο και θρησκεία σε μία αγροτική περιοχή στη Δ. Θράκη, *Επιθεώρηση κοινωνικών ερευνών*, 116 Α΄ pp. 79–110.

Zakour, A.B. (2004). Cultural differences and information technology acceptance. *Proceedings of the 7th Annual conference of the Southern Association for IS.*

Zenginis, E. (1994). *Οι μουσουλμάνοι αθίγγανοι της Θράκης.* Thessaloniki: Hemus Peninsula Institute of Studies.